Canadian Educational Leadership

Dr. Thomas G. Ryan

Canadian Educational Leadership

Library and Archives Canada Cataloguing in Publication

Canadian educational leadership / edited by Thomas G. Ryan.

Includes bibliographical references.
ISBN 978-1-55059-367-9

1. Educational leadership--Canada. 2. School management and organization--Canada. I. Ryan, Thomas G. (Thomas Gerald), 1960-

LA411.83.C36 2009 371.200971 C2009-900490-9

Detselig Enterprises Ltd.

210, 1220 Kensington Road NW
Calgary, Alberta, T2N 3P5
www.temerondetselig.com
Phone: (403) 283-0900 Fax: (403) 283-6947

We acknowledge the support of the Government of Canada through the Book Publishing Industry Development Program (BPIDP) for our publishing program.

We also acknowledge the support of the Alberta Foundation for the Arts for our publishing program.

SAN 113-0234
ISBN 978-1-55059-367-9
Cover Design by Shane Riczu

Contents

Introduction

The following pages contain the collective energies of several authors who were invited to write about leadership in Canadian education. Each author delivers a perspective that will trigger the reader to both question the text and thoughtfully examine the ideas put forward. While the topic at hand can be examined from many different vantage points, this text addresses Canadian education from a provincial and regional focus. The perspectives presented in this text are both timely and current, and we have made a concerted effort to included the voices of writers from across Canada who are themselves education leaders of considerable integrity and resourcefulness.

There are several good books on leadership in Canada currently available. One particularly good recent publication is *Made in Canada Leadership*, a study of leadership in Canada written by Amal Henein and Françoise Morissette. The authors identify what they call the five cornerstones of the Canadian leadership brand: harmony, integrity, quality, resourcefulness, and inclusiveness. Our text exchanges these cornerstones with similar yet unique foundational tenets. We situate Canadian educational leadership within a framework of redefinition, transformation, improvement, moral literacy, multiculturalism, emotions, and evolution. While the terms are distinct, there is overlap in that redefinition, transformation, improvement, and evolution concern change. Moral literacy and multiculturalism embrace the very distinctive qualities of the Canadian leader in education.

Chapter One, written by Ray Williams of St. Thomas University and Ken Brien of the University of New Brunswick, digs into the recent history of leadership reforms within New Brunswick to uncover four themes related to the misapplication of positivistic business models of leadership within the education system. Although these themes need to be examined to ensure that successful reforms are implemented, often they receive little consideration when politicians and bureaucrats attempt to reform education. In Chapter Two Yvette Daniel of the

University of Windsor presents two educational leaders who demonstrate the moral use of power. The portraits highlight the proactive ethical stance often required to support student success. In Chapter Three George Bedard of the University of Lethbridge details leadership practices and school improvement in Alberta. These details emerge from a survey of provincial school improvement projects that demanded visioning, goal setting, and internal and external support to advance teacher leadership in Alberta. Chapter Four moves the reader into Manitoba as Carolyn Crippen of the University of Manitoba describes how investing in moral literacy can be a positive initiative in educational leadership.

Duncan MacLellan of Ryerson University takes us into Chapter Five where we learn about the substantial changes that school boards in Canada have undergone and the challenges in educational leadership these changes have wrought. In Chapter Six Brenda Beatty, a long-time Ontario educator formerly of the University of Toronto's Ontario Institute for Studies in Education and now working out of Monash University in Australia, explains how we can develop school administrators who lead with the emotions in mind while making the commitment to connectedness in schools and education. Moving into Chapter Seven, Verna McDonald of the University of Northern British Columbia delves into the many voices within multicultural education leadership in order to alert the reader to several significant elements. Working with research conducted at Nipissing University, I report in Chapter Eight that evolving leaders can facilitate their own professional growth within an action research enterprise. Chapter Nine, penned by Jason Price of the University of Victoria, presents a lighter look at the future of educational leadership within Ontario.

In all, these efforts present a candid and discerning representation of Canadian educational leadership that is positioned within a framework of redefinition, transformation, improvement, moral literacy, multiculturalism, emotions, and evolution. Upon completion of this text please look into *Made in Canada Leadership: Wisdom from the Nation's Best and Brightest on Leadership Practice and Development*, by Amal Henein and Françoise Morissette, published John Wiley & Sons.

Thom Ryan

Chapter One

Redefining Educational Leadership for the Twenty-First Century

Ken Brien, Ed.D.
University of New Brunswick

Ray Williams, Ed.D.
St. Thomas University

The dawning of the twenty-first century forces us to focus on the changing economic and social patterns that we experience as global citizens. The industrial society is rapidly being replaced with a knowledge society and advances in technology are making the world a smaller place. Dramatic shifts in the job market due to the expansion of multinational corporations and the outsourcing of jobs place new demands on schools to prepare graduates for a future that can no longer be predicted with any certainty by inferring from our industrial past. Traditional patterns of schooling that had sufficed for an industrial society are no longer adequate (Hartle & Hobby, 2003). As change becomes the only constant, success both personally and organizationally is dependent on every individual's capacity to adapt and learn. As innovation and creativity become the driving forces for successful organizations, the hierarchical patterns of leadership flatten. Survival in the global economy requires companies to become learning organizations that can respond quickly and creatively to shifts in the international marketplace. As a result, leadership has been redefined from being a characteristic exhibited by relatively few individuals at the top to a capacity for improvement that permeated every level of the organization.

As in the past, schools are modeling their reforms on those that have succeeded in business. The challenge for educational leaders today is to adapt the corporate model of learning organizations to make schools places where continuous learning by teachers supports the improved learning of students. On its face this seems a relatively easy task but it is a challenge that should not be taken lightly. To understand this challenge we must examine the ingrained leadership traditions and beliefs that schools have already adopted from the corporate world. We will then describe the changing models of leadership for school reform and their connection to educational purposes of the twenty-first century. Finally, we will describe leadership and research for school reform in New Brunswick to illustrate the redefinition of educational leadership for the future.

Leadership as a Field of Study

While research into the leadership of educational organizations is far more limited than that in the corporate sphere, the studies that have been done point out some interesting patterns. Successful schools require strong leaders (Edmonds, 1979; Lezotte, Edmonds, & Ratner, 1974), and the principal is a key person in affecting school reform (Fullan, 1991; Hallinger, 1992). Proponents of educational change have therefore focused significant energy in determining why certain principals prove to be more effective leaders than others. Given the paucity of research on leadership within education, they looked to the corporate literature where the link between effective leadership and successful organizations has been a continuous topic of study (Argyris, 1961; Barnard, 1938; Bass, 1990; Bennis & Nanus, 1985; Pearce, 2004). A prominent theme in the corporate and education leadership literature has been the evolution from an emphasis on trait and situational considerations towards transactional and transformational theories of leadership.

Trait and Situational Theories of Leadership

The model of public education and the leadership patterns being used in schools today trace their origins to the early 1900s. The prevailing belief in the industrial society that characterized the period from the 1920s to the 1940s was that leadership was dependent on a assortment of personal traits that a leader possessed. The best way to provide strong leadership was to study successful leaders, identify the traits that made them successful, and look for these traits in leadership candidates. The theory associated with this belief became known as the *great man theory*. Bass (1990) pointed out that, despite the examples of Joan of Arc, Elizabeth I, and Catherine the Great, most great women were ignored. It is important to realize that this theory resonated with societal beliefs of the era. The mobilization of the military for two world wars and the achievements of the Canadian Pacific Railway proved that success could be attained if a few strong leaders were given authority over a workforce that would follow their direction. The organizational metaphor for the industrial society was the machine; workers were perceived as cogs in the machine while leaders were its designers and operators (Taylor, 1916/2005). As organizations got larger the metaphor morphed from the machine to the factory, which was basically several machines located within a confined space and maintained by a larger labor force working under a hierarchy of leaders. The great man theory was the subject of studies for several years and it continues to impact the selection of principals even today. The research on leadership traits, reviewed by Smith and Kruger (1933) and Jenkins (1947), provided a rich picture of strong leadership but it was unable to identify a consistent list of traits that characterized effective leadership. The mental model that developed was that leaders were born not made. More importantly, this meant that leadership could be emulated but it lacked a curriculum that could be taught.

During the postwar period, leadership experienced the impact of behavioral sciences as researchers (Argyris, 1961; Blake & Mouton, 1964) shifted their focus from personal traits to leadership behaviors and leadership styles. Halpin and Winer (1957) found that 83% of the differences between leaders' behavior could be accounted for by two factors – consideration for employees and the initiation of structures to achieve a task. This finding provided an empirical basis for the development of a leadership curriculum (Hersey & Blanchard, 1969; Reddin, 1970; Zaleznick, 1970) in that the leader's choices and ways of thinking about such choices could presumably be taught and learned. In 1967, Fiedler proposed an alternate theory of leadership. From his studies he determined that a man could be great in one situation but was not necessarily great in another. He saw leadership as a match between the leader's personal traits and the demands of the job. The situational leadership theory explained why a single list of leadership traits was so difficult to find. The metaphor for situational leadership remained the same but, as society became more egalitarian, the theory supported the belief that leadership was more broadly spread across society. The belief in situational leadership also persists today and is often used to explain why hiring committees look for different leadership styles when selecting principals for a city rather than a rural location, or an elementary rather than a high school position.

During this same period, the postwar baby boom forced school districts to build and staff countless new schools. These new schools were often larger and more complex organizations that required better trained administrators. Principals, who were often removed from the classroom to become middle-level managers within larger educational bureaucracies, based their leadership behaviors on successful business practices, and educational authorities adopted the administrative curriculum used by business management programs to prepare the new generation of school principals. Since the administrative curriculum adopted from business focused on organizational management, the measurement of successful principal performance centred on an individual's ability to manage a smoothly operating school.

Transactional and Transformational Leadership

Unlike their industrial management counterparts, principals in many Canadian schools found that they had little input into employment decisions such as hiring, dismissal, or salaries. Without this authority they were limited in their ability to manage effective teacher performance and were forced to adopt a transactional leadership approach to achieve their day-to-day responsibilities. Transactional leadership involves the exchange of resources for the appropriate performance of duties. This was characterized by principals' use of clinical supervision, a deficit model, to identify teacher weakness and prescribe expected improvement. Teachers who performed well received evaluations that would enhance career mobility through promotion; those who did not were documented and recommended for dismissal. The transactional leadership approach did provide the ability for principals to control schools, but it created a we/they mentality that boosted the popularity of teacher unions and increased the importance of teachers' collective agreements.

For more than three decades (1960s-1980s) the transactional approach was the primary leadership model in schools. Its success was based on the superior managerial capacity of principals and the authority vested in them by the hierarchical system. Toward the end of this period all of this changed. The effective schools movement (Edmonds, 1979; Lezotte & Bancroft, 1985) expanded the role of principals from school managers to instructional leaders. The leadership curriculum that had well prepared principals for their management role proved insufficient and, as principals attempted to transact instructional improvement, it became clear that it was impossible to force teachers to improve their instructional performance beyond a minimal competence. Once again schools followed the lead from the business world and adopted a new leadership approach. Successful businesses had learned lessons that schools were just beginning to learn: motivated and passionate employees dramatically outperformed their less motivated counterparts and that transactional management practices were insufficient to provide this motivation. Studies on motivation (Herzberg, 1968/2003) showed that the rewards typically used to encourage employees to work hard were ineffectual in encouraging them to excel. After a point, rewards such as increases in salary might even decrease worker productivity. In contrast to this, job satisfaction, employee pride, and empowerment had no such limiting effects. These factors, however, were not subject to employer-employee transactions and called for a style of leadership that inspired rather than directed improved performance.

The term transformational leadership was coined to describe this new approach. Transformational leadership taps into the employees' pride in their work and takes its name from the efforts that leaders exert to transform employees from followers into leaders. This approach to leadership is particularly powerful in education because, as a historically underpaid group of professionals, teachers had always been motivated by the pride they take in the success of their students. It also resonated with the changing societal perception of teachers as professionals. The rapidly expanding knowledge on both teaching and learning in the latter half of the century had led to a more qualified teacher workforce. This fact combined with the failures resulting from the unreasonable expectation that principals become instructional and curricular exemplars set the stage for a new definition of transformational leadership. Rather than describe a process by which principals transformed teachers, transformational leadership became a term to describe how the sharing of leadership between administrators and the teaching staff transformed schools into better learning environments (Fullan, 2006; Lambert, 1998; Schmoker, 2005).

The importance of knowing the history of school leadership is that it informs us of our unquestioned beliefs about effective leadership. Knowledge of the evolution of leadership provides us with a greater understanding of where the leadership structures that persist in schools came from and why principals behave as they do. It also helps us frame our own beliefs and provides a mirror against which we can reflect the leadership demands of the future.

Leadership in Education

As outlined above the approach to leadership in education parallels changes in the world beyond the school walls. These changes govern the evolution of leadership in education from three dimensions: organizational models of schooling, the purpose of educational leadership, and the leadership style that meets the structural and cultural demands of the times (Figure 1).[1]

Organizational Models of Schooling

The organizational model for schools for much of their existence has been a bureaucratic one. Beairsto (1999) outlines two types of organizational models that co-exist within schools: a machine bureaucracy and a professional bureaucracy. The machine bureaucracy is a remnant of the transformation of society from an autocracy to a democracy. Indeed, the impersonal nature of the machine bureau-

[1] These leadership style categories are explained in detail in Williams (2006).

Figure 1: Dimensions of Leadership in Education

Organizational Model	Leadership Purpose	Leadership Style
• Machine Bureaucracy	• Smooth Operation	• Directive/Behavioral
• Professional Bureaucracy	• Closing Performance Gaps	• Analytical
• Community	• Preparation for a Global Marketplace and Knowledge Society	• Conceptual

cracy, which many people find so offensive today, provided a level playing field for our ancestors. Bureaucracies, even ones as powerful as provincial governments, are still subject to public pressure. Although we entrust each province with the legislative control over education, more than once we have toppled these governments when they acted in a manner that displeased the public. Experience in the 1990s showed that matters dealing with education are commonly associated with that displeasure.

Schools may also be perceived as professional bureaucracies because both entry into teaching and subsequent promotion within the profession are based on the attainment of professional qualifications. Legislative and contractual language not only outlines what these qualifications are, but also the steps to be taken when they are lacking. As with other professions, we rely on formal programs at colleges and universities to maintain the integrity of teaching through their delivery of a curriculum that prepares graduates to enter the workplace. Each province ensures this integrity through a teacher certification process that defines the professional standards required for employment. This means that there is not only a clearly structured organizational system, but teachers must also meet a high standard of professionalism before they enter that system. The professional bureaucracy in education provides both a sense of security and a high degree of satisfaction with the quality of education provided by our schools. However, this security comes with a price because bureaucracies are built upon systems that maintain the status quo. This means that as organizational structures they are at a loss when faced with shifts in paradigms (Cranston, 2003). Bureaucracies are best suited for a stable environment rather than one replete with change. Leadership in the bureaucracy is more akin to management because control and uniformity take precedence over innovation and diversity. Although there are certain bureaucratic aspects of schools that we must retain, we must ask ourselves if we should continue to work from an organizational model and a leadership approach that no longer suit our rapidly changing environment.

Beairsto (1999) proposed a third organizational model for schools that builds upon the professional bureaucracy - the adhocracy. This model has a less rigid leadership approach that provides for shifting of leadership responsibilities according to varying levels of professional expertise. The adhocracy is not an entirely new concept and we are most comfortable with its most common form - the community. The community model recognizes both the commonality and diversity that exist among a group of interdependent individuals. It balances the stability of collectively established norms with the provision of opportunities for change. The move toward the community model for schools is closely aligned with the development of learning organizations in business. In a later section, we will elaborate on this model with reference to the New Brunswick context.

Purpose of Leadership

The purpose of school leadership depends greatly upon the type of organizational model we adopt. The school as a machine bureaucracy required a leader who could guarantee its smooth operation. Indeed, the measure of effective educational leadership prior to the 1980s was whether parents were satisfied with the schools their children attended. Other than the scare precipitated by Russia's launch of Sputnik, large-scale comparisons between schools were rare and the publication of school results was unheard of in most provinces. School reviews, annual reports, and PISA scores (e.g., Organisation for Economic Cooperation and Development, 2007) were not even part of the educational lexicon.

As noted previously, corporate globalization and the impact of technology dramatically has changed the purpose of schools and their leadership. The research into effective schools identified the extent to which schools differed from each other. Schools that were deemed effective became the benchmarks for those that were not. The purpose of school leadership shifted from keeping students' parents satisfied to closing the educational performance gap across each province. Politicians forecasted the dire consequences that underperforming schools would have on the economic stability of our nation. Governments in Ontario, Alberta, and New Brunswick embarked on centralized strategies to make schools the engines for economic success. As a consequence, leadership turned its focus to the improvement of school outcomes and the achievement of high standards became the measure of leadership success. The restructuring efforts by government held the potential to raise standards, but politicians who embraced a directive leadership approach seemed to doubt the professionals' motivation and capacity. At a time when the professional bureaucracy should have been ascendant, the political will in some provinces undermined teachers' potential to lead. Educational change in these provinces during the 1990s in many ways reflected the antithesis of what research supported as effective practice (Fullan, 1991).

The purpose of school leadership entered a new phase as the 1990s closed. The standards-based approach with its focus on top-down control had failed to produce the expected results and there was a general recognition that educational leadership had to change. This change, while continuing to support improved student achievement, focused on leadership that improved learning rather than teaching. As the leadership approach shifted from telling teachers how to teach to consulting with them about how to improve learning, the role of teachers in sharing leadership grew. At present, the primary purpose of school leadership is to mobilize staffs to work together to create a synergistic culture of co-learning and to build leadership as a school-wide capacity (Sackney & Mitchell, 2005; Sackney & Walker, 2006). Principals are being encouraged to share their leadership roles with teachers and to tap into the professional expertise that had been previously ignored (Anderson, 2002).

Alignment of Leadership Styles with Structures and Culture

The structure and culture of the educational systems in most provinces were significantly impacted by the reduction in the number of school districts and the amalgamation of small schools into larger schools that occurred in the 1960s. Although the entire system became more organizationally complex, the hierarchical structure remained relatively unchanged at both the school and the district levels. As units were amalgamated and the concentration of leadership positions increased, the linear chain of command survived intact. In most people's minds, the leadership style that best suited the changing situation in schools was a directive one. As staffs expanded and resources poured into the construction of new schools, districts looked for principals who were up to the task of directing school dynamics. Hiring committees relied on a combination of trait and situational theories of leadership when selecting new principals. Principal in-service and university coursework highlighted the skills and theory of effective management.

Two decades later, as principals were adopting their new role as instructional leaders, the focus on management training for school leaders gave way to the recognition that principals required a new set of skills. The complexity of the newly articulated responsibilities placed principals in the added role of curriculum coordinator and instructional supervisor within the building. The preference for the directive style for principals that worked so well in the less complex school environment shifted to an analytical leadership style (Williams, 2006). This style persisted until a growing belief surfaced that, contrary to all the efforts by provincial leaders, schools were still not performing effectively.

The restructuring reform of the 1990s – with its emphasis on centralized authority and decentralized responsibility – brought back a directive leadership style at the highest provincial levels. Expectations that standards would be achieved by edict and that hierarchical control could produce the professional collaboration necessary for school improvement characterized the new leadership mentality. In the provinces that adopted this directive leadership mentality the changes in structure worked counter to the development of an innovative school culture. For nearly a decade, many principals were adrift and more than a few reverted to the comfort of the directively managed school and the protection of their union. Now, after a decade of centralized authority's failure to achieve significant improvement in student results, many provinces are embarking on a different leadership approach – a transformational approach that underlies a learning community.

Leadership after 2000 has shifted to a transformational approach. Recognition of the complexity of not only the structure of schools but also the professional culture that defined teaching made it clear that, as Wheatley (1997) argued, "you can't direct people into perfection, you can only engage them enough so that they want to do perfect work" (p. 25). She went on to say that in times of complex change we need self-organizing systems built upon trust rather than control and that leadership must focus on "helping everyone stay clear on what we wanted to accomplish and who we wanted to be" (p. 25).

The leadership style most suited for building trust in the transformational model of schools as communities is one that balances both task and people orientation (Reddin, 1970), is capable of motivating teachers to excel (Herzberg, 1968/2003), and promotes meaningful collaboration (Williams, 2006). This is the leadership style that Beairsto (1999) describes as adhocratic, Fullan (1991) calls moral, and Williams (2006) depicts as conceptual.

The Changing Model of Leadership for School Reform

The quintessential role of leadership is to improve organizational performance. During each phase of its development the educational system has adapted to the changes in society in order to improve schools. To do so, educational leadership has adopted the successful attributes of leadership from business to accommodate the evolving structure and culture of schools. Our aspirations for creating successful schools for the twenty-first century hinge on our understanding the interplay between the shifting demands on educational leadership and the relative success we have experienced with school reforms in the past.

Demands on Educational Leadership

Any significant attempt at school reform must examine leadership not only at the school but the district and provincial levels as well (Fullan, Rolheiser, Mascall, & Edge, 2001). The varied forces at work at each of these levels drive quite different leadership styles. Provincial leadership focuses its energy on defining educational goals and relies extensively on a strategic planning model within a political context. The forces driving leadership decisions are political, financial, and interdepartmentally competitive. The goal of school reform is to produce measurable improvement in student achievement within the term of office of the party in power. Long-term leadership, while important, often gives way to demands for short-term results. In a system as complex as education, this often translates into well-intended but poorly executed reform initiatives. School districts inherit provincial goals that may or may not support or reinforce their own leadership goals. District leaders must therefore balance the need to maintain ongoing efforts that promise to produce long-term improvement with the need to align their actions with ever changing provincial directives. The forces that drive district-level leadership derive from a more local context of the communities they serve. District leaders are directed by strategic plans from the provincial bureaucracy, guided by publicly elected officials of the community, and confined by budgetary restrictions and the collective agreements of various unions. Districts are also in closer communication with, and are more accountable to, their schools. Schools form a third and also different level of leadership. While they are subject to forces from both the provincial and district levels, principals are faced with a very different leadership dynamic. They perform their leadership roles amid a situation where hundreds of people are playing out the reality of schooling. Like teachers, they are on the *front lines* of the educational system and must survive the vagaries of the continuous cycle of externally imposed change while maintaining an orderly place that is conducive to learning. Twice each year they face hundreds of parents and are held accountable for their actions. The forces upon principals are so numerous and diverse that few districts have been able to even delineate a principal's job.

As shown in Table 1, several factors combined to impact the leadership necessary for successful school reform during the past hundred years. The purpose of schools shifted as economic and social spheres expanded from a local to a global perspective. The source of leadership for educational reform expanded commensurately with this change in perspective. Research in effective leadership had an impact on the approach that leaders employed to achieve reform. Finally, an increasingly qualified teacher workforce raised the expectations on the quality of the leadership being provided.

Table 1: Changing Demands on School Leadership

	Pre-1960	1960s & 1970s	1980s	1990s	Post-2000
Reform Initiative	n/a	School constructions, district amalgamation	Effective schools	Restructuring	Learning Organizations
Purpose of Schools	Preparation for local jobs and college	Preparation for post-high school careers	Maximize the education of *all* students†	Prepare students for lifelong learning	Prepare students for lifelong learning and multiple careers
Source of Reform Leadership	Community Boards, Superintendents, Principals	Regional Boards, Provincial Leadership Associations‡	Provincial Departments, Provincial Leadership Associations‡	Provincial Departments, Provincial Leadership Associations‡, CMEC*	Provincial Departments, Provincial Leadership Associations‡, CMEC*
Leadership Approach	Transactional	Transactional	Transactional & Transformational	Transactional & Transformational	Transformational & Transactional
Minimal Teacher Preparation	One year of normal school	Two years of Teachers College	Four-year education degree	Undergraduate degree plus two-year education degree	Undergraduate degree plus two-year education degree

† Education for all students focused on the inclusion of special-needs children as well as multicultural populations.

‡ Provincial leadership associations include teacher associations, as well as professional associations of superintendents and learning specialists/school supervisors.

* Council of Ministers of Education, Canada

Impact of Leadership on School Reform

School reform consists of more than the first-order changes (Fullan, 1991; Uline, 2001) that accompany the adoption of a new curriculum or the redistribution of grades or schools across districts. True reform occurs when the educational system experiences second-order change. Examples of this order can be seen in two large-scale reform initiatives: the effective schools movement of the 1980s and school restructuring movement of 1990s. The true test of leadership effectiveness lies in an analysis of the success of these two reforms.

The effective schools reform met with some success in elementary schools because its goal for principals was achievable. Elementary principals who had experience as classroom teachers brought to the job a working knowledge of the curriculum across the range of subjects. In this situation, it was far more realistic to expect a principal to be familiar with the school-wide curriculum and instructional practices and, hence, to be able to provide teachers with instructional leadership. At the next two levels of the system, in junior high/middle schools and high schools, the situation was different. The diversity of subjects taught and the increasingly difficult and broader content combined with the typically larger school size meant that principals had to attain much more curricular expertise and provide instructional leadership to far more teachers. The situational complexity at these two levels was compounded by the very different behavioral challenges associated with older students and reduced involvement of parents. Two other situational concerns also plagued the effective schools research. Much of the research that identified the tenets of effective schools was conducted in elementary school situations and then extrapolated to other situational levels of the system. Furthermore, while the research was successful in identifying what contributed to school effectiveness, it failed to determine how effective situations had been achieved (Purkey & Smith, 1983).

The school restructuring movement of the 1990s was predicated on the centralization of authority for school change with the decentralization of responsibility for its achievement. It was based on a combination of total quality and site-based management principles. The centralized authority component depended greatly on the great person theory of leadership because the control of the reform rested in the hands of a few key individuals. The dismal record of restructuring efforts during the 1990s pointed to the fact that there were no great leaders who understood the educational system. Also, many of the failures were a result of attempting to mandate rather than facilitate educational change (Hargreaves, 2003). Provincial leaders failed to understand that the links between government offices and schools, and between the school office and the classrooms, were tenuous at best (Weick, 1976). The transactional efforts that epitomized the restructuring movement in New Brunswick represented a prime example of its ineffectiveness as a leadership approach. After dissolving school boards and creating a direct chain of command all the way from the school principals' to the premier's office, the efforts of Premier Frank McKenna to achieve improvement in student literacy were unproductive (McKenna, 1999).

Many of the ideas and goals that characterized the effective schools and school restructuring movements were very commendable. What we find, however, is that large-scale reform even with the best of intentions is extremely difficult to achieve. We argue that by failing to fully understand education as a complex system, educational leaders not only limited the success of these two reforms, but they also prevented educators from improving Canadian education. A better understanding of organizational models and the limitations of leadership styles might have led to better results. As we enter the new century, a third wave of large-scale school reform is emerging, one that will demand far greater changes in the leadership approach that currently exists at each level of the educational system. As we move forward with the development of professional learning communities for our educational model, we must use our knowledge of leadership theory and practice and do a better job at redefining educational leadership in Canada.

Educational Purpose of the Twenty-First Century

Why do schools exist? This is a question that haunts our profession but has never been resolved. The philosophical debate surrounds two somewhat conflicting purposes of either perpetuating the past or creating the future. Those who support the former argue that schools exist to ensure the survival of great literature and art, scientific breakthroughs, and the history of mankind's struggle. A focus on the perpetuation of historic achievements fits well within a model of school as an academy and the bureaucratic values of maintaining all that is best from the past. Individuals who support the latter perspective argue that schools are important vehicles for changing society and should be designed to promote creativity and innovation. A focus on creating the future means constantly questioning well-established values and making way for new practices. For some, it calls into question the need for the very existence of schools in their current form (Abbott & MacTaggart, 2008). Pragmatists' arguments for the purpose of schools see these two philosophical perspectives as complementary. They argue that we cannot ignore the reality of the impact of rapid change on society nor can we diminish the value of learning from all that was best from our past. Nowhere is this argument more important than in the field of leadership. Changing purposes and contexts call for a new organizational paradigm, a redefinition of educational leadership, and a reconsideration of the education of teacher leaders.

New Organizational Paradigm

Beairsto (1999) captured the paradigm shift in leadership by examining the evolution of schools from the *machine of professional bureaucracies* to their current manifestation as *organic moral communities*. Although his analysis of the changing demands upon public education argued for a new model for schools, he recognized the value of both forms of bureaucracies and the continued importance of the principal as the school leader. His conception of the principal, however, is very different from the heroic instructional leader espoused by proponents of the effective schools reform (Edmonds, 1979; Lezotte, Edmonds, & Ratner, 1974).

The recognition of schools as organic systems rather than factories is a far more complex shift than most people comprehend. An organic systems perspective runs counter to the positivistic mentality that has permeated educational organizations in Canada for decades, and the community model differs dramatically from the mechanistic factory model upon which many schools currently operate. This means that the organizational and leadership paradigms that define schooling must be substantially redefined.

In 1990, Peter Senge captured the essence of the systems paradigm in his groundbreaking book *The Fifth Discipline: The Art and Practice of the Learning Organization.* His fifth discipline, which repositions organizations as complex systems, is credited with redefining the essence of both private and public organizations. Stated simply, a systems approach posits that organizations must be treated as a whole rather than as a series of individual parts. Together with his first four disciplines – personal mastery, mental models, shared vision, and team learning – Senge redefined educational as well as corporate leadership. In his second book, which focused specifically on schools as learning organizations, Senge and his colleagues (2000) argued that, since knowledge and learning are living systems, teachers' beliefs and values about the nature of schooling are part of that system. He called for a change in what he termed the hard-to-see patterns of relationships among people. Foremost among these relationships are those that exist between school administrators and teachers – whether it is one of principal control over or collaboration with teachers. The changes associated with the adoption of a learning organization, commonly referred to in education as a professional learning community (Hord, 1997), represent what Fullan (1991) and Uline (2001) termed a second-order change. While first order changes improve the efficiency of current practices, a second order change fundamentally redesigns both the organization's structure and culture. If schools become professional learning communities, the hierarchical authority based relationship between principals and teachers must be replaced with a collaborative relationship characterized by co-learning interdependence among professionals. For this to be successful, we must revisit our mental model of school leadership because leadership figures as the most significant set of beliefs and values within schools.

Redefinition of Educational Leadership

Our position has been that leadership behaviors result from the beliefs and assumptions that we rely on even when we are not consciously aware of them. Senge (1990/2007) refers to these deeply ingrained assumptions and generalizations as mental models and he argues that they strongly influence how we perceive reality and play an important role in every decision we make. He cautions that because we are often not conscious of the mental models that guide our actions, it is incumbent on us to consciously examine what we too often take for granted as real or true. This is particularly pertinent when we examine the concept of leadership. Many who write about leadership combine it with management to form the collective term – administration (Beairsto, 1999; Hersey & Blanchard, 1988). In fact, principals are more commonly referred to as school administrators rather than school leaders. If we examine the mental model of school administration over several decades, however, we find very little that can be considered leadership and much that is more aligned with school management. Indeed, Webster's dictionary clearly defines administration as a management practice, not a leadership one: to administer is to manage or direct, where managing is a process used "to exercise control over" or to "influence someone so that he does as one wishes" (*New Lexicon Webster's Encyclopedic Dictionary*, 1988, p. 605). This mental model of the principal as an administrator has given rise to a job description that is predominantly one of control over teachers' actions.

The term principal derives from the title "principal teacher," the member of a staff who, as schools became larger and school districts were amalgamated, was charged with completing the paperwork for the school. As expectations on principals grew, their role as principal teachers shifted to that of school administrators and their relationship with teachers took on more of a control rather than a collegial interaction. Principals assumed direction on matters pertaining to structural issues such as teacher assignments, bell schedules, and the oversight of school finances. Pedagogically, principals managed the curriculum being taught, the supervision of teachers' instructional practices, and even the manner by which student achievement was assessed. Today, in some provinces, principals have been removed from the teacher associations and designated as members of the management team. It is this managerial role within which principals as school administrators operate that reinforces the bureaucratic chain of command and colors the relationship between themselves and teachers. It is this mental model that impacts many decisions that principals make.

We would argue that the traditional approach used by many school administrators does not constitute leadership. While some authors portray administration as a leadership function they continue to use a management mental model and describe the principal as a transactional leader (Stewart, 2006). We argue that transactional leadership is akin to control-centred management. Transactional principals exert control over teachers by rewarding effective teachers with recommendations for continuing contracts, more abundant resources, and opportunities for promotion. Less effective teachers are subjected to more frequent performance evaluations, documentation, and the threat of dismissal.

If we return to Webster's dictionary to examine how leadership is defined, we see a very different picture. A leader is defined as a person who "acts as a guide" or "who leads a group," and to lead is to "show the way to go by accompanying someone" or to "cause or persuade someone to do or believe something, or follow one's example" (p. 561). This characterization of leadership is more aligned with the concept of transformational leadership that we find in the literature (e.g., Leithwood, 2007; Stewart, 2006). Since a transformational principal leads by example rather than control, transformational leadership represents a vastly different mental model for the principalship. Transformational principals guide by example and assist teachers in assuming leadership roles that enhance their performance as teachers. Foster and St. Hilaire (2003) described this as sharing leadership while Lambert (1998) referred to these behaviors as building leadership capacity within the school staff. Transformational principals become leaders of leaders, who ultimately promote leadership not only among teachers but also among students, parents, and within the greater school community.

The history of school reform has taught us how important it is to *surface* our mental models of leadership and assess their appropriateness as we move into a third wave of second-order educational change. This is a process that is difficult to perform once we have become encultured within our profession. One way to encourage educators to examine mental models would be to focus on *reflection on action* as part of the programs we use to educate teachers and teacher leaders.

Education of Teacher Leaders

The education of teachers and by extension the preparation of teacher leaders has changed dramatically in the past fifty years. Table 1 shows that teacher education over that period increased from a single year of teacher training at a normal school (teachers' college) to six years of university education. A comparable increase in the professional qualifications of principals occurred as well. Principal selection in the 1960s was based predominantly on individual traits rather than professional coursework. With the increasing complexity of 1970s came expectations for principals to have graduate degrees that provided them with the managerial skills required to administer larger schools. The 1980s brought new expectations for principals to be instructional leaders, which were addressed by the introduction of curriculum-based programs at the graduate level. While the restructuring movement added few academic expectations, it did cement the practice of requiring principals to be certified as administrators. This translated into a requirement for coursework in administrative theory, curriculum theory, and supervision of instruction.

The current movement by schools to become professional learning communities will require even further changes in teacher and teacher leader education programs (Foster & St. Hilaire, 2003). The most significant change in both undergraduate and graduate programs will be a shift from a competitive to a collaborative approach for student work. This shift, which is fundamental in preparing university graduates for the collaborative culture of learning communities, will see student schedules based on a cohort rather than individualistic model. At the undergraduate level, this will be accompanied by an increase in team project work and opportunities for problem-based learning. The curriculum for methodology and assessment courses will model team collaboration for lesson planning, formative assessment, and the delivery of learning intervention strategies. The most challenging change will take place during the professional practicum when university-school partnerships provide teacher interns with collaborative opportunities during their initial classroom placements.

At the graduate level, the cultural shift to prepare teachers for their role in professional learning communities will be reflected in an emphasis on action research and assignments that embed academic learning in the ongoing professional development of practicing teachers. Curriculum in programs for principal preparation will balance the emphasis between managerial and leadership theory. The focus will shift from doing things right to doing the right things the right way. The most challenging change at the graduate level will be the redefinition of educational leadership. According to Cooner and Quinn (2008), the knowledge and skills needed by twenty-first-century principals will be as leaders of curricular change, data-driven decision-making, innovative and diversified instructional strategies, and the use of accountability models for staff and students. The line between programs in educational administration and curriculum and instruction will blur as students in both specialty areas take on the task of building leadership capacity for schools. Given the call for newer forms of leadership in schools, teacher educators have a central role to play in promoting, modeling, and critiquing leadership for change (Castle, 2001).

Another important change in teacher and teacher leader education will occur at the university – school classroom interface. The traditional perception underlying the professional bureaucracy is that university programs are discrete educational experiences that occur outside of public education. Even the practicum, which provides teacher interns with the practical experiences of the classroom, is perceived as an antecedent to becoming a professional. These perceptions are relics of the positivistic linear bureaucracy that has defined teacher and teacher leader education for a century (Lemisko, Griffith, & Cutright, 2001). In professional learning communities there is no separation between university preparation for the profession and the on-going improvement of classroom practices in schools (Dibbon, 2006). If we are to realize the potential of reflection on practice and continuous inquiry that separate professional learning communities from educational bureaucracies, there must be a closer relationship between universities and public education and a more effective alignment between what teachers learn and how they teach (Laferrière et al., 2001). The artificial separation between public schools and universities is no less a barrier to improving schools than the structural separations that exist within and between levels of provincial education systems.

View from New Brunswick

Leadership reform in education in New Brunswick in recent decades reflects the evolving views of leadership described earlier. As a small province, there has been a tradition of hierarchical and centralized control of the public education system. However, in the past decade, there have been initiatives taken at various levels of the system that reflect a move towards a new organizational and leadership culture. In this section, we will review the sharply contrasting leadership approaches of the 1990s with those of this decade, and describe some ongoing research on educational leadership for reform in New Brunswick.

Leadership in the 1990s

Attempts to restructure education in New Brunswick peaked during the period from 1989 to 1999 during Premier McKenna's term of office. As a strong proponent of education's capacity to invigorate and sustain the economic and social future of New Brunswickers, McKenna adopted centrally mandated educational reforms driven by an outcomes-based approach and measured by highly visible, standardized achievement testing. He was able to do this because New Brunswick already had the most centrally controlled provincial system of education in Canada (Bezeau, 2000). Centralization in New Brunswick began in the mid-1960s when the "Equal Opportunity" program of Premier Louis Robichaud emasculated local school boards by transferring all control over financial, transportation, and property matters to the provincial government. Thirty years later, the McKenna government abolished school boards completely, replacing them with elected school and district councils, all of which served primarily in advisory capacities (*An Act to Amend the Schools Act*, 1996, as cited in Bezeau). The day-to-day management of the schools, districts, and provincial department of education was streamlined to the point that all educational administrators were directly responsible to the premier. Professional associations of district supervisors and superintendents were dissolved and principals, who had long ago lost their professional councils, were forced to accept five-year term appointments (New Brunswick Teachers' Federation, 1997, s. 29.05). During his final years as premier, McKenna had an unprecedented degree of control over the province's schools and should have been able to achieve his intended reforms. Shortly after leaving power, however, McKenna (1999), while speaking at a national collegium of work and learning, lamented: "The school system in our province and across Canada on this issue [literacy] is little short of a national disgrace." Why then, did McKenna's reforms aimed at better preparing students for work in an information society fail? The answer lies in something other than adequate control over the existing educational bureaucracy – it lies in the manner in which the bureaucracy itself operates.

The bureaucratic structures and systems within which New Brunswick schools operate are based on a technical-rational perspective (Ogawa & Bossert, 2000). From this perspective, the metaphor for schools is the factory, authority is hierarchical, and individuals are both defined and restricted by their roles and relationships in a chain of command (Mintzberg, 1979). According to Sackney and Mitchell (2005), the traditional organization of schools is grounded in a mechanistic and bureaucratic worldview in which clearly defined roles are entrenched: administrators lead, teachers teach, and students learn (p. 276). Senge and his colleagues (2000), examining the persistence of technical-rational traditions in schools, commented that they "were the starkest example in modern society of an entire institution modeled after the assembly line," (p. 30) governed in an "authoritarian manner oriented above all else to producing a standardized product" (p. 31). His further observation is more reflective of the barriers this perspective presents. He noted that when pressured to reform, the "factory" responded the only way it knew how – by doing what it had always done, but harder!

The record of educational change in New Brunswick during the 1990s shows that reform efforts that were primarily top-down were unsuccessful in engaging teacher effort toward excellence (Williams, 2006). Mandate-based reform failed to consider the complexity of schools and the reality of classrooms, a failure that Senge and his colleagues (2000) argued has prevented school reform for decades. The failure of reform stemmed not from a lack of passion or positive intentions, but from a failure to examine our mental models, those underlying beliefs that define our culture and color our perspectives of reality. Political leaders who rely primarily on plans and policies to promote educational excellence would do well to heed Wheatley (1997) when she argues for the use of goals rather than "intricate directions, time lines, plans and organizational charts" (p. 6), stating that leaders who honor and trust the people who work with them "have unleashed startlingly high levels of productivity and creativity" (p. 4).

Current Leadership for School Reform

The government of New Brunswick continues to share McKenna's belief that schools hold the key to a more prosperous future. The approach being used, however, differs radically from the top-down mandates of the past. In 2002, the New Brunswick Department of Education initiated a process of transforming schools from teaching-focused bureaucracies to learning-focused communities (Williams, 2006). A year later, Hargreaves (2003) introduced the province's educational leaders to the concept of the professional learning community. This was followed by a mutually spearheaded effort by school districts and the provincial department to provide senior leadership with an understanding of professional learning communities.

During the ensuing five years several hundred educational leaders from schools, district offices, and the provincial department have attended sessions that provided both theoretical background and practical support required to adopt a professional learning community model for schooling. In its continuing effort to promote learning organizations, New Brunswick hosted an educational summit in August 2008 for another thousand educators.

The most recent education plan of the New Brunswick government, entitled *When Kids Come First*, recognizes the importance of collaboration at the school level and encourages the expansion of the professional learning concept throughout the K-12 system (Province of New Brunswick, 2007b). Current reform in New Brunswick can best be described as a combined top-down, bottom-up effort that merges the effective aspects of each. The progress made during the previous Progressive Conservative government (1999-2006) indicated that sustainable reform occurred when top-down leadership and support were combined with bottom-up engagement and accountability (Province of New Brunswick, 2007a). In *When Kids Come First*, the current government indicates that it is striving to maintain a balance between top-down and bottom-up approaches by its focus on teacher innovation and school accountability. As with any government initiative, however, success will depend on how well the provincial policy makers understand the culture of the system they are attempting to change. One of the most important lessons from past educational reforms is that changes in structures and policies alone are insufficient to change the organizational culture of schools (DuFour, 1998; Elmore, 1995; Honig, 2003).

New Brunswick's new education plan (Province of New Brunswick, 2007b) calls for significant changes in the way schools operate. Teachers and principals who were prepared, hired, and evaluated for their capacity to follow well-defined curricula and who have worked in relative isolation without questioning central authority are being asked to become entrepreneurs of educational excellence. The cultural shift required to accomplish this change is monumental. It is a shift that strips away the security of working independently, following prescribed curriculum, and relying on traditional practices. The intentions articulated in the plan to "create a culture that makes leaders of outstanding teachers and principals" (p. 19) and to support "innovative projects led by teachers and school teams" (p. 19) will demand more than a belief "in our people on the front lines of learning" (p. 19) and more than the "opportunity and resources to share best practices" (p. 19). This vision must be accompanied by a deeper understanding of the cultural constraints of the previous system that prevent collaboration, innovation, and mutual accountability. While many of these constraints are localized within the school, those that exist at all levels of the system must also be considered.

Perhaps the greatest challenge that must be addressed is the lack of organizational trust that teachers have in the educational system (Hoy & Kupersmith, 1985). The cultural changes proposed in the New Brunswick government's education plan must therefore be informed by the literature on organizational trust. Deming (1993, as cited by MacNeil, Spuck, & Ceyanes, 1998) wrote, "Trust is mandatory for the optimization of a system. Without trust there cannot be cooperation between people, teams, departments, or divisions" (p. 3). As Fukuyama (1995) noted, "a high trust [organization] can organize its workplace on a more flexible and group oriented basis . . . low trust [organizations], by contrast, must fence in and isolate their workers with a series of bureaucratic rules" (p. 31). The evidence that schools have been operated as low trust organizations is far more apparent than the converse. It would be wise for the architects of the current plan to reflect on how the traditional school organization has conditioned teachers.

The broadly embraced standards-based reforms of the 1990s are testimony to the lack of trust government had in teachers (Cohen, 1995). Raising academic standards was a simplistic answer to improving student achievement and, although this solution created as many problems as it solved, assumptions were made that success was achievable if teachers would just take responsibility and work together to raise standards. It was this form of mandated collaboration that Hargreaves (1991) appropriately coined *contrived collegiality*. In a more recent study connecting teacher collaboration and school improvement, Slater (2004) warned of the consequences of contrived collegiality: "Collaborative activity that was imposed by others often resulted in participants expressing feelings of frustration, betrayal, uselessness, cynicism, disappointment, pain and anger" (p. 5). Slater found, however, that teachers would work together and contribute their time and energy to improve schools if they felt that they were making a difference in the education of children. This is precisely what the current New Brunswick plan intends to accomplish with its vision of teachers working together "to make the sharing of good ideas second nature in our system" (Province of New Brunswick, 2007b, p. 19). Vision-based intentions are a beginning, but cultural change requires action. Perhaps the most far-reaching action proposed in the plan centres on transforming schools into learning organizations. Honoring its commitment to enhance quality teaching, the plan "ensure[s] the professional learning communities concept is expanded throughout the K-12 system" (p. 14). We believe that the collaboration embodied in this approach can become the engine that generates teacher innovation.

The implementation of the learning community concept is, however, more than a simple strategy to promote quality teaching. It represents an essential understanding that the alignment of intention and reality requires a shift to the professional learning culture and leadership practices in New Brunswick schools. This understanding builds on several years of collaboration among provincial, district, and school leaders to create the level of trust required to transform the systemic culture toward a community model. Since 2003, key provincial leaders have been working to inform, encourage, and support a move toward professional learning communities. Although still at a preliminary stage in many schools, the evolution towards learning communities represents an excellent example of how top-down and bottom-up initiatives can be successfully combined to shift school culture in meaningful ways. It is a process that has eschewed mandated change by relying instead on a trust-based emergent model for achieving common goals.

Researching Leadership in New Brunswick

In spite of encouraging research elsewhere and the provincial government's espoused support for the adoption of professional learning communities in schools, concerns about leadership practices in New Brunswick schools persisted. The genesis of our study occurred when Morehouse and Tranquilla (2005) unveiled the findings of the province's school review process. Their report showed serious concerns with school leadership and the overall teaching and learning processes in schools, both of which could be improved through greater professional collaboration. This report coupled with a study of principal leadership styles (Williams, 1997) led to an investigation as to why principals who favored a collaborative leadership style were not fostering collaboration within their schools. This result was due in part to the frustration principals have expressed when, on one hand, they are expected to be collaborative with their staffs while, on the other, they are given little input into directives originating at the district and provincial levels. After three years of effort to transform schools into learning communities the provincial results showed that most schools had changed very little. Principals continued to model their leadership practices on those that persisted at the upper levels of the system because, while goals and expectations for schools had changed, the policies and practices in district offices and in the provincial department of education had remained the same (Williams, 2006).

Subsequent conversations with the assistant deputy minister and other colleagues regarding the impact of educational policies and practices on school reform efforts prompted a system-wide examination of the provincial educational system. Following Fullan's (2005) call for tri-level educational reform, we argue that the implementation of professional learning communities is being hindered because education reform tends to focus only on the school level. If district and provincial education officials truly wish to transform schools into learning communities, educational reform initiatives and research need to move beyond the school as the primary unit of change (Louis, Toole, & Hargreaves, 1999). The success of the current reform depends upon changing the leadership culture throughout the system (Anderson, 2002). *Institutional Barriers to Tri-level Educational Reform*, a study begun in 2006 and jointly funded by Social Sciences and Humanities Research Council (SSHRC) and the New Brunswick Department of Education, set out to develop instruments that could measure barriers at the school, district, and provincial levels that prevented the implementation of professional learning communities.

We have reported elsewhere on the creation of assessment instruments for the school level (Williams, Brien, Sprague, & Sullivan, 2008) and the district level (Brien & Williams, 2008) as well as preliminary results from 50 schools that used the school instrument to assess their professional learning community readiness (Williams, Brien, & LeBlanc, 2008). These instruments were designed for use as tools to help the educators at a school or within a district to identify strengths and barriers affecting their readiness to operate as learning communities. Included in our instruments were survey items related specifically to leadership practices at the school and district levels. The range of responses to these items reflects the evolving nature of educational leadership described earlier.

School-Level Research

Our school-level instrument was developed by working with teams of teachers at four schools in two New Brunswick school districts (Williams, Brien, Sprague, & Sullivan, 2008). Based upon our review of the literature and our work with the school teams, we proposed four main themes for our school instrument: culture, leadership, teaching, and professional growth and development. Within the leadership section, we chose five key statements about leadership at the school level:

- School leadership in this school is grounded in effective organizational practices.
- Building the leadership capacity among both teachers and support staff reinforces learning for both teachers and students in this school.
- The sharing of leadership strengthens the leadership capacity of this school.
- Decisions in this school are based on careful analysis of school-based data on student performance.
- Decisions regarding resource allocation are made by those most involved in their use.

Each of these statements was measured using three or four specific survey items presented with a five-point Likert scale for responses. Written descriptors were provided for responses 1, 3, and 5 of each item to increase instrument validity. In general, the descriptors for response choice 1 represented traditional bureaucratic leadership styles, while the descriptors for response choice 5 represented the collaborative, shared leadership practices associated with professional learning communities. We will describe the instrument items used for each statement and we will also report on the findings from our initial use of the school instrument with fifty New Brunswick schools (Williams, Brien, & LeBlanc, 2008).

With respect to effective organizational practices at the school, our research led to three survey items for our instrument. We asked about the extent to which the school had a vision that guided decision-making. The second item measured the degree of coordination between classroom operations and the work of teachers in the school. The third item provided respondents with the opportunity to indicate whether their energy was expended mostly on preserving the status quo, reacting to external pressures, or identifying and pursuing their own goals. In our study of fifty schools responding to these items, the majority of teachers in 46% of the New Brunswick schools indicated their school leadership was grounded in effective organizational practices (Williams, Brien, & LeBlanc, 2008). Respondents in 68% of schools reported that they had a vision that directed decision-making. Classroom operations and teachers' work were clearly coordinated in 38% of schools and in 30% teacher energy was expended in the proactive pursuit of their own goals. In these schools, the majority of teachers (>60%) were collaborating and working together on strategies to achieve teacher-developed goals that reinforced the school vision.

The second statement in the leadership section of our school instrument was associated with the building of leadership capacity among school personnel to reinforce learning for teachers and students. As described earlier, the shift from the traditional bureaucratic and transactional leadership styles towards transformational leadership requires the intentional development of leadership capacity among the teachers and support staff in a school rather than the concentration of leadership in the hands of one great leader or a few key people. Our research suggested three appropriate survey items dealing with the extent to which leadership was distributed among staff members, the degree to which teachers possessed expertise in collaborative skills, and the amount of input that school personnel contributed in the selection of a new principal. We found that, in 20% of the schools studied, a majority of teachers reported that efforts to build leadership capacity reinforced learning among teachers and students (Williams, Brien, & LeBlanc, 2008). This was due mainly to the fact that in 40% of schools a majority of teachers shared leadership responsibility. Leadership capacity was impacted to a lesser degree by the level of teacher expertise in collaborative skills (12%) and teachers' ability to impact the selection of a new principal (6%). This last statistic is important because it was reported by a majority of teachers in 52% of schools as a significant barrier to the development of professional learning communities. When staff are excluded from the principal selection process their efforts for school improvement are devalued, often reducing their engagement and in some situations fostering a counter-culture that subverts the sharing of leadership. More importantly, the practice of making principal appointments without staff input undermines the smooth transition of the new principal and threatens the sustainability of the overall reform processes within the school.

The practice of shared leadership is related to the building of leadership capacity among a school staff. As noted earlier, the sharing of leadership is a means of strengthening the leadership capacity within a school (e.g., Foster & St. Hilaire, 2003; Lambert, 1998). Our survey items probed for the extent to which principals collaborated with teachers on pedagogical and school policy matters, as well as the willingness among teachers to participate in decision-making on school-wide issues. In our study, respondents indicated a high degree of shared leadership (Williams, Brien, & LeBlanc, 2008). In 64% of the schools, a majority of teachers indicated that principals frequently collaborated with staff on matters pertaining to both pedagogical and policy matters. In the same percentage of schools the majority of teachers indicated a consistent choice to participate in decision-making on school-wide issues.

The fourth leadership statement dealt with the use of data in decision-making. In the learning community approach to schooling, the purposeful and effective collection, analysis, and use of data is a key component (e.g., DuFour, 2004). While the bureaucratic model of leadership thrived on stability and standardized decision-making practices, the complexity of today's school environment demands that leaders pay close attention to changing circumstances by collecting and responding to relevant data to inform decision-making. Our survey items on this topic probed for the extent to which teachers used school-based and external data to inform decision-making and whether a lack of expertise in data handling represented a barrier to data-based decision-making. In 44% of the schools, the majority of teachers indicated that they gathered and analyzed school data to inform their decision-making. More than 60% of teachers in twenty-five of the schools were able to access external data in a timely manner. Notwithstanding the availability of student data, teachers in only 30% of schools indicated its high use when making instructional decisions. This may be due to the indication that only 40% of schools were able to overcome the barrier created by the lack of expertise among staff to analyze data (Williams, Brien, & LeBlanc, 2008).

The final school leadership statement referred to the often contentious issue of resource allocation. Consistent with the understandings of shared decision-making described earlier, those most involved in the use of resources need to be involved in these decisions. Of course, as noted earlier, it can be difficult for leaders to relinquish control over resources, especially those operating from a transactional perspective, since the allocation of frequently scarce resources is often the only effective control mechanism available to some principals. Shared leadership demands a high level of organizational trust, a quality that takes time and deliberate effort to build in schools. We chose decision-making practices regarding resources such as purchasing, the teaching timetable, and the assignment of non-teaching staff as proxies for the trust between school administrators and the staff (Williams, Brien, & LeBlanc, 2008). Our results showed that, while in over 40% of schools the majority of teachers indicated that the purchase of resource materials was a collaborative process, only 30% of the schools had a majority of teachers who were actively encouraged to be part of the teacher timetabling process. This figure dropped to 12% when it came to collaboration on non-teaching staff assignments.

The data gathered from a study of fifty schools indicated that readiness levels for schools to adopt a professional learning approach for instructional decision-making, while not uniformly high, was far more positive than that portrayed by the surveys conducted by Morehouse and Tranquilla (2005). Interestingly, first-level analysis of the data indicated district-based differences on key items. This analysis reinforced the premise of Fullan and his colleagues (2001) that school success in adopting a fundamental reform such as the professional learning community approach is intricately tied to the leadership dynamics at the district and provincial levels of the system.

District-Level Leadership

The second stage of our research focused on the development of an instrument that would examine district leadership and its impact on the process of transforming schools into learning communities. As it turned out, we would need two instruments, one that examined the internal machinations of the district itself and another that examined the district – school interface, both of which substantially impacted school leadership practices. This stage of our research was based on Fullan's (2005) argument that it was unreasonable to expect schools to change their leadership culture significantly and to sustain that change within the confines of a larger district system that continued to operate according to the principles of a traditional bureaucracy. We called the first instrument the Internal District Instrument (IDI) because it focuses on the professional dynamics among educators working at the district office and the principals of the district schools. It is important to note that our research identifies these individuals collectively as the educational leaders of the district and examines them as a single group who share the leadership of the district. In doing so, we set up an expectation that the district move from a bureaucratic to a professional learning community approach for at least some of its leadership behaviors. The second instrument, called the District Support to Schools Instrument (DSSI), examines the interactions between the district and the schools. Both instruments are designed to be completed by district office educators as well as school principals, and both instruments include a section related to leadership.

The IDI was completed in 2007 and is currently being piloted in a large urban district in New Brunswick. The design of the IDI is similar to that of the school instrument. It contains four sections dealing with the following themes: district culture, district structure and operations, district leadership, and district professional development. The examination of district leadership utilizes the following five descriptive statements:

- The leadership approach in our district fosters empowerment.
- In our district we build leadership capacity among educational leaders.
- In our district we strongly support growth and positive change.
- Our district's policies and practices promote educational leadership.
- The District Education Council (DEC) sets district goals and trusts district leaders to manage the system.

Just as the leadership of a principal has a major influence on the development of school-based professional learning communities, it seems likely that the leadership practices of superintendents would have an analogous effect at the district level. Following Sackney and Mitchell's (2005) concept of a community of leaders within schools and Lambert's (2003) call for enhanced teacher leadership, we posed questions to determine the extent to which district leaders modeled and encouraged shared leadership in their interactions within the district office and with principals. As with the school instrument, each of these statements is measured by three Likert-style survey items. We will describe the instrument items for each statement and show how they reflect the evolution in leadership associated with the concept of professional learning communities.

The first leadership statement on the IDI deals with empowerment. Three survey items were created to measure district efforts to foster empowerment among district office staff and principals. These items include questions about the degree to which respondents were encouraged to take initiatives and how often they collaborated with other educational leaders in the district and how often they took leadership roles in district-wide initiatives. In posing these questions, we were particularly interested to learn whether principals were treated as leaders at the district level or whether they were viewed more as school managers under the traditional hierarchical paradigm, working in isolation in their schools and having little opportunity to collaborate and share leadership with district office educators.

The second IDI leadership statement flows from the first by examining the leadership capacity building process within the group of educational leaders of the district. The three items we developed focus on the attribution of leadership within district teams and workgroups, district efforts to improve the district's educational leadership, and expectations of respondents for developing their leadership skills. While the descriptors associated with a more traditional bureaucracy emphasize leadership based on seniority and leadership skills possessed at the time of hiring, those associated with the emerging leadership models focus on leadership skills distributed among all members of the group and developed through training, mentoring, and collaboration.

The third IDI leadership statement addresses change. These three items measure the extent to which district efforts support growth and positive change. One question probes the extent to which respondents focussed their efforts on maintaining existing practices or on achieving district-defined learning goals. The second question deals with the change initiatives originating from the provincial department of education, with the response choices ranging from resistance to these external changes through compliance to actual contribution to these changes. The third question gives respondents the opportunity to indicate how new initiatives have affected their assigned responsibilities. In all three questions, we were looking for evidence of purposeful, goal-oriented, and learning-centred actions associated with change. As described earlier in this chapter, dealing with change forces – both internal and external – is a key requirement for twenty-first-century leadership.

The fourth IDI statement is concerned with the promotion of educational leadership. The three questions we posed are associated with the job description of school principals, the expectation to act as educational leaders in the district, and the provision of training to fulfill a district-wide leadership role. These questions provide indications of the extent to which there were clear expectations and support for all district office staff and principals to exercise educational leadership, rather than a concentration of leadership among a select few respondents.

The final statement related to leadership on the IDI is predicated on the governance model for New Brunswick school districts. Under the New Brunswick *Education Act* (1997), educational governance is provided by a District Education Council (DEC) whose members are elected by eligible voters residing within each school district (s. 36). The authority and responsibility of DECs are primarily related to the creation of a district education plan and the associated policies required at the district and school levels to implement that plan. Day-to-day delivery of education within the district is the responsibility of the superintendent, who is accountable to the DEC. The survey items in this section were chosen to measure the extent to which DECs entrusted day-to-day administrative, personnel, and pedagogical matters to superintendents and their district educational staff.

The second district instrument, the DSSI will be completed in late 2008 and piloted in 2009. This instrument examines the interaction between the group of district educational leaders and the schools. It addresses the following four themes: leadership for school improvement, two-way communication, instructional support for schools, and operational support for schools. Once again, we followed the format used for the school instrument. As with the IDI, the intended respondents were all members of the group of educational leaders in the district. For the theme of leadership for school improvement, we provided the following descriptive statements:

- Educational leaders in this district demonstrate effective leadership for establishing professional learning communities in schools.
- Educational leaders in this district ensure that staffing decisions support professional learning community implementation.
- In this district the development of teacher leadership is encouraged.
- Decisions at the district level reinforce and support school-based professional learning communities.
- This district recognizes the importance of transforming schools into professional learning communities.

The leadership theme of the DSSI deals with efforts by educational leaders to promote the implementation and sustainability of learning communities in schools. For learning communities to develop and grow in schools, districts must provide clear articulation and direction for the reform initiative, while ensuring that such principles as collaboration and shared leadership are respected in the process (Fullan et al., 2001). As both Morrissey (2000) and Mehan, Datnow, and Hubbard (2003) have pointed out, district support for reform at the school level is crucial for its sustainability.

The first and second DSSI leadership statements centre on the effectiveness of district efforts to ensure reform implementation. The first statement is concerned with the extent to which respondents provided necessary information and direction to schools with respect to reform implementation. Similarly, the second DSSI leadership statement addresses the alignment of staffing decisions with the reform initiative. The instrument items identify the extent to which responsibility for leading the reform has been clearly assigned to a member of the district office staff and also the degree to which school-level staffing decisions that enhance PLCs were supported. The importance of these items lies in the need for leaders to articulate clearly the purpose and nature of a reform and to provide the necessary staff to ensure its effective implementation.

The third DSSI statement addresses the development of teacher leadership. As described earlier in the chapter regarding emergent leadership styles, and as addressed on the IDI, we wanted respondents to identify district-level efforts to encourage teacher leadership. The items used to measure this statement refer to modeling the importance of teacher leadership, assisting schools in building teacher leadership, and including these efforts in the performance assessment of educational leaders in the district. The inclusion of these items highlights the need to redesign school evaluation criteria and focuses the district assessment of schools on community rather than solely bureaucratic parameters.

The fourth and fifth DSSI statements both relate to district leadership efforts towards the transformation of schools and their leadership culture. The fourth statement is assessed using questions about the district plan, district decision-making practices, and the extent to which these support and sustain school-based reform. Towards the same end, the fifth statement examines district goals, timelines, and resource allocation decisions. All of these items were chosen to determine whether leadership decisions made at the district level were encouraging, modeling, and reinforcing the reform expectations for schools. This type of alignment between espoused purpose and corresponding action by educational leaders would represent the type of leadership that Hallinger (2006) described as "inspirational and skillful, moral and practical, process-driven and results-oriented" (p. 2). In the complex and changing educational environment, district-level leadership must reflect this type of leadership to sustain reform for improvement.

Each of the three instruments described above is designed to gather data on potential barriers that prevent the development and sustainability of professional learning communities. The preliminary data from fifty schools indicate that the instruments are also useful in determining the strengths that exist in the system. For either purpose, each instrument is designed to be used by the individuals who provide the data. The statements and items were carefully selected and specifically worded to reinforce organizational growth through personal reflection of the respondents rather than for external evaluative purposes. Furthermore, the methodology used to collect the data ensures the anonymity of individual respondents. The purpose for this approach is twofold: to increase the legitimacy of the responses and to instill trust for the process by using a method that characterizes the philosophy of a professional learning community. One step in the research process remains. Fullan and his colleagues (2001) have depicted systemic reform as a tri-level endeavor. Our final task will be the development of a third tier of instruments, mirroring those at the district level, which will examine the impact of leadership practices within the provincial department of education. This work will provide further evidence of evolving redefinition of Canadian educational leadership.

Conclusion

In this chapter, we have traced the evolution of Canadian educational leadership in the face of increasing change and complexity in our world. We began by illustrating the influence of well-established leadership theories from the business world on educational leadership. This was followed by a description of the changing models of school leadership during periods of large-scale reform and their alignment to educational purposes and context of the twenty-first century. We then illustrated this evolution in leadership for school reform using our ongoing research in the New Brunswick school system.

Effective educational leadership continues to be an essential prerequisite to school improvement. The lessons learned through the study of organizational leadership show us that our current practices are based on a mixture of theories and beliefs from both the past and the present. While we continue to search for individuals who exhibit desirable leadership traits and acknowledge that both the traits and types of individuals we seek vary from one situation to another, we are just starting to realize that heroic leadership is no longer the answer in our increasingly complicated organizations. Leadership has evolved from being an amalgam of personal characteristics to become a system-wide capacity requiring every individual in an organization to accept leadership responsibility.

The metaphor of the organization as a machine may work well in a relatively stable environment, and the bureaucratic approach may be well suited for maintaining the status quo, but the rapidly evolving world of the twenty-first century demands that schools and the systems developed to support their effectiveness adopt new leadership approaches. As the globalization of educational pursuits and the emergence of a knowledge society force us to adapt to the forces of change, educational leadership must be fundamentally re-examined. Once more we take our lead from successful leadership beyond the educational realm. More than ever we need to revisit our past and incorporate leadership practices that combine the strengths of that past with practices that we need to move into the future. The main difference is that this process is no longer the purview of the few. The success of educational leadership in Canada's future depends upon our ability to develop it as a systemic capacity and our willingness to accept it as the responsibility of every individual in our profession.

This chapter provides four common themes that we believe are given little consideration when politicians and bureaucrats attempt to reform education:

1) Business management principles significantly influence leadership practices in education.
2) It is important to learn why business models must be adapted rather than adopted by educators.
3) Provincial education is a complex system that cannot be reformed using positivistic mental models.
4) Leadership of complex systems is an interdependent construct resulting from a broad leadership capacity that permeates the system.

Each of these themes may be recognized in passing through casual comments but they are seldom given the depth of study they deserve.

Each of these themes is driven by subconscious beliefs of which most of us are blissfully ignorant. Because of our failure to examine and learn the lessons they contain, we once again face a large-scale reform, full of the best intentions but unprepared to provide the leadership to turn our hopes into reality.

Questions

1. What three important lessons about educational leadership can we learn by studying corporate leadership?
2. How does leadership in an organic system differ from that in a mechanistic bureaucracy?
3. In what ways have the changes in schools led to demands for new kinds of leadership?
4. Describe the leadership of your school if it were to become a fully functioning professional learning community.
5. Why will schools always need a bureaucratic component to their organizational structure?

References

Abbott, J., & MacTaggart, H. (2008). *Overschooled but undereducated: Society's failure to understand adolescence.* Bath, UK: The 21st Century Learning Initiative. Retrieved on Aug. 19, 2008, from http://www.21learn.org/publications/books/overschooled.php

Anderson, K. (2002). Why teachers participate in decision-making and the third continuum. *Canadian Journal of Educational Administration and Policy, 23.* Retrieved Mar. 14, 2006, from http://www.umanitoba.ca/publications/cjeap/articles/anderson.html

Argyris, C. (1961). Organizational leadership. In L. Petrullo & B. M. Bass (Eds.), *Leadership and interpersonal behaviour.* New York: Holt, Rinehart, & Winston.

Barnard, C. (1938). *The functions of the executive.* Cambridge, MA: Harvard University Press.

Bass, B. (1990). *Bass & Stogdill's handbook of leadership: Theory, research and managerial applications* (3rd ed.). New York: Free Press.

Beairsto, B. (1999). Learning to balance bureaucracy and community as an educational administrator. In B. Beairsto & P. Ruohotie (Eds.), *The education of educators: Enabling professional growth for teachers and administrators.* Tampere, Finland: University of Tampere.

Bennis, W. G., & Nanus, B. (1985). *Leaders: The strategies for taking charge.* New York: Harper & Row.

Bezeau, L. M. (2000). *Structural reform of the New Brunswick education system in the 1990s.* Fredericton, NB: New Brunswick Centre for Educational Administration. Retrieved on Mar. 14, 2006, from http://www.unb.ca/centres/nbcea/nbeduc90.html

Blake, R. R., & Mouton, J. S. (1964). *The managerial grid.* Houston, TX: Gulf.

Brien, K., & Williams, R. (2008, June). *School districts as professional learning communities: Development of two district-level assessment instruments.* Paper presented at the Annual Conference of the Canadian Society for the Study of Education, University of British Columbia, Vancouver, BC. Retrieved on Aug. 20, 2008, from http://ocs.sfu.ca/fedcan/index.php/csse/csse2008/paper/view/341/218

Castle, J. B. (2001). Teacher education and leadership for change: Exploring faculty perspectives. *Alberta Journal of Educational Research, 47*(2), 108-122.

Cohen, D. (1995). What is the system in systemic reform? *Educational Researcher, 24*(9), 11-17, 31.

Cooner, D., & Quinn, R. (2008). Becoming a school leader: Voices of transformation from principal interns. *International Electronic Journal for Leadership in Learning, 12*(7). Retrieved on Aug. 22, 2008, from www.ucalgary.ca/~iejll/

Cranston, N. C. (2003, November - December). *Game, set and match: Bureaucracy 1, schools 0: Time to change the rules?* Paper presented at the International Education Research Conference of the AARE and NZARE, Auckland, New Zealand. Retrieved on Aug. 18, 2008, from http://www.aare.edu.au/03pap/cra03151.pdf

Dibbon, D. (2006, November). *Sustaining and imaging futures for the work of teachers: Using professional learning communities to facilitate learning in teacher education programs.* Paper presented at the International Conference on Teacher Education, University of Calgary, Calgary, AB.

DuFour, R. (1998). Schools as learning communities: Learning-centered schools grow from strong cultures. *Journal of Staff Development, 19*(1).Retrieved on Aug. 23, 2008, from http://www.nsdc.org/news/articleDetails.cfm?articleID=311

DuFour, R. (2004). What is a "professional learning community"? *Educational Leadership, 61*(8), 6-11.

Edmonds, R. (1979). Effective schools for the urban poor. *Educational Leadership, 37*(1), 15-24.

Education Act, S.N.B. 1997, c. E-1.12. Retrieved on Aug. 23, 2008, from www.canlii.org/nb/laws/sta/e-1.12/20080715/whole.html

Elmore, R. F. (1995). Structural reform and educational practice. *Educational Researcher, 24*(9), 23-26.

Fiedler, F. E. (1967). A theory of leadership effectiveness. New York: McGraw Hill.

Foster, R., & St. Hilaire, B. (2003). Leadership for school improvement: Principals' and teachers' perspectives. *International Electronic Journal for Leadership in Learning, 7*(3). Retrieved on Aug. 19, 2008, from http://www.ucalgary.ca/~iejll/volume7/foster.html

Fukuyama, F. (1995). *Trust: The social virtues and the creation of prosperity.* New York: The Free Press.

Fullan, M. (1991) *The new meaning of educational change.* New York: Teachers College Press.

Fullan, M. (2005). Professional learning communities writ large. In R. DuFour, R. Eaker, & R. DuFour (Eds.), *On common ground: The power of professional learning communities* (pp. 209-223). Bloomington, IN: National Educational Service.

Fullan, M. (2006). *Turnaround leadership.* San Francisco: Jossey-Bass.

Fullan, M., Rolheiser, C., Mascall, B., & Edge, K. (2001). *Accomplishing large scale reform: A tri-level proposition.* Retrieved on Aug. 24, 2008, from http://www.michaelfullan.ca/Articles_01/11_01.pdf

Hallinger, P. (1992). The evolving role of the American principals: From managerial to instructional to transformational leaders. *Journal of Educational Administration, 30*(3), 35 – 48.

Hallinger, P. (2006). Scholarship in school leadership preparation: The unaccepted challenge. *Journal of Research on Leadership Education, 1*(1). Retrieved on Aug. 23, 2008, from http://www.ucea.org/JRLE/pdf/vol1/issue1/Hallinger.pdf

Halpin, A. W., & Winer, B. J. (1957). A factorial study of leader behavior descriptors. In R. M. Stogdill & A. E. Coons (Eds.) *Leader behavior: Its description and measurement.* Columbus, OH: Ohio State University.

Hargreaves, A. (1991). Contrived collegiality: The micropolitics of teacher collaboration. In J. Blase (Ed.), *The politics of life in schools: Power, conflict, and cooperation.* Thousand Oaks, CA: Corwin Press.

Hargreaves, A. (2003, March). *Sustaining professional learning communities.* Paper presented at the meeting of New Brunswick Educational Leaders, Saint John, NB.

Hartle, F., & Hobby, R. (2003). Leadership in a learning community: Your job will never be the same again. In B. Davies & J. West-Burnham (Eds.), *Handbook of educational leadership and management* (pp. 381-393). London: Pearson Longman.

Hersey, P., & Blanchard, K. H. (1969). The management of organizational behavior. Englewood Cliffs, NJ: Prentice Hall.

Herzberg, F. (2003). One more time: How do you motivate employees? *Harvard Business Review, 81*(1), 87 – 96. (Reprinted from *Harvard Business Review, 46*(1), 53-62. Original work published 1968)

Honig, M. I. (2003). Building policy from practice: District central office administrator's roles and capacity for implementing collaborative education policy. *Educational Administration Quarterly, 39*(3), 292-338.

Hord, S. M. (1997). Professional learning communities: What are they and why are they important? *Issues. . . About Change, 6*(1). Retrieved on Aug. 21, 2008, from http://www.sedl.org/change/issues/issues61.html

Hoy, W. K., & Kupersmith, W. J. (1985). The meaning and measure of faculty trust. *Educational and Psychological Research, 5,* 1-10.

Jenkins, W. O. (1947). A review of leadership studies with particular reference to military problems. *Psychological Bulletin, 44,* 54-79.

Laferrière, T., Bracewell, R., Breuleux, A., Erickson, G., Lamon, M., & Owston, R. (2001, May). *Teacher education in the networked classroom.* Paper presented at the Pan-Canadian Education Research Agenda Symposium Teacher Education/Educator Training: Current Trends and Future Directions, Laval University, Quebec City, QC. Retrieved on Aug. 21, 2008, from http://www.cmec.ca/stats/pcera/symposium2001/LAFERIERE.O.EN.pdf

Lambert, L. (1998). *Building leadership capacity in schools.* Alexandria, VA: Association for Supervision and Curriculum Development.

Lambert, L. (2003). Leadership redefined: An evocative context for teacher leadership. *School Leadership & Management, 23*(4), 421-430.

Leithwood, K. A. (2007). Transformational leadership in a transactional policy world. In *The Jossey-Bass reader on educational leadership* (2nd ed.) (pp. 183-196). San Francisco: John Wiley & Sons.

Lemisko, L. S., Griffith, B., & Cutright, M. (2001). Reshaping teacher education in a knowledge society: Chaos and Collingwood. *Journal of Teaching & Learning, 1*(2), 33-45.

Lezotte, L. W., & Bancroft, B. A. (1985). Growing use of the effective schools model for school improvement. *Educational Leadership, 42*(6), 23 – 27.

Lezotte, L. W., Edmonds, R., Ratner, G. A. (1974). *Final report: Remedy for school failure to equitably deliver basic school skills.* East Lansing, MI: Department of Urban and Metropolitan Studies, Michigan State University.

Louis, K. S., Toole, J., & Hargreaves, A. (1999). Rethinking school improvement. In J. Murphy & K. S. Louis (Eds.), *Handbook of research on educational administration* (2nd ed.) (pp. 251-276). San Francisco: Jossey-Bass.

MacNeil, A. J., Spuck, D. W., & Ceyanes, J. W. (1998, October). *Developing trust between principal and teachers.* Paper presented at the Annual Convention of the University Council for Educational Administration (UCEA). Retrieved on Aug. 17, 2008, from http://ceyanes.com/UCEA.pdf

McKenna, F. (1999, June 16). Round table discussion on literacy hosted by the Collegium of Work and Learning, Toronto, ON. Retrieved on Mar. 10, 2006, from http://www.abc-canada.org/public_awareness/literacy_matters_round_table.asp

Mehan, H., Datnow, A., & Hubbard. L. (2003). Why educational reforms sustain or fail: Lessons for educational leaders. In B. Davies & J. West-Burnham (Eds.), *Handbook of educational leadership and management* (pp. 461-477). London: Pearson Longman.

Mintzberg, H. (1979). *The structuring of organizations.* Englewood Cliffs, NJ: Prentice-Hall.

Morehouse, A., & Tranquilla, D. (2005). *Planning for improvement.* Fredericton, NB: New Brunswick Department of Education.

Morrissey, M. S. (2000). *Professional learning communities: An ongoing exploration.* Austin, TX: Southwest Educational Development Laboratory. Retrieved on May 9, 2008, from http://www.sedl.org/pubs/change45/plc-ongoing.pdf

New Brunswick Teachers' Federation. (1997). *Agreement between Board of Management and The New Brunswick Teachers' Federation, September 1, 1997 to August 31, 2000.* [Collective Agreement]. Fredericton, NB: Author.

The new Lexicon Webster's encyclopedic dictionary of the English language (Canadian ed.). (1988). New York: Lexicon.

Ogawa, R. T., & Bossert, S. T. (2000). Leadership as an organizational quality. In *The Jossey-Bass reader on educational leadership* (pp. 38-58). San Francisco: Jossey-Bass.

Organisation for Economic Cooperation and Development. (2007). *OECD's PISA survey shows some countries making significant gains in learning outcomes.* Paris, France: Author. Retrieved on Aug. 19, 2008, from http://www.oecd.org/document/22/0,3343,en_2649_35845621_39713238_1_1_1_1,00.html

Pearce, C. L. (2004). The future of leadership: Combining vertical and shared leadership to transform knowledge work. *Academy of Management Executive, 18*(1), 47-57.

Province of New Brunswick (2007a). *Briefing notes: Assessment results for provincial literacy.* Fredericton, NB: Author.

Province of New Brunswick. (2007b). *When kids come first: A challenge to all New Brunswickers to build Canada's best education system.* Fredericton, NB: Author. Retrieved on June 17, 2007, from http://www.gnb.ca/0000/pubications/4578_report_E.pdf

Purkey, S. C., & Smith, M. S. (1983). Effective schools: A review. *The Elementary School Journal, 83*(4), 426-452.

Reddin, W. J. (1970). *Managerial effectiveness.* New York: McGraw Hill.

Sackney, L., & Mitchell, C. (2005). Leadership for a community of leaders: Developing capacity for a learning community. In H. D. Armstrong (Ed.), *Examining the practice of school administration in Canada* (pp. 275-291). Calgary, AB: Detselig Press.

Sackney, L., & Walker, K. (2006, October). *Leadership for knowledge communities.* Paper presented at the Commonwealth Council for Educational Administration and Management (CCEAM) Conference, Nicosia, Cyprus. Retrieved on Aug. 19, 2008, from http://www.topkinisis.com/conference/CCEAM/wib/index/outline/PDF/SACKNEY%20Larry.pdf

Schmoker, M. (2005). Here and now: Improving teaching and learning. In R. DuFour, R. Eaker, & R. DuFour (Eds.), *On common ground: The power of professional learning communities* (pp. xi-xvi). Bloomington, IN: National Educational Service.

Senge, P. M. (1990). *The fifth discipline: The art and practice of the learning organization.* New York: Doubleday.

Senge, P. M. (2007). "Give me a lever long enough . . . and single-handed I can move the world." In *The Jossey-Bass reader on educational leadership* (2nd ed.) (pp. 3-15). San Francisco: John Wiley & Sons. (Original work published 1990)

Senge, P., Cambron-McCabe, N., Lucas, T., Smith, B., Dutton, J., & Kleiner, A. (2000). *Schools that learn: The fifth discipline fieldbook for educators, parents, and everyone who cares about education.* New York: Doubleday.

Slater, L., (2004). Collaboration: A framework for school improvement. *International Electronic Journal for Leadership in Learning, 8*(5), 1-12. Retrieved on Aug. 20, 2008, from http://www.ucalgary.ca/~iejll/

Smith, H. L., & Kruger, L. M. (1933). *A brief summary of literature on leadership.* Bloomington, IN: Indiana University, School of Education Bulletin.

Stewart, J. (2006). Transformational leadership: An evolving concept examined through the works of Burns, Bass, Avolio, and Leithwood. *Canadian Journal of Educational Administration and Policy, 54*, 1-29. Retrieved on Aug. 18, 2008, from http://www.umanitoba.ca/publications/cjeap/pdf_files/stewart.pdf

Taylor, F. W. (2005). The principles of scientific management. In J. M. Shafritz, J. S. Ott, & Y. S. Jang (Eds.), *Classics of organization theory* (6th ed.) (pp. 61-72). Belmont, CA: Thomson Wadsworth. (Original work published 1916)

Uline, C. L. (2001). The imperative to change. *International Journal of Leadership in Education, 4*(1), 13-28.

Weick, K. E. (1976). Educational organizations as loosely coupled systems. *Administrative Science Quarterly, 21*(1), 1-19.

Wheatley, M. (1997). Goodbye command and control. *Leader to Leader Journal, 5*, 21-28. Retrieved on Aug. 21, 2008, from http://www.pfdf.org/knowledgecenter/journal.aspx?ArticleID=147

Williams, R. B. (1997). *The relationship between personal characteristics and situation complexity and decision-making style flexibility in New Brunswick school principals.* Retrieved from Dissertation & Theses database. (AAT 9729635)

Williams, R. B. (May, 2006). Leadership for school reform: Do principal decision-making styles reflect a collaborative approach? *Canadian Journal of Educational Administration and Policy, 53.* Retrieved on Aug. 17, 2008, from http://www.umanitoba.ca/publications/cjeap/articles/williams.html

Williams, R., Brien, K., & LeBlanc, J. (2008, June). *Transforming schools into learning organizations: Supports and barriers to educational reform.* Paper presented at the Annual Conference of the Canadian Society for the Study of Education, University of British Columbia, Vancouver, BC. Retrieved on Aug. 19, 2008, from http://ocs.sfu.ca/fedcan/index.php/csse/csse2008/paper/viewFile/433/304

Williams, R., Brien, K., Sprague, C., & Sullivan, G. (2008). Professional learning communities: Developing a school-level readiness instrument. *Canadian Journal of Educational Administration and Policy, 74,* 1-17. Retrieved on Aug. 18, 2008, from http://www.umanitoba.ca/publications/cjeap/pdf_files/williamsspraguesullivanbrien.pdf

Zaleznick, A. (1970). Power and politics in organizational life. *Harvard Business Review, 48*(3), 47 – 60.

Chapter Two

The Quest for Equity and Excellence in Public Schools: A Portrait of Transformative Leadership

Yvette Daniel, Ph.D.
University of Windsor

In an era of accountability and global competition, school leaders and administrators face immense pressures to ensure that students in their schools are meeting standards of success as demonstrated mainly through tests and other measurable indices. Concurrently, there is a call for educational leaders to take on the role of public intellectuals dedicated to transformative practices in the quest for social justice and equity (Daniel, 2007). This call poses special challenges in a milieu of increasing diversity and demographic shifts in which isolated stabs at inequities will not suffice (Marshall, 2004). Further, in the thrust for accountability, equity often times has had to take a back seat; however, equity and excellence are not in competition nor are they mutually exclusive. In fact, accountability makes educational inequities visible and raises the standards for student success (Skrla & Scheurich, 2001); hence, we can no longer ignore or explain away under-achievement of students from disadvantaged backgrounds. Most jurisdictions are demanding for a narrowing of these achievement gaps in education.

The school administrator is the person who has to provide leadership in this area. Despite several progressive policies, inequities continue to exist. Many obstacles, including deeply systematic problems, halt progress made towards the goal of equality. Specifically, school leaders often become "caught up in the meta-narrative of accountability" (Grogan, 2004, p. 224) that reinforces the status quo. The *habitus of assimilation* in which school leaders focus on complying diligently with directives and operate from the ideology of sameness will not address inequities (Goddard & Hart, 2007).

The majority of books, monographs, articles, and research projects that examine the notion of educational leaders as transformative intellectuals focus on the landscape in the US with its specific challenges, but only a few capture a Canadian vantage point. A recent study by Goddard and Hart (2007) of Canadian administrators found that most of them took a keen interest in equity and were aware of supportive policies, but most felt overwhelmed by the plethora of initiatives they have had to implement. Their study concluded that the insistence on sameness and avoidance strategies to minimize differences did not address systemic challenges confronted by students from disadvantaged backgrounds who lack the social, cultural and economic capital. They stated:

> As key administrators at the school level, principals must take the lead role in meeting the demands of these social, economic and demographic changes. Principals exhibit varying degrees of success in providing the leadership required to adapt to the pluralistic society (p. 8).

Therefore, this chapter aims to fill this gap by presenting an evolving portrait of transformative leadership as displayed by two leaders in the local public educational context of Windsor, a mid-sized town located in the Southwestern Ontario. In the first section, the objectives of the study are delineated. In the second and third sections, the theoretical framework and the methodology are outlined respectively. In the fourth section, a portrait of transformative leadership is presented.

Objectives of the Study

The purpose of this study was to capture and portray exemplary transformative leadership in action in public educational institutions in Windsor, Ontario. A mid-sized, blue-collared border town of 220,000 inhabitants, Windsor is heavily reliant on the auto-making industry as a main source of employment. The decline of this manufacturing sector has had a strong negative impact upon the local economy, resulting in higher unemployment (than usual) and a sharp decline in the already faltering real estate market. All these factors have affected students and schools. The local school boards are cash-strapped due to declining enrollments: the Ministry of Education's funding formula is based on per-student funding to local school boards. In this milieu, educational leaders must be able to forge new alliances with other agencies, address the impact of the rapid changes in technology and communications on schools, and respond to the increasing diversity in the student body manifested in immigrant status, income disparities, language barriers, and variation in learning abilities, to list a few.

This study set out to investigate the nature of inclusive practices and the manner in which they were played out in the lived reality of schools while also examining the strategies employed by leaders in their quest for social justice and equity in schools. These strategies included an interrogation into the way data was used, not only to identify strengths, but also to bring issues to the forefront in order to target areas where improvement was critical. The following key questions framed this study: What role do these leaders play in discrediting pathologies of silence and deficit thinking and to what extent are they able to achieve their visions and goals for equity? What hurdles do they face and how do they attempt to overcome them? The questions that guided the study were not meant to glorify these leaders, but rather aimed to become a search for *goodness* that was framed by a balanced and probing perspective of the lived complexity of the task of educating our young people in a complex milieu of diversity and competing demands. These renditions underscored the challenging nature of the work of leadership in service to the community to present a portrait – an authentic narrative that is receptive yet challenging.

Theoretical Framework

Shields (2004) states that transformative leadership focuses on the ethical and moral dimensions, and acknowledges the centrality of relationships. Educational leaders as public, transformative intellectuals have to take a critical approach to both the rhetoric and reality of addressing issues of diversity and difference in their schools (Riehl, 2000). Grogan (2004) calls for an ethic of critique in which "we have a moral responsibility to ask probing questions about who benefits from our educational policies and practices" (p. 223). Educational leaders need to investigate and pose questions for the issues that generate inequities (Dantley & Tillman, 2006). In order to critique and interrogate existing structures, leaders need to develop

> a proper understanding not only of how educational institutions and systems are positioned within the social and economic dynamics of urban contexts, but also how they might engage with and impact upon those dynamics to promote greater educational equality (Raffo & Dyson, 2007, p. 265).

Consequently, two theoretical concepts frame this investigation. The first is the concept of equity audits (Skrla, Scheurich, Garcia, & Nolly, 2004) that require school leaders to confront and address inequities that remain invisible due to pathologies of silence (Shields, 2004) and deficit thinking (Valencia, 1997). The concept of pathologies of silence, as delineated by Shields emphasizes that school leaders were silent about inequities and chose to ignore their existence.[1] Deficit thinking is described as "a ubiquitous description-explanation-prediction-prescription cycle" (Skrla & Scheurich, 2001, p. 236). This mode of thinking is especially pervasive as it relates to urban schools. Educators and others in the field described these deficits/shortcomings in students from disadvantaged backgrounds, and then explained these deficits by blaming the victims arguing that the problem resided with students and their families. Thus, deficits are perceived as individual problems rather than societal or structural ones. This perception, in turn, is followed by predictions guided by self-fulfilling prophecies that lead to prescriptions designed to ameliorate these deficits. In contrast to silence and a deficit-thinking worldview, the equity of teacher and programmatic quality are confronted front and centre in equity audits as part of societal and structural responses in the quest for achievement equity.

The concept of equity audits introduced by Skrla and her colleagues (2004) into the current literature is a leadership tool that can be used to unmask existing inequities in the school system. The focus is on the key areas of equity in teacher and programmatic quality. Addressing these inequalities results in achievement equity, which is one of the main goals in transformative leadership. Teacher equity audits are built upon the premise that "high quality teachers are key determinants of students' opportunities to be academically successful" (Skrla et al., 2004, p. 142). Some of the indicators for teacher quality are level of expertise and training, years of experience, teacher mobility, among others to ensure that schools located in low SES and urban areas benefit from the experience and expertise for a sustained period of time. For programmatic equity audits, the authors above have identified four key areas: special education, gifted education, bilingual education (for the Ontario context this translates to English language learners), and student discipline. Such audits bring to the forefront the issue of over or underrepresentation of students from different backgrounds in each of these areas. Leaders in schools and school districts can then take measures to remedy these discrepancies and inequities.

The second theoretical concept of Kumashiro's (2000) four approaches to anti-oppressive education also plays an essential role in the process of examining programmatic quality. He advocates that programmatic equity encompass the following four approaches to anti-oppressive pedagogies: (1) education for the other; (2) education about

---

[1] It is important to note that many school leaders have acknowledged the pervasiveness of deficit thinking and pathologies of silence and have made programmatic and organizational changes to address these issues.

the other; (3) education that is critical of privileging and othering; and (4) education that changes students and society. Embedded in the quest to address social inequities through anti-oppressive pedagogies is the concept of care, both at the institutional and at the individual level (Noddings, 1995). The ethic of caring actions stems from a personal and deep-rooted belief in the importance of relationship building centred on respect for the diversity in human abilities and the notion of service to others (Gabro, 2002).

Methodology

Portraiture is a creative qualitative research approach employed in studying leaders, institutions, and groups in action. It was made famous by Sarah Lawrence Lightfoot in her 1984 AERA award-winning book, *The Good High School* in which she used a *verbal canvas* to provide a thick, rich description of the elements of good schools. In portraiture, the researcher as portraitist seeks to document and interpret the perspectives and experiences of the people and places they are studying by documenting voices, artifacts, visions, and context. Aspects of ethnography, case study, and narrative methodologies are embedded in portraiture (Gabro, 2002). The portrait is created through a process of relationship building and negotiation between the participant (subject) and the researcher as the portrait is evolving and is being shaped. Lightfoot (1984) states that "artists must not view the subject as object, but as a person of myriad dimensions" (p. 6). Specifically, the following parameters for the canvas are established: (1) people and their relations with each other; (2) knowledge and educational design; and (3) schooling and social change (Daniel, 1997).

The researcher takes four different stances or voices when creating portraiture, all of which are integral and occur concurrently to build the evolving portrait. Lightfoot & Davis (1997) list these as: (1) witness, in which the researcher/portraitist is an observer trying to capture the ecology of the place and its inhabitants while he/she is sufficiently removed and sitting on the sidelines; (2) interpreter, in which the researcher is trying to make sense of these observations; (3) pre-occupation, in which the researcher's voice is evident in the interpretation that is influenced by the researcher's own assumptions and biases; and lastly, (4) autobiography, in which the researcher reflects on her/his life experiences to enhance the interpretation in creating the portrait. As researchers, it is important that we are continually cognizant of these stances that guide and give shape to our research findings. And we acknowledge that biases exist and that our biases and assumptions are not meant to obscure, but serve to enhance the portraits we are creating. Lightfoot and Davis (1997) have phrased this idea eloquently:

> She must use the knowledge and wisdom drawn from these life experiences as resources for understanding, and as sources for connection and identification with the

> actors in the setting, but she must not let her autobiography obscure or overwhelm the inquiry (p. 95).

As such, data collection included surveys with school staff, students, parents/guardians, and semi-structured, open-ended interviews with school leaders, teachers, community organizations, and support staff at these schools. The approach taken to analyzing interviews was mainly phenomenological – meaning that interviews were not seen as a means of gathering data but rather as opportunities for conversation and interpretation. These conversations were attempts "to gain access to the inner world of personal experience – in this case, the personal experience of those with special responsibilities for the education of the young" (Evans, 2005, p. 45). Various policy documents such as Ministry of Education directives and school-related policies were also analyzed. Observational data includes description of the local context, cultural identities, economic and social activities, cultural artifacts, school newsletters, school data, test scores, decorations, displays, announcements, school-related activities, and school-community activities.

The Portrait

This chapter drew from a larger study that provided extensive and detailed portraits of two educational leaders and the context in which they conducted their work. The challenge, for the purpose of this chapter, was to capture the essence of transformative intellectuals within the limited space provided. Hence, more vivid and in-depth details had to be condensed. In creating the portrait, I also provide the context and climate to paint an integrated verbal canvas of both individuals. Since both work for the same school board and share many of the same challenges and experiences, albeit in different capacities (one is the school principal and the other is a supervisory officer in charge of secondary curriculum and student success), often times, the reader will find the description moving from one to the other. Overall, the portrait depicts administrative practices rooted in the understanding that "if strong relationships with all children are at the heart of educational equity, then it is essential to acknowledge differences in children's lived experiences" (Shields, 2004, p. 110). At the same time, the portrait depicts practices that are also pedagogically sound while attempting to encapsulate the tact, humility, and pedagogical wisdom (Evans, 2005) that make them transformative individuals.

The Researcher's Perch

As explained in the methodology section, the researcher's standpoint and the four stances or voices need clarification. Throughout my career in education, I have worked in various capacities in urban school districts, and therefore, I have a vested interest and passion in interpreting the lived reality of schools and in studying transformative practices in action. Besides having served in several leadership positions in this context, I have an in-depth understanding of how. despite good intentions, the pressures of the day-to-day challenges in schools become rather overwhelming, hence pushing transformative practices into the background. As I walked through the hallways of the school and observed leadership in action at Catholic Central High, my background and interests allowed me to understand and analyze these challenges and obstacles while concurrently searching for goodness – not as perfection, but as a quality with all its imperfections, uncertainties, and vulnerabilities (Lawrence-Lightfoot, 1984).

The Context: Catholic Central High School (CCH)

Portraiture relies heavily upon the understanding of context. CCH is a large high school opened in the mid-1980s with over one thousand students and sixty-five teaching staff in addition to a large number of auxiliary personnel. CCH is located in a small working class neighborhood with narrow streets and mature tress for the most part, although the school is situated on one of the main streets in the city. CCH has a highly transient and multi-ethnic student body. Although the building is old, it is well maintained and clean. It exudes a certain old-world charm when compared to the brand-new school buildings across town. Overall, it has the appearance of a well-used and cherished facility. As the school expanded, portables were built and additional space was acquired in a nearby building. The teaching staff is very friendly, and the attrition rate is not high. As I walked toward the school building, I saw that most students had uniforms. One of the students held the front door open for me and asked me if I needed assistance. The hallways of the school are adored with student work, trophies and other accomplishments – typical of most schools in the region. The office staff is very attentive and they take good care of their visitors.

In their recent Ontario Secondary School Literacy Test (OSSLT), CCH scored below the provincial average. The OSSLT is a standardized test administered to all Grade 10 students across the province of Ontario. While the province–wide passing rate for students who passed both reading and writing was 70%, CCH had a pass rate of 51%, which was much lower than the school board rate of 72% (EQAO results published on the web). A factor contributing to this result is the increasing number of English language learners (ELLs) at CCH. According to the Ontario Ministry of Education (2007) guidelines and policies, ELL learners are students whose first language is other than English or is a variety of English significantly different from that used for instruction in Ontario schools. Under the umbrella of English Language Learners there are two categories of programs: The first category, English as a Second Language (ESL) programs are for students who have had educational opportunities to develop age-appropriate, first-language literacy skills. The second category, English Language Development (ELD) programs are for students who have had limited access to education. Mostly, these are students who come from countries where their academic and language development was inconsistent, disrupted, or unavailable. As a result, they arrive in Ontario schools with a significant gap in their language and literacy development. In order to meet the specific needs of these students, many creative and individualized programs have to be set up.

Two Personalities, One Goal

Ms. Darlene Kennedy, principal at Catholic Central High School, is a gregarious, friendly, compassionate, and welcoming person. She is a sharp intellectual with a quick wit. She emanates an aura of warmth and a zest for life and all that is good in it. She is a genuine individual who is driven by her faith and her strong belief in service to the community, especially to the students in her school. Yet, this caring and faith she demonstrates is devoid of arrogance, sometimes perceived on the part of the care-giver in the caring/leadership relationship. She is strong, yet she can be soft; she is persistent, yet she can also be yielding and flexible. One of my colleagues called her Mother Teresa and Mike Tyson rolled into one. She captured my attention from the very first moment I met her. During my numerous visits to the school, she did not wait for the office staff to take me to her office but came out to greet me. During these conversations and by participating in some of the initiatives at CCH, I recognized very quickly that she embodied and lived the reality of the transformative intellectual that I had read so widely about and wanted to meet.

Earlier this year, Darlene was named one of Canada's most outstanding principals along with thirty-two others from a pool of 30 000. She was inducted into the National Academy of Canada's Outstanding Principals. In order to understand how this honor came to be bestowed upon her, one needs to be familiar with her journey. From the time she finished high school in the 1960s in Windsor, she has been teaching children and working in community service. She worked with the diocese of London, Ontario on youth programs and also with programs to assist welfare recipients in acquiring the knowledge and skills to become employable. No matter where life's journey took her, her heart remained at CCH, and eventually she returned to become principal. An article in the local newspaper stated that Darlene is an integral part of CCH, "as much as its battered lockers, marbled floors, high ceilings, and of course, the student body" (*Windsor Star*, Jan. 11, 2008).

Linda Staudt is a supervisory officer responsible for secondary curriculum and Student Success at the school board. She has had extensive experience in leadership positions both at the local and provincial level. She is a disciplined and dynamic leader who is highly respected by students, staff, and all those with whom she works. She is an excellent listener, quick-witted, and has a calm and friendly disposition. She is thoughtful and reflective and, when presented with a challenge, moves beyond bifurcated thinking to come up with creative and novel solutions. She is a forward thinker and an intellectual who understands the importance of educational practices grounded in theories and research. As such, she has created strong alliances with the academic community both at the local and provincial level in order to obtain grants for innovative programs in collaboration with Darlene to benefit the diverse and high-needs community serviced by CCH. She worked as a biology teacher, school vice principal, and principal at CCH before moving on to a senior position. She works closely with administration and teaching staff in supporting new initiatives to build and sustain a caring community school that nurtures student success. She takes her responsibility for caring for students seriously. She recalls her time as a school vice-principal, specifically one defining event that changed her perspective:

> Our work with students is complex. So in the role of administrator, you were worried about whether a student came on time, and then you got hung up on the detentions and all of that stuff. Sometimes you didn't even bother to ask why the student was late. And I still remember a case where we had this one particular student and now she was late for the fourteenth, fifteenth, sixteenth time. So I had some time that morning so I asked her for a reason for her tardiness. Then she told me that she was taking care of her grandmother who was suffering from Alzheimer's. Her mother was also sick and, in addition, she was also in charge of her youngest brother who was in elementary school. What I realized then was that we were lucky that she was even here today. If she showed up in the school, we were fortunate because there was so much to detract her, to prevent her from coming. And I think we have to take a look at where they are and what we can do to assist them. It gave me a totally different mind set.

Both Linda and Darlene are strong leaders with brave and passionate hearts who realize that school administration and leadership is a uniquely moral enterprise (Greenfield, 1995). They are working hard to support a relationally oriented school that fosters caring connections and meaningful and rigorous academic programs while promoting equity. They have conducted a deeper analysis of data to make fundamental changes in structure and form. They open themselves up to learning, personalized education, and operate from an egalitarian ethic. It was apparent from my very first encounter with them that both leaders did not espouse deficit thinking to view the underperformance of children from disadvantaged backgrounds as inevitable (Skrla & Scheurich, 2001). They did not consider the lack of resources as obstacles; on the contrary, they used their resourcefulness to create innovative programs for students. They realized the enormous responsibilities and moral imperative they shouldered. Unlike many leaders in position of power and influence, both Linda and Darlene did not feel uncomfortable or consider it politically risky to confront educational inequities. They appreciated that the push for accountability is much needed and would result in better education for students (Skrla & Scheurich, 2001), especially for those who were underserviced by the current system.

Moreover, Darlene and Linda have intimate and first-hand knowledge of the school and the system with all its complexities and challenges; hence they avoid the *gunslinger model* of leadership in which an external leader rides into town to reform the system (Eisinger & Hula, 2004). Darlene can be extremely persistent and will not hesitate to pursue her demands with senior administration. Both Darlene and Linda firmly support and are committed to putting in place creative programming and initiatives that benefit all students. Among the plethora of outstanding initiatives under the leadership of Linda and Darlene at CCH, for the purpose of this partial portrait, I chose to focus on two major programs: Retrieving Early Leavers Initiative and Supporting English Language Learners in Mainstream Classrooms.

Retrieving Early Leavers

The Ontario Ministry of Education is committed to understanding the phenomenon of early school leaving and to finding ways to remedy the situation. The King (2004) report indicated that up to one-quarter of students might not graduate from high school in Ontario. Further, a series of research studies regarding early school leavers was initiated by the current Ministry of Education which resulted in a comprehensive report entitled *Early School Leavers: Understanding the Lived Reality of Student Disengagement from Secondary School* (2005) also referred to as the Ferguson report. The findings from these studies have served as the impetus for several remedial policy initiatives, such as *6 Pathways to Student Success in High School, Dual Credit, Expanded Co-Op Program*, as well as additional funding to school boards to support implementation. These initiatives have been widely adopted across the province, resulting in several programs aimed at the successful reintegration of early school leavers.

In September 2007, the Windsor-Essex Catholic District School Board (WECDSB) under the leadership of Supervisory Officer Ms. Linda Staudt, and in collaboration with the secondary school administrators, department heads of guidance, and Student Success teachers designed and implemented a bold initiative aimed at taking a proactive stance by responding to the early warning signals leading to student drop-out and also reaching out to retrieve the early leavers. Two teachers from the school board's Student Success Teacher allocation were assigned to board-wide Continuous Intake Cooperative positions.

These positions were put in place to support students within the board who were at risk of dropping out of school and also to contact students who had left the board without a high school diploma. Under the leadership of Linda, the board undertook a proactive approach in contacting these students rather than waiting for them to find their own way back to a high school diploma. Two outstanding teachers were appointed to retrieve students who had yet to complete their high school diplomas. These teachers were given full support by Linda in carrying out this task. These teachers stated that the trust and confidence bestowed upon them enabled them to take initiatives and allowed them to reach out to students. Further, they explained that many families were surprised to be contacted. Mostly, when students left (or dropped out), it was up to them to make their way back if they wished. Here, two dedicated teachers went the extra mile and took a personal interest in each and every student and his or her unique circumstances. These teachers mapped out a personal plan for each student, found appropriate placements for each one, and monitored their progress.

From September 2007 through to April 2008, over one hundred students returned to high school, and of this group thirty five attained their Ontario Secondary School Diploma. Some of these students who have attained their high school diploma are also actively seeking support from the school system to help them gain admission to post-secondary destinations previously not available to them. Currently, negotiations are underway with the local university to enable these returning students to take a university course that is designed especially for them and earns them partial credit. The credit will be banked and taken into account should the student wish to pursue a university degree. The intent is to open up possibilities for higher education, something that was not on the horizon for these students. In fact, some of the students were so excited that they contacted the university office themselves to inquire about this option.

Supporting English Language Learners (ELLs) in the Mainstream Classroom

Programming for secondary ELLs within the school board is centralized at CCH, which had an increasing number of incoming students requiring ELD support. These students have very weak first language literacy skills and have experienced significant gaps in their education. In the 2007-08 school year alone, out of the fifty-six students who entered CCH from a country outside of Canada, thirty-five required ELD support. Currently, the school has over ninety students enrolled in ELD programs. The results from the March 2006 Ontario Secondary School Literacy Test (OSSLT) showed that only 21% of the first time eligible students were successful as compared to the provincial average of 51%. In terms of numeracy achievement, the results were not much better. Again, in the Grade 9 applied assessment test only 6% succeeded as opposed to the provincial average of 18%.[2] Thus, it was obvious that urgent measures were needed.

Linda and Darlene examined these statistics and declared that neither silence nor deficit thinking would suffice. Their passion and caring for student learning and achievement led them to inquire and make decisions about how they could address the more pressing needs. Linda applied for a Ministry of Education Student Success Lighthouse grant to start a program to support the integration of language and content instruction for ELLs. Her proposal was based on a sound theoretical and research-based understanding on the need for this program at CCH. This program has two full-time support teachers: one teacher is an expert in language and literacy and the other in numeracy, math, and science. The framework for this program rested upon collaboration between mainstream and ELL teachers in order to build upon the strengths of expertise of each one. While the mainstream/classroom teacher was responsible for the curriculum, the ELL teachers identified students who were experiencing language and/or content difficulties; thus they were better able to provide appropriate support.

In general, the following strategies were employed: (1) integrate academic and language literacy skills with subject matter concepts and higher-order thinking skills; (2) assist ELLs acquire the pertinent vocabulary and language skills they needed to be successful in the content area; (3) support classroom teachers in designing differentiated instruction and assessment tools; (4) provide individualized instruction and mini-lessons to small groups comprised of students with similar needs; and (5) support students in the use of a variety of learning strategies. The Ontario Ministry of Education (2007) interim report noted that a total of ninety-three students across the school were impacted as a result of this project. The two teachers assigned to this project were very enthusiastic and spoke passionately about their work with students. Students approached them and were eager to sign up for individual sessions with them. The sign-up log indicated that the demand was much greater than the hours allocated, and these teachers often times went the extra mile so as not to turn away a single student who needed their assistance. They had also established an excellent rapport with the staff. They were always welcomed into the various classrooms they visited in order to provide collaborative assistance to students in their subject areas/classrooms.

This program is now in its second year. The overarching goal is to promote cross-cultural understanding and appreciation for diversity and difference based on respect, caring, and trust. The key long term goal is to measure the increase in credit accumulation and student success due to the establishment of this program. Further, the purpose

---

[2] For a detailed report of these results go to: http://www.eqao.com/results/results.aspx?grade=10&year=2002&Lang=E&submit=View+Resultsissues.

of this program is to empower teachers with strategies and resources so that they are successful in meeting the unique needs of ELL learners in their classrooms. These two appointed teachers meet regularly with school staff to create units of study that are subject specific and cognizant of the needs of ELL learners. They also deliver professional development sessions and create appropriate, culturally relevant support materials for students and teachers. Last, the goal is to fully embed the program within the school so that it becomes an integral and essential feature of CCH.

Emerging Themes

The Task Force on Research in Educational Leadership (Leithwood & Reihl, 2003) identified a core set of leadership practices that form the basics of successful leadership. This core set is comprised of three main dimensions: (1) setting directions; (2) developing people; and (3) developing the organization. This core set of practices is most appropriate in identifying the themes emerging from this portrait of Darlene and Linda. In the following section I will use these three dimensions to examine the transformative leadership demonstrated by these two through there continual engagement in the pursuit of equity and school renewal.

Setting Directions

In this dimension of leadership, the focus is on inspiring others to create a shared vision and meaning through skillful communication to foster high performance expectations. In order to monitor and assess organizational performance, astute leaders use multiple indicators, ask critical questions, and provide constructive feedback, ongoing encouragement and support. Both Darlene and Linda are focused and have a passion for continual improvement to enhance student learning, especially for those who are underserved in the current system. They use the statistics provided by standardized testing to set the course for school improvement. They seek out the most experienced and enthusiastic teachers to lead these specialized programs. Furthermore, they trust these designated individuals to the fullest, by providing space for them to develop their ideas to the fullest. Linda often spoke about leadership as an emerging design and not as something rigid and predestined. According to one teacher:

> When Linda first gave us this special appointment, we did not know what to expect. As teachers we were accustomed to following directions. Here, we soon discovered that they trusted us to take initiatives by gauging the needs of our students in the day to day lived reality, and we had the freedom to shape the program to meet these needs. It was awesome and it inspired us to do more.

In one of my conversations, Linda reiterated the main principle that drives her leadership practices:

> I would say, it would be impossible to micro-manage because there are too many things going on. My philosophy is that you have to trust the people you are in charge of. This was true for the two teachers heading the ELL program. I don't know the needs of individual ESL students. I know that we need to do more to support them. In terms of the various strategies to be implemented, these teachers are living in the building and know first hand the needs of the students. We met frequently to collaborate and work with the ideas as they evolved. One idea in particular that the teachers developed, I thought, was totally brilliant in terms of an innovative professional development plan for teachers.

Developing People

This is another dimension of successful leadership that occurs concurrently while directions are being set. In fact, they are integral and integrated as part of the core set. It is obvious that the work of educating our young people cannot be accomplished without the efforts of people involved in the organization: "Effective educational leaders influence the development of human resources in their schools" (Leithwood & Reihl, 2003, p. 4). They accomplish this by offering intellectual stimulation that nurtures innovation, by allowing people to understand the complexities of change and by providing appropriate modeling through their example. They provided care that was responsive and responsible. Darlene states:

> As a matter of fact, I never forget this – education comes from the Latin word which means to gently lead forward and it's always with the presumption that with every person we meet that there is something there. Our responsibility is to be able to provide an environment where you can allow that individual to bring out what they can share with or have to offer to the community. Even the quiet or reluctant ones – everybody has something to contribute and give. Sometimes it just takes a while to get to them and they have to feel safe, they have to feel needed and that they have something valuable to contribute.

Together Linda and Darlene stress the importance of teacher leadership as a way of nurturing personal and professional growth. Their comments are clear indicators of their shared belief that unless teachers are provided with the support and the freedom, it will not be possible to move beyond mere compliance to create transformative pedagogic practices. This process is, of course, messy and fraught with tension and resistance, and these leaders have their fair share of challenges. However, they accept these challenges with courage and resilience to forge ahead in service to students and community.

Developing the Organization

Setting direction and developing people are integral components to developing the organization as a professional learning community of practice (Wenger, 1998). Communities of practice have three defining characteristics: mutual engagement, joint enterprise, and a shared repertoire. At CCH, these two leaders are continually engaged in developing Wenger's notion of communities of practice. School staff, teachers, and students are all engaged in sustaining interpersonal contact with each other around their practices as was observed during discussions in formal and informal settings. For example, the two teachers in the ELL program held ongoing conversations with classroom teachers around their practices and sought ways to further support ELL learners in their classrooms and beyond. The second characteristic of a community of practice is manifested in the pursuit of a joint enterprise. Under the direction of these leaders, the educational community was engaged in improving teaching and in supporting the learning for all students. They did this by addressing the challenges through a process of dialogue and negotiation to find innovative ways to meet the needs of students and the community. The pursuit of a joint enterprise inevitably led to the creation of a shared repertoire of routines, stories, concepts that become the culture and climate of the school. At CCH, the pursuit of a joint enterprise is noticeable in the hallways, in the conversation with students, and in listening to passing conversations among students and between students and staff. Darlene's comments summarize this idea comprehensively:

> And I've found it here – also found in other schools, but especially at Catholic Central because you have students who come to us with a variety of backgrounds and who come to us – I find when you get to know them – with barriers that are unimaginable that I would have never had in my life. And they are able to rise above them and go on. In many ways, it's because there are people here who care, who are not only excellent in their teaching but they provide every possible experience for the students to be able to go on whether it is in terms of belief, sometimes it's financially, whatever – to be able to have them succeed.

They have created a collaborative culture that includes, teachers, students, staff, and all other stakeholders in the school community. They have developed and strengthened a positive school culture that sets the tone and context within which equity work, although messy and contentious, can be nurtured and sustained. They set the direction for structural changes, oftentimes disrupting institutional conformity to establish a climate that is inclusive and conducive to learning and growth through caring affirmative relationship building.

Significance

This study captures transformative leadership in its impact on the educative environment to underscore the power of human encounters. This portrait is unique and is not intended to be a template to be copied. Moreover, the portrait created of these transformative intellectuals does not paint a picture of perfection. Rather, it offers intriguing and valuable lessons about goodness in educational leadership practices that account for strengths and weaknesses to compose holistic and realistic accounts of struggles and triumphs. The struggle to reach all students at CCH continues, but Darlene and Linda are relentless. Their moral conviction and sense of service has imbued them with passion and commitment to the education of all children. Darlene stated it thus, which was echoed by Linda:

> Of course, there's a lot more to be done at CCH. The work here is far from over. But we strongly believe in all children – not just the ones who are doing well. We don't let the test scores discourage us into thinking that schools cannot do it. We use the test scores to light the way for improvement and change. But, I know that all children can achieve their fullest potential – and I am not using it as some sort of slogan, but it is the belief that guides our every waking moment.

Conclusion

The portrait I've presented of these two leaders is congruent with Bogotoch's (as cited in Shields, 2004) definition of educational leadership as a "deliberate intervention that requires the moral use of power" (p. 110). Both leaders recognize the power and personal dimensions of their work. The portrait highlights the proactive ethical stance Darlene and Linda have taken to support student success. In their capacity as leaders in administrative positions, they have not separated the administrative tasks from the educative ones (Evans, 2005) because they regard every administrative task as educative. These leaders have broken through the barriers of deficit thinking and pathologies of silence to demonstrate creativity and passion in designing unique programs and services to meet the needs of the diverse student body. They are engaged in an interactive process involving attentiveness, caring, responsiveness, and competence (Cassidy & Bates, 2005), one that fits with the notion of service that undergird their work in education and beyond.

In addition, the personal involvement and dedication of educators in leadership roles is making a huge difference in the lives of many students in this high school. They acknowledge the contributions of their team/staff in these endeavors. Both Linda and Darlene emphasize the importance of relationship building. Darlene explained:

> I've got wonderful people working here. There is so much talent and potential. And you nurture and you let them have these great ideas in terms of what they want to do, you allow them to do it and you support them. And if they make a mistake, that's okay too, because we learn from our mistakes. Nobody is perfect.

A quote from one participant epitomizes the essence of relational pedagogy that is inherent in transformative leadership:

> In many cases, it's our way of caring and paying attention to these kids so that they don't stop coming to school. Both work with passion and dedication that goes beyond the dictates of the position. It's not the job; it's not the title that makes the program. People with passion are the driving force.

The research literature on transformative intellectuals in school leadership in Canada is sparse. This chapter illustrates exemplary practices within my local context in an effort to address this gap in the literature. Most leaders and those aiming for leadership positions are well-intentioned professionals. It is the responsibility of preparation programs at the university and provincial level to provide them with the appropriate skills and strategies by infusing these programs with the necessary theoretical constructs, practical applications, and examples from the local context of creative, thoughtful, and transformative leadership practices.

Questions

1. Can you describe the Canadian transformative leader?
2. What do we mean by the words *researchers perch*?
3. How can this *perch* impact research?
4. What are the strengths and needs of the participants in this research?

References

Cassidy, W., & Bates, A. (2005). "Drop-outs" or push-outs": Finding hope at a school that actualizes the ethic of care. *American Journal of Education, 112*, 66-102.

Daniel, Y. (1997). *Public schools: Themes of goodness and empowerment.* Unpublished Masters Thesis, York University, Toronto, ON.

Daniel, Y. (2007). School administrators as public intellectuals: Rethinking leadership preparation. In W. Smale & K. Young (Eds.), *Approaches to educational leadership and practice* (pp. 41-57). Calgary, AB: Detselig.

Dantley, M., & Tillman, L. (2006). Social justice and moral transformative leadership. In C. Marshall & M. Oliva (Eds.), *Leadership for social justice: Making revolutions in education* (pp. 16-30). New York: Pearson.

Eisinger, P., & Hula, R. (2004). Gunslinger school administrators: Nontraditional leadership in urban school systems in the United States. *Urban Education, 39*(6), 621-637.

Evans, R. (2005). *The pedagogic principal.* Edmonton, AB: Quail Institute Press.

Gabro, C. (2002). *Portraits of caring elementary administrators: A qualitative study of the caring behaviors of three elementary school administrators.* Doctoral dissertation, Graduate School of Austin State University, TX.

Goddard, T., & Hart, A. (2007). School leadership and equity: Canadian elements. *School Leadership and Management, 27*(1), 7-20.

Greenfield (1995). Toward a theory of school administrations: Informal learning outcomes. *Education Administration Quarterly, 21*(4), 99-119.

Grogan, M. (2004). Keeping a critical, post-modern eye on educational leadership in the United States: In appreciation of Bill Foster. Educational Administration Quarterly, Vol. 40, No. 2, pp. 222-239.

King, A. (2004). *Double cohort study: Phase 3 report for the Ontario Ministry of Education.* Retrieved Feb. 17, 2004, from http://www.edu.gov.on.ca/eng/document/reports/phase3/report3.pdf

Kumashiro, K. (2000). Toward a theory of anti-oppressive education: Four approaches to anti-oppressive education. *Review of Educational Research, 70*(1), 25-53.

Lawrence-Lightfoot, S. (1984). *The good high school: Portraits of character and culture.* New York: Basic Books Inc.

Lawrence-Lightfoot, S., & Davis, J. (1997). *The art and science of portraiture.* Jossey-Bass: San Francisco.

Leithwood, K., & Riehl, C. (2003). *What we know about successful school leadership.* Philadelphia, PA: Laboratory for Student Success, Temple University.

Marshall, C. (2004). Social justice challenges to educational administration: Introduction to a special issue. *Educational Administration Quarterly, 40*(1), 3-13.

Noddings, N. (1995). Teaching themes of care. *Phi Delta Kappan, 76*(5), 675-697.

Ontario Ministry of Education. (2005). *Early school leavers: Understanding the lived reality of student disengagement from secondary school. Final report prepared by Community Health Systems Resource Group – The Hospital for*

Sick Children for the Ontario Ministry of Education and Training, Special Education Branch. Toronto, ON: Author.

Ontario Ministry of Education. (2007). *English language learners: ESL and ELD programs and services: Policies and procedures for Ontario elementary and secondary schools, kindergarten to grade 12.* Retrieved on Jan. 11, 2008 from http://www.edu.gov.on.ca

Raffo, C., & Dyson, A. (2007). Full service extended schools and educational inequality in urban contexts – New opportunities for progress? *Journal of Education Policy, 22*(3), 263-282.

Riehl, C. (2000). The principal's role in creating inclusive schools for diverse students: A review of normative, empirical, and critical literature on the practice of educational administration. *Review of Educational Research, 70*(1), 55-81.

Shields, C. (2004). Dialogic leadership for social justice: Overcoming pathologies of silence. *Educational Administration Quarterly, 40*(1), 109-132.

Skrla, L., & Scheurich, J. (2001). Displacing deficit thinking in school district leadership. *Education and Urban Society, 33*(3), 235-259.

Skrla, L., Scheurich, J., Garcia, J., & Nolly, G. (2004). Equity audits: A practical leadership tool for developing equitable and excellent schools. *Educational Administration Quarterly, 40*(1), 133-161.

Valencia, R. (1997). *The evolution of deficit thinking: Educational thought and practice.* London: Falmer.

Wenger, E. (1998). *Communities of practice: Learning, meaning, and identity.* Cambridge, UK: Cambridge Press.

Chapter Three

Leadership Practices and School Improvement in Alberta

George J. Bedard, Ph.D.
University of Lethbridge

Introduction

In this chapter I try to connect some of the dots between leadership practices and school improvement projects in the province of Alberta. The data upon which I draw is from two province-wide surveys that targeted administrators, teachers, and district coordinators, supplemented by findings and analysis of two Master's theses. The surveys were designed to allow respondents to assess the efficacy of practices to create and sustain school improvement projects (Bedard & Aitken, 2004). Respondents were asked to rate (numerically) leadership practices and encouraged through semi-structured questions to articulate the reasons for their choices.[1] The specific time frame for consideration is the first cycle of the Alberta Initiative for School Improvement (AISI), 2000-2003, but we also included items that probe what organi-

[1] We designed a different semi-structured questionnaire for coordinators only.

zational learning, if any, was garnered in the first three-year cycle and applied to subsequent ones. The University of Lethbridge Research Fund supported this research.

Within this chapter, leadership applies to those with *formal* designations, such as principals, vice-principals (administrators), and district level coordinators, as well as those with *informal* leadership roles, such as teacher leaders. Leadership is defined as the practices that *influence* the processes and outcomes of school improvement projects (Leithwood, Jantzi, & Steinbach, 1999) This definition of leadership implicitly entails that success or failure in this enterprise resides not only with those formally accountable but also with those who work in the core of schools, the teachers (Elmore, 2000; Lambert, 1998).

About AISI

Alberta Education outlined the objectives of AISI as follows:[2]

> The goal of the Alberta Initiative for School Improvement (AISI) is to improve student learning and performance by fostering initiatives that reflect the unique needs and circumstances within school jurisdictions. . . . [AISI] is a bold approach to supporting the improvement of student learning by encouraging teachers, parents and the community to work collaboratively to introduce innovative and creative initiatives (Alberta Education, n.d.).

Alberta Education allocated $198 million to school districts and authorities over the course of AISI Cycle I. All school jurisdictions opted to take part in the first cycle of AISI, 2000-2003. To many in the system, this funding was particularly welcome after several years of cutbacks to programs and salaries (1994-1997). Upon the conclusion of the first round of three-year projects, funds for Cycle II were announced. This second set of completely new projects was launched during the 2003-2004 school year, and completed at the end of 2006, with Cycle III spanning 2006 to 2009. Not all AISI funding has found its way to school improvement projects, however. Anecdotal evidence suggests that some funds were diverted as a "catch-up" mechanism to offset funding cuts, to support additional staffing, to purchase resources, and even to subsidize educators pursing graduate degrees in education.[3]

A description of AISI projects speaks of "partnership, catalyst, student-focused, flexibility, collaboration, culture of continuous improvement, evidence-based practice, research-based interventions, inquiry and reflection, building capacity and sustainability, and knowl-

---

[2] Alberta Education is used throughout the text of this chapter for the sake of consistency, although for the first cycle of AISI the correct term is Alberta Learning (the latter combined K-12 and post-secondary education). Citations, however, differentiate between Alberta Learning and Alberta Education.

[3] See The University of Alberta (2004, June) for a comprehensive report prepared for Alberta Education on the lessons learned from AISI's first cycle.

edge" (Alberta Learning, 2004, pp. 6-7). This is the language of school improvement and re-culturing, staples of educational research in the 1990s and beyond (Heck & Hallinger, 1999). It is certainly the rhetoric of a preferred future about the work of professional educators but whether it reflects a bold new reality needs to be established by more empirical research.

A Tough Nut to Crack

There is a problem if we embrace this AISI rhetoric as reality. Simply put, the traditional idea of schooling with teaching as a semi-covert activity and administration largely as an exercise in administrivia – remains a mighty resilient model. The *grammar* of the traditional model (policies, processes, and forms of organization) has largely survived in tact over the span of several generations despite waves of erstwhile reform (Tyack & Tobin, 1994).

In the traditional model, the teaching and learning process goes relentlessly on, but is rarely observed or commented upon by administrators or by peers. The relationship between administrators and teachers reflects a norm of non-interference that also encompasses teacher-to-teacher relationships (Feiman-Nemser & Floden, 1986; Goldstein, 2003). When grievance procedures, real or threatened, are used to discourage administrators from visiting classrooms, the norm of non-interference is bolstered by micro-politics. Structural issues in large schools may also contribute to a sense of balkanization (by subject departments), and teacher isolation (Hargreaves, 1994) that inhibit collective and group-centred action. Silins and Mulford (2001) affirm that the "traditional structural arrangements in schools, particularly high schools, have long been recognized as impediments to change and the collective learning required for continuous improvement" (p. 3).

Attending to *collective learning* in the context of school improvement, other commentators would suggest, requires a fundamental overhaul of traditional notions of "the way we do things around here," and reframing the organizational culture of schools: Implementing change is a gradual process rather than a direct adoption process. The transition is pervasive and requires change in almost all aspects of the organization, including roles, structures, rules, and practices, as well as the knowledge and skills of the participants (Wohlstetter & Mohrman, 1994, as cited in Wan, 2005, p. 858).

The organizational challenge is to promote more administrator and teacher collaboration. Success in this endeavor can be achieved through a process of mutual adjustment and adaptation, a focus on innovation rather than pigeonholing routines (Mintzberg, 1979), a widening of the net of leadership, and an orientation towards continuous improvement.

But in practical terms, moving Alberta schools in the direction of the alternative model is a very tough nut to crack, constrained by some very durable variables. These same variables have produced a very checkered history for school improvements over decades in North America. In explaining the complexities of restructuring, Newmann (as cited in Brandt, 1995) over a decade ago stated that as few as ten percent of schools that undertook improvement initiatives were successful. Successful exemplars, he noted, focused on teaching that "changed and responded to restructuring as a growth process, pursuing change through a reflective dialogue – as opposed to mandated change – and schools that measured their success by improved learning through changed classroom practice" (p. 71). A more recent large-scale study of school improvement projects in schools across Ontario and New York State came to a similarly pessimistic conclusion: Sustaining school improvement initiatives is systemically undermined by significant "change forces," typically beyond the control of schools, and is ultimately stagnated by standardization in educational policy-making (Hargreaves & Goodson, 2006). Omitted from Hargreaves and Goodson's discussion is how collective bargaining agreements enforce a standardized uniformity that may serve association/union members well, but not necessarily the evolving needs of students (Lawton, Bedard, MacLellan, & Li, 1999).

Beach and Lindahl (2004) argue that sustainable wide-scale school improvement consists of three phases: planning, implementation and institutionalization. For institutionalization to coalesce, improvement initiatives must have authentic beginnings within the organization, commitment and ownership among teachers, flexibility, adequate resources, and policy alignment (Datnow, Hubbard, & Mehan, 2002). Many school improvement initiatives fail to reach the stage of institutionalization precisely because these variables are found wanting.

What do we expect to find when schools move away from the traditional model to the school improvement model? Silins and Mulford (2001) provide the following answer:

> These schools have agreed upon goals that include developing a trusting and collaborative environment. Processes and structures that support open communication, sharing of information and participatory decision-making are necessary for a school to work as a team of learners and build their capacity for organizational learning. The trusting and collaborative climate factor confirms the need to promote collective learning for continual improvement. Schools require structures that encourage the development of learning communities that value differences, support critical reflection, and encourage members to question, challenge and debate teaching and learning issues. (p. 11)

In the new model, relationships, processes, and structures are realigned in order to create a tighter fit between professional activity (the means) and student learning outcomes and development (the ends).

Accountability

Peeking beneath the school improvement focus of AISI, one finds a framework for accountability, built on three core initiatives: (1) refocusing policy on regulating performance by outputs, such as student achievement, rather than by input or process standards, such as hours/minutes of instruction and qualifications of staff; (2) the articulation of standards for student achievement; and (3) the linking together of policies for curriculum frameworks, assessments, accreditation, performance reporting, rewards, sanctions, certification, and licensure (Cibulka & Derlin, 1998). These three core thrusts could be construed as modes of standardization, the lament of Hargreaves and Goodson notwithstanding.

The accountability agenda was further advanced by the findings and recommendations of the Alberta Commission on Learning (ACOL) (2003). ACOL commissioners found that leadership preparation was sorely lacking both focus and standards; hence, two recommendations were made aimed at ensuring that principals are adequately prepared in core competencies required for school improvement. ACOL recommended, first, that educational stakeholders develop a quality practice standard that would identify the knowledge, skills, and attributes required for principals to reflect current realities (p. 122) and, second, that a new program be established to prepare and certify principals (p. 123). A Stakeholders' Committee from 2006 to 2007 articulated the quality practice standard, with seven leadership dimensions, in response to ACOL's recommendations. Even so, how this standard will be applied, and the organizational framework needed to support it, still await formulation and implementation by Alberta Education.

AISI Cycle I Survey

Conceptual framework

In preparing the AISI Cycle I survey, my colleague and I chose Ken Leithwood's model of transformational leadership as our conceptual framework (Leithwood, Jantzi, & Steinbach, 1999). For over thirty years, Leithwood and his colleagues have analyzed the work of formal and informal leaders as they attempt to influence the values, attitudes, and behaviors of others in schools and districts. Leithwood's seven dimensions of transformational leadership are:

> building school vision; establishing school goals; providing intellectual stimulation; offering individualized support; modeling best practices and important organizational values; demonstrating high performance expectations; creating a productive school culture; and developing structures to foster participation in school decisions. (Leithwood, Jantzi, & Steinbach, 1999, p. 9)

The notion of transformational leadership sees leaders as agents whose commitment to organizational change goes well beyond superficiality (Hargreaves, 2003). Within this concept, *leading* means going beyond administrivia to move schools in the direction of significant, large-scale improvement (Beach & Lindahl, 2004). In Leithwood's model, formal leaders are expected to exercise their influence on members by focusing on three core tasks: setting direction, developing people, and redesigning the organization. The aim is – from a facilitative, not a control-centred perspective – to align roles, practices, cultures, structures, and work processes to reflect values, visions, and goals as articulated by the school community. We adapted these three core tasks in our surveys to focus on visioning and goal setting, internal and external support, and promoting teacher leadership. Another important issue that lies beyond the scope of this discussion is discerning how school improvement initiatives are connected by leadership practices through engaging students, parents, and the larger community.

Design and Methods

This mixed methods design consisted of one quantitative survey (with some anecdotal items), one qualitative survey, and findings from two Master's theses (Darroch, 2006; Thiel, 2006) that I supervised. Data collection was generated from a number of sources and instruments that met university and district guidelines for human subject reviews. The first of these was a web-based survey with items designed by Bedard and Aitken (2004) with administrators and teachers as respondents. The intent of this survey was to provide a clearer picture of specific leadership practices of this group and their relationship to AISI projects. Twenty-two Likert-type questions enabled us to pursue a quantitative analysis of the data, and six anecdotal items provided additional data that we analyzed qualitatively for patterns and themes. We also developed a different survey for AISI coordinators (district level) that featured eleven semi-structured, open-ended questions that produced anecdotal responses. For this voluntary study a total of 227 subjects responded from 20 school districts: 118 administrators, 88 teachers, and 21 district coordinators. Of these, 55 subjects worked in K-6 schools and 151 worked in middle or high schools. A total of 206 schools were represented with 156 schools classified as rural and 50 designated as urban schools (for the Alberta context, this means larger towns and cities).

In addition to web-based surveys, our data is supplemented by the findings and analysis of two Master's students whose thesis topics were closely related to the theme of leadership practices and the development and sustainability of AISI projects. Thiel (2006) researched three districts in central Alberta and developed a written questionnaire that was responded to by twenty-two AISI participants. From these responses, nine interviews were conducted. These interviews were conducted with two elementary teachers, four high school teachers (including one counselor and one student support teacher), one vice-principal of a K-9 school, one high school vice-principal, and one high school principal. In addition, a focus group was conducted consisting of an AISI coordinator, three administrators at the Preschool to Grade 9 level, and one Grade 7-9 teacher. In all, twenty-seven subjects were queried in this project. Darroch (2006) worked from one southern Alberta school district and interviewed fifteen AISI contacts, of which thirteen were administrators. Between these two projects, an addition 42 respondents were queried, bringing the total number of respondents to 269.

Survey Characteristics

Respondents were asked to indicate their level of agreement with 22 different statements, using Strongly Agree (1), Agree (2), Neither (3), Disagree (4) and Strongly Disagree (5) response categories. Upon entry into SPSS, all responses were reverse coded (e.g., a 1 response was entered as a 5). Survey items were grouped into four different categories: Vision (4 items), Goal Setting (7 items), Teacher Leadership (3 items) and Internal Support (8 items). Scores for each of the items in each of these categories were summed to create four variables for analysis: Vision, Goal Setting, Teacher Leadership and Internal Support. A fifth variable, entitled Overall Leadership Practice, was created by summing rating scores across all 22 items. External support items consisted of semi-structured questions that required written responses.[4] The *sense making* of both qualitative and quantitative data was very much a collective and protracted enterprise, involving two professors and a research assistant. We undertook data collection and analysis from spring 2004 (surveys) to fall 2006 (to include thesis findings).

Findings

Administrators and Teachers :Not Quite on the Same Page

Before I discuss the specific practices of vision, goal setting, internal and external support, and teacher leadership, I should note that we found that administrators and teachers were statistically significant different groups, with administrators rating their practices consistently higher than teachers rated administrator practices. Administrators and teachers were also consistently different on which items on the scales were considered to be more important to them.[5]

---

[4] Results from the reliability analysis performed on each of the four scales indicate that the scale items have adequate internal consistency: Cronbach alpha scores were as follows: Vision .78, Goal setting .86, Teacher Leadership .796 and Internal Support .899. The survey scales and questions in their entirety are found in the Appendix of this chapter.

[5] The numerical details of this discrepancy can be found in the Appendix.

Why did administrators rate their leadership practices consistently higher than teachers? One possible explanation is that teachers' work keeps them at least partially out of purview of what administrators do, and thus they do not know what administrators are actually doing, nor do they care to take on even more work to find this out. While this possibility may have some bearing here, it is difficult to assume that core activities such as vision, goal setting, and internal support can be exercised without teachers being aware of them, since their implementation implies administrator-teacher interaction. Another possible explanation is suggested by a study of Alberta principal effectiveness by Townsend and Adams (2003). Noting that self-report surveys are particularly vulnerable to subjective, if not self-serving, assessments, they suggest that the penchant for higher self-ratings by principals may "reveal some obvious gaps between principals' espoused theory and theory-in-use" (Argyris & Schön, 1974), as well as a "greater generalized misalignment between their *skills espoused* and *skills applied*" (p. 2). Consequently, I found the comments of district-based coordinators most helpful in adding another perspective on leadership practices as their purview included many schools, administrators, and teachers.

Vision and Goals

Leithwood, Jantzi, and Steinbach (1999) note that vision and goal setting are important because they help set the general direction that a staff agrees should be embarked upon and the specific targets for improvement. In his model they are two of the more powerful levers that formal leaders have *direct* influence over, as opposed to an *indirect* influence on core teaching and learning functions that are embedded in teacher-student interactions. Vision and goal setting require protracted, deep, on-going discussions among staffs in order to generate

> personal agreement with the importance of those directions, a sense that the directions have considerable value or moral weight, and motivaticn to develop whatever new capacities might be required to successfully progress towards them. Organizational directions acquire such authentic meaning only through processes that are relatively extended, and that permit individual reflection, as well as dialogue and discussion among school members. (p. 70)

In our survey, vision items asked respondents to quantify and verbalize their perceptions about shared beliefs, mission statements, current visions and contexts, processes to determine instructional and school-wide effectiveness, and communication patterns to support them. Items that inquired about goals focused on the use of data in goal setting, collective and group discussions, target setting, timelines for achievement, identification of resources to support goals, action plans with identified actors, and communications with stakeholders about goals.

For teachers, the mean ratings for Vision and Goal Setting were 3.1 (SD = 0.7), and 2.9 (SD = 0.8), respectively. The mean ratings for administrators on these same variables were 3.4 (SD = 0.5) and 3.4 (SD = 0.5).

While visioning and goal setting may be important considerations in various leadership models, their application in settings such as AISI projects does not neatly fit a tidy pattern in which visioning and goal setting *precede* and give direction to the planning process, most particularly at the school level. In the AISI framework, the district supervises projects through the approval process, reporting to the School Improvement Branch of Alberta Education, and it is the district that receives the funding which it shares with participating schools. Thus, much of what we heard about visions and goals was centred on district-level activity. In some cases, districts involved school level staff in the process. One respondent captures this process succinctly:

> Vision and goals for the district were developed in a strategic plan – established in a collaborative process by various stakeholders. The district vision/goals helped to direct how . . . the project was organized. Senior level administration was actively involved in constructing the project collaboratively with teachers.

Sixteen respondents pointed out that the focus on goals and vision was the glue that held the project together, gave it purpose, and contributed to the overall success of the project, as one noted:

> It [the project] was based on mission, vision and shared beliefs. It involved teacher leaders. The project was collaboratively determined. Appropriate funding was provided to allow for teacher in-service and resource acquisition. We have a fantastic staff dedicated to ensuring student success.

On the other hand, district-level leadership and administrator involvement and support of AISI in visioning and goal setting seems suspect at best in several districts, according to several respondents:

> The potential of leadership at the district level and at the school level to have a very strong positive impact on our AISI project is there, but it has been hindered by a lack of knowledge and understanding. As knowledge and understanding increases, so does the influence that leadership at these levels has.

> Senior leadership has not understood the value of articulating the vision and mission. Leadership at that level is philosophical and moral, but not necessarily strategic. Leadership at the principal level is absent for the most

> part. They neither grasp the idea that their role is two fold – spread the message and change the context (i.e., make it happen). Those occupying the chairs of leadership seem to see the work as someone else's. Hence, teachers are filling the gap. This is now causing power and authority issues as people raise the question: Who is in charge?
>
> The most challenging part of leadership has been getting school principals to go through the process with their teachers and take an "active" role in the learning and action part of the process. We had strong leadership at all the other levels but, in some schools where the principal was sitting on the sideline and just giving lip service, very little was happening. . . . The principal is still the key to making things happen in a school and paving the way, removing obstacles, etc. Teachers who are keen need to feel truly supported in every way by the principal or it is not enough for the teachers and myself to be committed.

While some evidence suggests a merging of top-down and bottom-up approaches to visioning and goal setting, this was by no means the universal practice. In several school districts, school-level staff were unsure about how the district arrived at the visioning and goal setting process. Nonetheless, some schools incorporated district efforts with very little or no indication of resentment by their staff, while the staff in other schools within similar contexts chafed at projects they felt were imposed from above over which they had little say in defining (Thiel, 2006). However, even where staff resentment was low, respondents were clearly at a loss to explain in a direct way the relationship of vision and goals to the AISI process because they had little or no say in the visioning and goal setting process. As Darroch (2006) explains:

> Nine of the fifteen interviews indicated, in varying degrees, that a vision had been developed within their schools and there was some alignment between their AISI projects and their visions. The responses, though positive, were quite vague. Rarely did explanations go into any depth, and more lengthy responses usually addressed other school needs unrelated to vision or mission. Elements of the AISI projects were a complement to the instruction and programming already available in schools, rather than an extension of the central vision of the school community. (Darroch, 2006, p. 38).

In some cases, the imposition of district-defined projects rankled school-level staff, and, as the following implies, very little cooperation between the district and schools on visioning, goals, and plans could be expected:

> Participants in District 2 school staff projected an, "us versus them" attitude, clearly holding negative perceptions towards district office. School staff felt district personnel were "out of touch" with what was going on, not having "been in the trenches" for some time. Participants were overwhelmed with the number of initiatives being "handed down" to them. These attitudes reveal strained relations between district office and school personnel and these perceptions were damaging at the school level as they permeated staff and school culture, creating a negative atmosphere, affecting staff and students alike. (Thiel, 2006, pp. 133-134)

Some survey respondents recognized that *goal articulation* was important but was not a central feature of their Cycle I projects. Many of the suggestions for improvement in subsequent cycles were linked closely to school goal-setting processes. Teachers typically offered that success could be enhanced if there were more involvement at the ground level and planning stages of the project. They suggested

> clearly stating and sharing the goals to the whole staff. Allowing people to get started now. Not mandating top down projects. Professionals need to take charge of their own practice, not be bored by others not on the same page, or stifled with others whose goals are ridiculously low. We need to have clear objectives with specific goals to achieve. More input and clarification from project. I am still not clear of exactly what it is or the goals that it has.

Similarly several administrators allowed that goal-setting improvements needed to be improved and implemented to enhance the success of AISI projects:

> Involving all the staff from K to 12 and regularly reviewing the goals and outcomes, and celebrating our successes as a school team.

> More clearly defined goals and outcomes for the program. More collaboration from staff members at our school. Getting feedback from the students in a more official manner.

There was a recognition that more should be done to ensure that this process was informed by the discussion of data, not just perceptions. We found scant evidence to suggest that baseline data was used to inform the goal articulation process and that goals were measurable. Many of the projects were designed around a perceived need rather than being data-driven decisions:

> This was a district-level project so schools had no input except through the strategic plan. Goals were designed on PAT scores and analysis, factoring in contextual variables.

> School data did not play a large role in AISI goal-setting. Goals were established through a process of perceptions rather than data.
>
> (Data use) varied greatly in schools. Some utilized available data well, others developed programs/goals based on perceived need.

Several respondents noted that the lack of measurable goals during Cycle I precluded making informed judgments about whether AISI projects were having any positive impacts, and they drew a direct link to this lack and the cancellation of projects. By Cycle II, some districts and schools made a more concerted effort to define, implement, and evaluate measurable goals, as an AISI district coordinator articulates, but even this was uneven in its application across subject areas:

> When AISI projects were first introduced in our district they were introduced at the school level with no district support on how to design a project that had observable and measurable indicators of success. Part way through the first cycle most of the school-level projects were discontinued because none of the school principals were able to articulate how school level AISI projects were being successful and no effort was being made on their part to collect data. . . . In addition it was clear that no changes in teaching practice were taking place in this initial stage. In Cycle ll, we moved to district projects with clearly articulated measures of success. AISI continued to provide an extra source of funding for professional development but the funds were directed towards targeted areas. In our early literacy projects our indicators of success have clearly demonstrated we are achieving our goals and there has been an observable change in teaching practice. With our other projects it has been more difficult to demonstrate the impact on student learning.

By Cycle II (2003-2006), we noted that some participants formed a greater appreciation of the role professional development could play in supporting the articulation and achievement of goals (particularly in areas like student assessment) and equipping educators with empirical means of evaluating a project's success or failure. Thiel (2006), however, cautions in her study that knowledge of project evaluation techniques for AISI projects was generally weak among the administrators in her sample from three districts. Thus it is not surprising to learn that that few projects in these districts were evaluated as to their efficacy even well into Cycle II.

Vision and Goals: The Bottom Line

The pattern that emerges here is that while visioning may be a fixture of school improvement literature, the first cycle of AISI proceeded largely without much work in this direction, at least at the school level. A vision was built into the promise and rhetoric of AISI, perhaps, but my colleagues and I find no abundance of evidence that districts and schools made visioning an explicit part of their planning process for AISI (with some notable exceptions). While confusion on this issue is somewhat understandable (why bother with vision when it's already been handed down by provincial bureaucrats?), the palpable indifference to goal setting (where do we want to go, how will we get there, and how will we know when we have arrived?) is more difficult to accept as a practice. It is impossible to chart improvements in student achievement (AISI's rationale) without setting measurable goals, creating baseline data (the before picture), developing a multifaceted understanding of student assessment techniques (going beyond sole reliance upon provincial achievement assessments), and connecting teaching practices to student learning and achievement (while refraining from using student achievement as the sole benchmark for evaluating the overall efficacy of leadership and teaching practices). This requires, among other things, applied knowledge and skills in data analysis (disaggregating the data) and opening up classrooms to shine a light on the realities of teaching practices. Educators need a more sophisticated knowledge of assessment techniques and these need to be plugged into the instructional process: "When teachers' classroom assessments become an integral part of the instructional process and a central ingredient of their efforts to help students learn, the benefits of assessment for both students and teachers will be boundless" (Guskey, 2003, p. 10).

Recognition of these needs did prompt some changes in Cycle II strategies, but evidence from the first cycle is that generally neither administrators or teachers understood the conceptual implications of a strategic approach to school improvement nor were they skilled in goal setting and assessment techniques necessary for this type of enterprise. Moreover, when some administrators chose to absent themselves from the school improvement process and treated projects as "giveaways" to be shouldered by their staffs, then the issue becomes not a matter of lack of knowledge or skills but rather a fundamental indifference to the very notion of school improvement. Deal and Peterson (1999) suggest that a leader must "realize that what is appreciated, recognized and honored, (and) signal the key values of what is admirable and achievable" (p. 207). Administrators who deem school improvement projects as peripheral to their own agenda signal to their staffs that they might just as well follow suit.

Internal support

Silins and Mulford (2001) suggest that leadership practices attending to internal support are built around the reciprocity of positive relationships, openness to discussion, willingness to learn about teaching and learning practices, a mutual commitment to capacity building through professional development, and processes and structures that enable a greater orientation to collective decision making and reflection. All of these practices are directed towards improving student achievement and development. New and creative approaches to providing internal support are necessary to help educators "navigate the difficult space between letting go of old patterns and grabbing on to new ones" (Deal, 1990, p. 11).

For this study, we defined internal support to encompass a wide range of actions carried out by leaders to motivate staff and build capacity for goal achievement. Survey items included the extent to which administrators and other members of the leadership team supported AISI projects by: monitoring discussions about action steps for change and about progress towards objectives; encouraging professional development built around the project's aims; discussing new knowledge and pedagogy emanating from the projects; accessing and discussing relevant research; leading an inquiry focus; supporting innovations through frequent classroom visits and follow-up discussions; offering encouragement; and valuing discussion and reflection on AISI projects.

For teachers, the mean ratings for the Internal Support variable were 3.0 (SD = 0.8) and the mean ratings for administrators on this same variable were 3.3 (SD = 0.6). Again, teachers rated administrators' practices lower than did administrators. Twenty AISI coordinators also responded to semi-structured questions about internal and external support.

Close to 200 comments from administrators and teachers provided an array of reasons why AISI work in the school was productive and many directly relate to internal support items.

Twenty-eight of these responses cited the direct link to student learning as the key reason for the success of the project. As an example:

> Every child has a different learning style and the AISI project allowed a handful of students to access their learning style and enjoy learning and their time in school to a greater extent.

Another common rationale for project success focused on teacher collaboration. For example:

> It has helped us develop teaching teams that are supportive and have grown into strong collegial groups.

> It allowed for prime time collaboration. Various colleagues began to discuss the theories and practical applications of material read or knowledge gained through focused PD. Dollars were provided to help facilitate purchasing resources and attending PD.

Some ran with the collaboration idea but articulated that the collaboration was a means to an end:

> All staff were operating from the same premise and were working together to achieve the goals set out. There developed a common sense of purpose within the school. We made it fun for the students and parents. A majority of the money was spent directly on resources for the students to use.

Only eight teachers responded that research practices enhanced their project, but there were several implied comments that suggested that high-level approaches such as reflective practice, a cycle of enquiry, and purposeful professional development were becoming part of the repertoire. For example:

> It has allowed me to become more reflective of my teaching practice and to question "why" I do things in the way that I do them. It has also benefited my students by . . . offering them greater choice in and ownership of their own learning.

> It has "opened" our classroom doors and has given us the opportunity to become a working member of the "whole school." It allowed us the luxury of time to research and discuss findings and new directions before having to implement these new focuses. From our research, we have been able to explore and implement new and exciting teaching practices that bring strong benefits to the children.

> The productive part of the AISI work was that we researched, implemented, and professionally developed teachers in a specific topic. The teachers started doing their own research and the dialogue was rich and student centered. Teachers began looking at the data to drive their instruction. They began to realize that their data was not significant. The initial project involved and changed as the staff looked at the data and realized that there wasn't enough. They wanted more information. They began to ask the questions.

The following comment illustrates a collaborative process of dialogue and inquiry made possible because AISI funds were used to enable it. As in many comments from our respondents, the use of *time* as a critical factor in collaboration is highlighted:

> We identified an area of weakness and worked together to improve the situation. We gained insight into and a greater understanding of each teacher's classroom situation (i.e., expectations for students). Regular focused conversations about our AISI project created a safe environment for teachers to seek assistance in areas they felt inadequate to deal with on their own. Regular, scheduled meeting times devoted to AISI allowed us to begin and finish conversations without interruption. Prior to AISI meetings we had no common planning time and therefore had snippets of conversations in hallways at recess break. Our efforts have produced results in the classroom – our students have improved their reading skills. Our efforts have produced results in teacher collaboration – we see each other as partners and network much more with each other.

In some cases, collaboration and inquiry led staffs to reconsider their attitudes about student learning and about the need to rethink their teaching practice. For example:

> AISI . . . set into motion a large group of teachers who have the skills to teach children more effectively and successfully, as well as have much higher expectations for what students can actually do. Staff no longer can use the excuse that it is the community, family, student that is the problem when students do not succeed – it has made us reflective and aware of best practices and the continued need to hone our craft based on the research that is available.

Only a few other respondents chose to comment on the actual student achievement result. For instance:

> Student participation was unusually high; test results showed improvement beyond expectation and usual student learning.

> Our school saw an increase in students earning a high school diploma. Many of these individuals were considered at risk students and would not have earned a diploma without the AISI program.

Some coordinators stressed just how essential the support of the principal is to the successful outcome of the project:

> There is a strong correlation between the principal's active interest and support and the success of the project. Almost all of our school projects demonstrated strong interest and support.

Shared or distributed leadership was cited by a few as an effective way to support the initiatives:

> Many of the principals delegated the project to a school lead teacher and then provided support for that position. This seemed to work very effectively.

Indeed, one coordinator suggested that when the principal takes the lead on a school improvement project that the initiative will not likely succeed:

> In schools where the principal took the primary leadership role, the AISI project tended to have less importance and less buy-in with staff.

A few coordinators indicated that the principal's support took the form of playing a key role in communication. For example:

> Principals who were engaged in the writing of the project continued with the project in one role or another. This involved attending monthly meetings with leaders from all of the schools in the project as well as participation in steering-committee meetings.

Thiel (2006, pp. 101-104) underscored the importance of three main categories of leadership practices that were positively perceived by her respondents as buttressing internal support for AISI projects: promoting teamwork, relationship building, and time management. Leaders promoted teamwork through the development of collaborative teams, professional learning communities, and staff meetings, ensuring the alignment of PD opportunities with professional growth plans and promoting interschool networking and relationships. Relationship building involved nurturing a culture of trust, encouragement, shared decision-making and transparency. Time management included creating spaces outside of preparation time where teams and whole staffs could reflect and evaluate their school improvement efforts. In this scenario, staff meetings became less focused on administrivia and more centred on project related activities.

One hundred-two teachers and one hundred-thirty administrators also shared with us their views on why projects were deemed unsuccessful. Just as a focus on student and teacher success, adequate resources, and a commitment to work on shared goals need to be evident for successful projects, the absence of those same attributes will contribute to the demise of the project. Most suggestions for better internal and external support of improvement projects mirrored parts of the following expansive list of factors offered by teachers:

- poor administration
- lack of looking at school data
- lack of looking to research for best practice
- lack of support from colleagues
- lack of communication for all steps in the process of change
- lack of school visioning and norms

- lack of significant student achievement gains within the first year expectations for only small increases (i.e., little by little things will get better – but by setting the bar only a bit higher lets you off the hook so to speak to be responsible to find something, (and it's out there), that will get the majority of kids)
- lack of communication between stakeholders
- lack of appropriate funding and assistance for the project
- no collaboration or PD for teachers
- money spent on staffing rather than PD
- non-reflective or short term professional development
- ineffective evaluation criteria
- project is top down rather than defined by those doing the project

Only a few teachers were introspective about viewing the project in terms of a broader set of needs, or in other words, thinking systemically. The following teacher comments illustrate the importance of operating within the larger context and operating without a dependency on external financial support as a motivator. This critique centred on projects that:

- serve as a band-aid approach for an instructional need
- require continuous funding (no matter how valuable)
- are carried out in isolation of what is happening at a school
- are not linked to the overall instructional network of the school in some way

Administrator respondents tended to express multiple needs and suggested enhancements in a variety of focus areas. For example, the following comments addressed several areas of concern related to internal support items, particularly related to the instructional leadership role:

- greater flexibility for the administrator to visit classes
- more staff members serving on the instructional leadership team so we could share the load
- better communication with the community about the focus that we have
- more instructional time devoted to collaboration for staff and more in depth discussion of how our teaching can change with the adoption of best practices
- better data display

In particular, most administrator comments were resource related. Apart from the anticipated time and money remarks, administrators ventured into a number of other resource-related needs. They spoke about the need for effective consultants, workable evaluation processes, focused coordination, emerging teacher leadership, and the need to promote teacher dialogue.

Internal Support: The Bottom Line

Teachers and administrators most often attributed the success of their projects to the connections that the initiative made with student learning. While a few respondents were able to cite specific student achievement goals as a result of their AISI projects, most did not. The asymmetrical rate of project development, with some districts and schools clearly lagging behind some others, suggests that some projects had not coalesced enough to produce any noticeable gains. Given the difficulties in establishing baseline data for achievement and in developing measurable goals (discussed in vision and goal setting), it would have been problematic to establish a positive connection to student learning in any case. In addition, poorly conceived and managed projects, of which we have much evidence in Cycle I, were doomed to a very short shelf life.

Collaboration was frequently cited as the reason why projects were successful and it is clear that AISI provided space, time, and resources for this collaboration to take place but only if administrators attended to these issues. Gibb, Gibb, Randall, and Hite (1999) noted, "The progress of collaborative paradigms of leadership is evidence that educators are emerging with their own definitions of what it means to lead in the schoolhouse" (p. 21). A collaborative culture is where

> teachers feel confident and are able to exercise judgment and power as professionals. Enabling centralization is flexible, cooperative and collaborative. . . . School administrators in such structures use their power and authority to help teachers to design structures that facilitate teaching and learning; in brief, they empower their teachers. (Sinden, Hoy, & Sweetland, 2004, p. 464)

Staffs collaborated in many forms: planning, discussing data and research, reflecting on practice, assessing practice, and planning professional development. While this collaborative orientation may have opened some classrooms to visits from teacher colleagues, we note that administrators had little to say about whether AISI had actually opened up classrooms for their visits, and some indicated that they would like more of an opportunity, and a more welcoming atmosphere, in this direction. It is clear that many teachers had never experienced the level of collaboration that AISI afforded and that many school leaders created the opportunities for this to happen through team and relationship building and creative scheduling. Our findings on collaboration and collegiality tend to support Barth's (1990) assertion:

> The literature suggests that a number of outcomes may be associated with collegiality. Decisions tend to be better. Implementation of decisions is better. There is a higher level of morale and trust among adults. Adult learning is energized and more likely to be sustained. (p. 31)

Focused professional development directly related to school needs and staff empowerment. Moreover, a much greater orientation towards reflective practice emerged as critical internal supports in schools where AISI projects were perceived to be successful. Management of time also emerged as an important aspect of successful implementation:

> Incorporating time up front in the change process for teachers to study new materials, practice new instructional techniques, and weigh the possibilities of new organizational arrangements is a critically important step in successful school reform efforts, but one that is more often than not given short shrift. The all-too-common pattern in educational reform has been and continues to be a leap from a planning phase . . . to an expectation of a full-blown implementation and documentation of positive results within two or three years. (Adelman & Walking Eagle, 2007, pp. 107-108)

External Support

External support for school improvement comes from two levels: provincial (Alberta Education) and districts. At the provincial level, it is important that an array of educational policies such as accountability, curriculum and assessment and funding mechanisms lend their weight behind school-based initiatives (Cohen & Hill, 2001). An alignment of policies towards this end is also needed:

> Successful school improvement requires a policy environment which creates and supports the basic conditions for professional learning communities and ongoing capacity building in schools in ways that increase the extent and deepen the degree to which teachers inquire into and discuss with their colleagues how best to raise standards of student learning. Capacity building is an inalienable condition of school improvement and this is undermined by short-term strategies based on compliance and control. (Hargreaves, Shaw, et al., 2000, p. 14)

District-level support is critical to initiate and sustain school-based initiatives, helping to develop purpose and direction, and to build capacity for fundamental change. Several researches have expressed the importance of this support. Musella (1995) comments that "[district-level] work created many of the organizational conditions giving rise to quality education, particularly through its contribution to the improvement of school-level administrator effectiveness" (p. 225). Ansell (2004) goes on to state that "you need to use external people in such a way as to say to the school, 'You are OK. I am going to empower you to sort this out.' External people need to build capacity in the school, not stifle it" (p. 15). Leighwood, Jantzi, and Steinbach (1999) also note that "teachers' commitment to change is subtly but significantly influenced by district-level conditions" (pp. 147-148).

Respondents were also asked to rate or comment upon how well districts and Alberta Education supported school-based AISI work. One hundred-and-one teachers (101) and 127 administrators provided responses to these cues. While some did cite both district and Alberta Education as positive external supports, most administrators and teachers were critical about the availability of resources and with the support provided by Alberta Education. Time and money were the main culprits linked to resources while Alberta Education was cited ten times for not providing sufficient funding, or for reducing funding.

One teacher said,

> The limited AISI funds did not allow the provision of resources and personnel in greater depth, across the full K-12 instructional spectrum.

Administrators tended to direct their criticism at the structure, tenure, and reporting requirements of the program. For example, one administrator saw the three-year cycle as an impediment. "The requirement that projects be changed every three years, even if something is effective, [was a limiting factor]." Another administrator summed up frustration, shared by a number of other administrator respondents, with the accountability role of Alberta Education,

> Trying to fit within Alberta Education's "rules" and jump through hoops. Having to justify that we really do qualify for this funding is offensive, given that it is our responsibility (and the Alberta government's) to educate and support our students.

Administrators were in agreement with teachers in terms of the most important areas that were needed to externally support projects. Some however used this question to express some of their frustrations with central office coordination,

- project dictated by non-classroom personal i.e., central office
- leave money in the schools where the students are and not to pay salaries for organizational type people, [for] travel funds, conferences, substitute teachers because teachers are not in the classrooms to teach their classes

The perceived lack of sustainability clearly bothered some teachers and some comments indicated that school improvement seemed to require continued external support as an incentive.

> This project needs to be sustained at the division level. I saw teachers turning off when they saw the project coming to an end. The teacher didn't feel they had the expertise and knowledge capable of continuing on their own. I wish I could get it through [to] our board to con-

> tinue this specific type of in-service and sustain it at the division level.

Many responses, from both teachers and administrators, clearly indicated a frustration with time availability. For example, the following comment was typical of teachers' concerns: "Time – not sufficient during the course of a day or week to permit teachers to plan, share, and discuss." Interestingly, some saw the little time that was allocated as a gift rather than a problem. This administrator comment seemed to sum up that particular sentiment:

> Teachers have an opportunity to work together once a month—meeting to share best practices, resources, look at student work, develop writing rubrics, identify key areas for instruction to enhance students' writing—more time for teachers to work together would be valuable. More opportunities for inter-visitations would also support staff. With more funding, we could plan more of this!

There were suggestions that colleague interest in the projects was often lacking. Ten percent of respondents indicated that there were difficulties creating interest among colleagues. Included in these remarks were suggestions that there was a necessity to try to *sell* the AISI ideas and projects to others. For example, "Some teachers saw this as just another thing being put on their plates – and thus had a difficult time seeing any benefits gained." Others acknowledged that staff were willing to support the projects, but were only able to do so in a limited way based on their perceived relevance of the project: "Staff did participate and their involvement varied due to individual recognition and willingness to use something that they were not currently using." To disaffected teachers, AISI projects were perceived as yet more impositions foisted upon schools by districts and Alberta Education.

AISI district coordinators offered a more positive take on external support than that offered by administrators and teachers. Our data suggests that district-based coordinators performed a number of roles as part of the external support for AISI: working extensively and communicating with project leaders; gathering data and analyzing results; designing structures to gather relevant information; reporting directly to boards, to the superintendent, and to principal groups, as well as to Alberta Education; and they often took on a primary role in coordinating and facilitating teachers' professional development. Coordinators also possessed a district-wide, detailed perspective on the evolution of school-based projects, growing pains, and hits and misses, that no other respondents, by virtue of their positions, could match.

Almost without exception AISI coordinators acknowledged that senior level district leaders supported the projects by implementing some form of district-wide coordination. Many added that the level of coordination and support was of a high quality. For example:

> Excellent. Strong support and in fact, an increasing level of involvement and support from the superintendent . . . AISI is on the Board agenda more frequently and on the agenda for administrators' meetings.

> Our school district has learned a tremendous amount regarding AISI leadership during this second cycle. We are currently writing recommendations for project design change (through leadership, individual school collaboration) in anticipation of Cycle III. At the district level, the areas that had the most impact were a) strong central office support, b) support for and formation of professional learning communities at the school level, c) strong support for individual school professional development plans, and d) formation of the AISI Lead teacher role at each individual school.

Another coordinator's comment illustrated the "start the ball rolling and get out of the way" approach:

> Once the projects were underway, there was little involvement from district leaders outside of the coordinator—although the superintendent responsible for AISI was kept appraised of development of each project. Support for projects was always in the forefront.

One coordinator's comment illustrated the diverse nature of the coordinator's role in supporting school-based projects:

> [The district] provided time for system coordination of the 21 AISI projects. This proved to be a very valuable use of funding to support AISI coordination, liaison with Alberta Education and other districts. The central coordination provided projects with assistance in the development of measures and tools, collection of data, financial procedures, tracking, reporting, selection of projects, revisions of projects, coordination for group projects, communication, celebrations, advocacy, etc.

But not all coordinators concluded that their support efforts were appreciated at the school level:

> While the coordinators gained significant capacity in many areas to help improve teaching, the process and system, we are regarded as not having any value generally. We spent the largest portion of time in paper work, often acting as travel agents, or event hosts.

On the other hand, most coordinators reported that they were heavily involved in facilitating teachers' professional development as it supported the project; some saw it as an on-going component of their job and others described it as the central part of their role. One was most eloquent in describing professional development work as a transformative experience:

> I am not the same person that I was at the beginning of my involvement with AISI. Our project focused on facilitating teacher professional development. By working with others toward a clear goal, by having on-going professional relationships with others in the project and by having access to fabulous resources, we became a strong professional learning community. As one of our principals said, "Our monthly meetings are the best PD that I get."

Still other coordinators commented that their coordination of professional development was based on a ground-up approach. For example:

> I encouraged teachers to engage in related PD, provided regular collaboration sessions, and the time and resources to expand their leadership and knowledge base.

External Support: The Bottom Line

External support for AISI, judging from the data, seems to be a case of the glass being half-empty or half-full: many administrators and teachers chafed at levels of funding (deemed inadequate) and time frames for projects (each new cycle of AISI requires starting new projects regardless of the promise, or degree of development, of ongoing projects) as well as other miscellaneous external impositions. It was also apparent that some concerns about the future of the school improvement were connected to an expectation of continued support – from Alberta Education, district leadership, and from colleagues. Coordinators had a more sanguine perspective, with a few exceptions, about their working relationships with Alberta Education, the role of the district, and their own efforts to provide support to schools engaged in AISI. The most critical external support in this process would appear to be the almost ad hoc development of AISI coordinators' role in motivating and encouraging staffs, identifying and developing relevant projects, communicating with stakeholders at three levels of the educational system, reporting results, and identifying and helping to provide professional development needs related to specific projects. All of this was in addition to their formal job description.

Teacher Leadership

Teacher leadership is important because it has the strongest influence on school improvement planning and school structure and organization, and this influence has been empirically demonstrated to be stronger than the principal's influence along these dimensions (Leithwood, Jantzi, and Steinbach, 1999). According to these researchers, teacher leaders often display the following capacities and dispositions: well-honed interpersonal and communication skills; technical and organizational skills for program improvement; broad knowledge base about policy, subject matter, the local community, and students; a realistic sense of what is possible as they actively participate in administrative and leadership work; and they are supportive of others' work. Like formal leaders (ideally), teacher leaders provide colleagues with intellectual stimulation and individualized support, they model best practices, they help develop structures that encourage shared decision making, they adopt a visionary perspective, and they consistently give extra effort (chap. 8, Leithwood, Jantzi, & Steinbach, 1999).

How can administrators support and foster teacher leadership? Leithwood and his colleagues (1999) suggest several ways: clarification of roles (but not overly prescriptive); gaining a realistic perspective on use of teacher time; creating training opportunities out of leadership tasks; providing support for challenging leadership assignments; building a culture of collaboration; and selecting teachers that already have leadership qualities that are hard to develop.

For the Teacher Leadership variable the mean rating for teachers was 2.9 (*SD* = 0.8). The mean rating for administrators for this same variable was 3.3 (*SD* = 0.7), which is to say that administrators rated their efforts in promoting teacher leadership higher than did teachers.

When asked to directly comment on the role that leadership plays in the AISI projects most respondents saw a positive relationship between the project and emerging teacher leadership as lead teachers tasked with AISI responsibilities and/or as teacher teams collaborating on one or more projects.

Thiel (2006) reports that *lead teacher* participation in school improvement projects was high, combining liaison, communication, consulting, and supporting instruction. She notes that this relatively new role, a form of distributed leadership included: serving as the inter-agency liaison by disseminating information among provincial, district and school level representatives and authorities; being proactive in promoting the initiative; ensuring communication between various stakeholders within the initiative; and communicating news and developments at the provincial level that affected their projects. Lead teachers also served as specialists or consultants on whom teachers relied for expertise and knowledge. She concluded that lead teachers' roles were often perceived by other teachers as more valuable and supportive of school improvement initiatives than the efforts of administrators (formal leaders). Lead teachers have been described as having a "mediating role" (Harris & Muijs, 2003) whereby they are "important sources of expertise and information . . . able to draw critically upon additional resource and expertise if required and to seek external assistance" (p. 5).

The teacher leadership *team approach* often emerged in schools where projects had captured the interest of colleagues. "The underlying idea behind all these forms of interaction is that shared expertise is more likely to produce change than individuals working in isolation" (Darling-Hammond, 2004, p. 1070, as cited in Elmore & Burney, 1997). The team approach may also open up the teaching and learning process to a more collective scrutiny and shared responsibility:

> Collaborative conversations call on team members to make public what has traditionally been private – goals, strategies, materials, pacing, questions, concerns, and results. These discussions give every teacher someone to turn to and talk to, and they are explicitly structured to improve the classroom practice of teachers – individually and collectively. (Dufour, 2004, p. 9)

Echoing Darling-Hammond and Dufour, a teacher notes:

> Our AISI project would not have been successful if the leadership team had not been supportive. We provided encouragement and praise to the teachers, helped develop the project and monitored its success and progress on a continual basis. We were also a sounding board for the teachers and coordinator.

One administrator's comment addressed the power of teacher empowerment and the subsequent benefits of such practice:

> Our project brought a significant amount of financial resources directly to each school. Teachers had a clear mandate to follow, but great freedom in how they actually took up the work. I saw teachers change right before my eyes. Initially a teacher or two would come to me (as a school-based administrator) with a form in their hands asking if it was okay to do something. In short order, they started coming and telling us where they were headed. It was very empowering for them. It was wonderful for them to attend a professional learning activity and then to have the funds to purchase necessary resources and then to have the money available to provide subsequent "sub" time or other resources so that their students benefited from what they had learned.

Several saw that AISI was a supportive, multi-level framework that spurred teacher growth in the area of leadership. For example:

> Watching and seeing the individual confidence of those teachers grow over the past three years because of the opportunities AISI was able to offer was outstanding.

> In our AISI project the teachers all felt a sense of power to be involved in improving what they do in the classroom and in sharing that magic with their colleagues. I

don't think I see this as leadership. However, it does fit the newer definition of leadership. Many other staff members wanted to share our learning and findings. This excitement in teaching is truly magic.

AISI encouraged many teachers to take on leadership positions who might not have otherwise:

> It has let us see the value of the variety of types of leadership, the various roles that we can all play and has brought about an awareness that leadership is not the sole responsibility or domain of the school administration.
>
> I have had the pleasant opportunity to be involved in AISI from its beginnings. I have grown as a teacher: through questioning my teaching practices, and allowing choice and decision making for my students. The learning opportunities through AISI and the workshops I've attended have all helped to provide me with greatly improved leadership skills.
>
> The AISI project has provided opportunities for teachers to take on leadership roles in some capacity that they may or may not have otherwise done. Through collaboration with peers, teachers have been able to share expertise and knowledge with each other.
>
> I am forever grateful for the opportunities that I have experienced over the past five years: I not only am a much better teacher, but my inquiry has spurred me on into taking my masters degree. I feel like I have a cohort of teachers that I can hone my own teaching practices with, I have taken on leadership roles within and outside of the district, I have and am presenting at international conferences sharing what we have learned . . . the list could go on in the ways that [I] and my students have benefited. I am grateful that our district had fantastic leadership at the level where training and the study of data were occurring.

Administrators also acknowledged the emergent nature of teacher leadership directly attributable to the school improvement initiative:

> Leadership capacity is the partial focus of our next project. Expanding leadership roles should include the students and staff as an integral part of the development of the AISI project. This should increase the ability to sustain the momentum and direction of the project.

Administrators who did *not* take an active role in leading and supporting projects, on the other hand, were perceived as obstacles to project success and a damper on the growth of teacher leadership.

> Effective leadership is essential. Our district leadership was phenomenal . . . but to transfer that to the school level – that showed varied success across the district. If new teaching practices/training/repertoire or whatever is provided for teachers, administration MUST also become involved to the degree that they too are experts. It is a joke to have administrators who do not know what is going on with an initiative that has been in their school for over 3 years. Teachers that do take leadership roles are often seen as the district "expert" or "pet," and are treated much differently (and often negatively excluded). If administrators were on board and supportive, this would likely be less blatant or prevalent.

Finally, one teacher urged that more work needed to be done to support teacher leadership, "to provide accredited training for staff members to feel competent and comfortable designing and presenting AISI proposals" and to "set up an AISI support network for people considering involvement."

Coordinators reported a variety of levels of teacher involvement in leadership practice. The diversity of responses to this question reveals the centrality of contextual issues (school culture, support for the project, sharing practices, etc.). An underlying element of most of coordinator responses linked shared leadership and teacher leadership to the success of the project. One coordinator gave this response: "I believe that distributed leadership was crucial to the success of our projects." Another coordinator expanded this idea: "In projects that were successful, teacher leadership was most evident. Teachers took the idea and implemented the concepts." Another response addressed the importance of sharing information and involving peers in the success of the project:

> In most of our projects the AISI teachers became leaders in their schools. In many of the projects these teachers were also asked to provide professional development to their peers.

A few coordinators added that assuming a leadership role did not necessarily suit everybody, noting that some teachers preferred to stay "low-profile," and other coordinators cited time constraints to be an impediment to teacher-leadership practice.

Teacher Leadership: The Bottom Line

AISI has no doubt contributed to an unprecedented growth of teacher leadership and spurred an appreciation for more distributive forms of leadership. Lambert (2002) notes that "the old model of formal, one-person leadership leaves the substantial talents of teachers largely untapped. Improvements under this model are not easily sustainable" (p. 37). AISI, our respondents would suggest, has spurred a departure from this old model and tapped into teacher leadership. Teacher leadership tends to blur the distinctions between formal and informal conceptions of leadership as lead teachers, teams, and administrators work together to plan and implement projects, to support instruction through discussion of practice, and to create professional development opportunities that are linked to projects. When administrators encourage and support this process, and when district knowledge and resources are used to support it, these teacher leadership roles appear to blossom. On the other hand, when administrators are not themselves engaged in the school improvement process and teachers assume leadership roles by default, it is not difficult to understand why these new forms of leadership never really take root and status quo oriented teachers remain unmoved. Teacher leadership needs to be sustained by an active administrator presence: in motivating staffs to take on new responsibilities, in creating time and space to allow for staff communication and reflection, and in aligning professional goals and professional development to fit the context of new roles and the particular needs of school-based projects.

Conclusions and Implications

Cycle I AISI projects, and subsequent cycles, clearly induced a steep learning curve in regard to leadership practices, including visioning and goal setting, internal and external support, and promoting teacher leadership. Where undertaken in more than a superficial manner, the school improvement process required a fundamental rethinking about the sources and forms of potential leadership within districts leaders, school administrators, lead teachers, and teacher teams. In these cases, district coordinators developed new roles and patterns of communication to support the process of change. Our findings also suggest that the transition from the traditional model of schooling to the school improvement model requires a shift in how we understand and support leadership practice in the context of the change:

1) School improvement requires learning and applying *new* sets of knowledge and skills. Not all formal leaders and staff members were committed to this learning, but many were. Where progress was made, respondents made it clear that the work of school improvement engaged them, professionally and emotionally, in ways very different from their previous, pre-AISI experiences. The growth of teacher and distributed leadership, spurred by AISI, is perhaps the strongest indicator that doing this work required a sharp departure from "business-as-usual" values, attitudes, and behaviors. Sustaining the development of a new knowledge and skill base requires district and university preparation programs of various formats and duration

that are informed both by leadership standards and by a thorough understanding of the school improvement process.

2) School improvement is a complex and protracted exercise that demands people who are cognitively and affectively able to deal with the rigors and vagaries of the change process. Potential leaders, particularly formal leaders, need to be identified and intentionally developed to understand what school improvement is all about and they also need the emotional intelligence to lead others to do the same (Goleman, Boyatzis, & McKee, 2002).

3) The school improvement process is continuous and context-specific. Once begun, it demanded new procedures, structures, and scheduling to allow for a more collective approach to learning, for redefining and sharing leadership tasks, and for inquiry and reflection geared for the particular needs of each school. This timeline extended from Cycle I to Cycle II and into Cycle III. The Alberta Education requirement that each cycle be defined by new projects is perhaps not helpful in allowing significant projects to be developed from start to finish.

4) The school improvement process is incremental. While creative scheduling allowed for more – and much appreciated – time for planning, dialogue and reflection, these were undertaken within the constraints of a traditional school year organization and collective bargaining agreements. Within this framework, school improvement took the form of many small steps, not quantum leaps. As noted by Darroch (2006) and Thiel (2006), the enterprise of school improvement may require a fundamental rethinking of how the school year is organized, to allow staffs to use larger blocks of time, outside of their classroom and administrative responsibilities, to plan, implement, and evaluate the work of school improvement.

5) The school improvement process is heuristic, meaning learning is largely on-the-job as participants discover what they know and don't know and adapt accordingly. For example, after it became apparent in many schools that *measurable* goals were needed to get a handle on student achievement, the need to address assessment and project evaluation in a much more focused fashion became recognized, if not implemented, in more schools and districts. A greater appreciation for the role of creating capacity building from the inside-out, supported by professional development more closely tailored to school needs, was also garnered in this learning process.

6) The school improvement process is unfinished. Our evidence would suggest that much of the school improvement agenda in Alberta, at the district and school levels, has thus far been attending to developing more appropriate *means* (practices, structures, cultures, procedures) for school improvement, but that the link between the efficacy of these means to the *ends* – improved student improvement and development – still needs largely to be established. To make that

linkage requires, among other things, a more robust orientation towards research and inquiry within school districts and schools, deeper knowledge and skills about student assessment (see Parker, 2006), and about project evaluation (Thiel, 2006). Most importantly, connecting the link between means and ends requires opening up teaching and learning processes for a more critical and collective examination than has hitherto been pursued. Accomplishing this task requires all involved to confront the norm of non-interference head on. This is the toughest nut to crack in the school improvement repertoire.

Questions

1. What does the phrase "A tough nut to crack" refer to in this chapter?
2. Given the balance of support and level of need to improve AISI, is this a process that should continue? Why? Why not?
3. Are the results credible given the research design and analysis used? Explain?

References

Adelman, N., & Walking-Eagle, K. (1997). Teachers, time and school reform. In A. Hargreaves (Ed.), *Rethinking educational change with heart and mind* (pp. 92-110). Alexandria, VA: Association for Supervision and Curriculum Development.

Alberta Commission on Learning. (2003). *Every child learns. Every child succeeds. Report and recommendations.* Edmonton, AB: Author.

Alberta Education. (n.d.). *AISI Background.* Retrieved Jan. 11, 2009, from www.learning.gov.ab.ca/k_12/special/aisi

Alberta Learning. (2004). *AISI: Improving student learning.* Edmonton, AB: Author.

Ansell, D. (2004). *Improving schools facing challenging circumstances: Perspectives from leading thinkers.* Nottingham, UK: National College for School Leadership. Retrieved Nov. 29, 2005, from http://newportal.ncsl.org.uk/media/F7B/95/randd-impr-challenging-circs.pdf

Argyris, C., & Schön, D. (1974). *Theory in practice: Increasing professional effectiveness.* San Francisco: Jossey-Bass.

Barth, R. (1990). *Improving schools from within.* Jossey Bass: San Francisco.

Beach, R., & Lindahl, R. (2004). Identifying the knowledge base for school improvement. *Planning and Changing, 35*(1 & 2), 2-32.

Bedard, G., & Aitken, A. (2004). *Exploring the linkage between leadership practices and selected school improvement projects under the umbrella of the Alberta Initiative for School Improvement (AISI).* Unpublished manuscript, University of Lethbridge, Lethbridge, AB.

Brandt, R. (1995). On restructuring schools: A conversation with Fred Newmann. *Educational Leadership, 53*(3), 70-73.

Cibulka, J., & Derlin, R. (1998). Accountability policy adoption to policy sustainability: Reforms and systemic initiatives. *Education and Urban Society, 30,* 502-515.

Cohen, D., & Hill, H. (2001). *Learning policy: When state education reform works.* New Haven, CT: Yale University Press.

Datnow, A., Hubbard, L., & Mehan, H. (2002). *Extending educational reform: From one school to many.* New York: Routledge.

Darroch, A. (2006). *Effective school leadership practices supporting the Alberta initiative for school improvement (AISI).* Unpublished master's thesis, University of Lethbridge, Lethbridge, AB.

Deal, T. (1990). Reframing reform. *Educational Leadership, 47*(8), 6-12.

Deal, T. E., & Peterson, K. D. (1999). *Shaping school culture: The heart of leadership* (1st ed.). San Francisco: Jossey-Bass.

Dufour, R. (2004). What is a "professional learning community?" *Educational Leadership, 61*(8), 6-11.

Elmore, R. (2000). *Building a new structure for school leadership.* Washington, DC: The Albert Shanker Institute.

Elmore, R., & Burney, D. (1997). *Investing in teacher learning: Staff development and instructional improvement in Community School District #2, New York City.* New York: National Commission on Teaching and America's Future.

Feiman-Nemser, S., & Floden, R. E. (1986). The cultures of teaching. In M. C. Whittrock (Ed.), *Handbook of research on teaching* (3rd ed., pp. 505-526). London: Collier-Macmillan.

Gibb, S. A., Gibb, G. S., Randall, V. A., & Hite, S. (1999). *From "I" to "we": Reflections about leadership.* (ERIC Document Reproduction Service No. ED432059)

Goldstein, J. (2003). Making sense of distributed leadership: The case of peer assistance and review. *Educational Evaluation and Policy Analysis, 25*(4), 397-421.

Goleman, D., Boyatzis, R., & McKee, A. (2002). *Primal leadership: Realizing the power of emotional intelligence.* Boston: Harvard Business School Press.

Guskey, T. (2003). How classroom assessments improve learning. *Educational Leadership, 60*(5), 6-12.

Hargreaves, A., & Goodson, I. (2006). Educational change over time? The sustainability and nonsustainability of three decades of secondary school change and continuity. *Educational Administration Quarterly, 42*(1), 3-41.

Hargreaves, A. (1994). *Changing teachers, changing times. Teachers' work and culture in the postmodern age.* New York: Teachers College Press.

Hargreaves, A., & Shaw, P., et al. (2000). *Networks for change: Supporting secondary teachers in interpreting and integrating secondary school reform.* Final Report to the Ontario Ministry of Education and Training.

Harris, A. (2002). Effective leadership in schools facing challenging contexts. *School Leadership & Management, 22*(1), 15-26.

Harris, A., & Muijs, D. (2003). Teacher leadership: Improvement through empowerment? An overview of research. Educational Management. *Administration and Leadership, 31*(4), 437-448.

Heck, R. H., & Hallinger, P. (1999). Next generation methods for the study of leadership and school improvement. In J. Murphy & K. Seashore Louis (Eds.), *Handbook of research on educational administration* (2nd ed., pp. 141-162). San Francisco: Jossey-Bass.

Lambert, L. (1998). *Building leadership capacity in schools.* Alexandria, VA: Association for Supervision and Curriculum Development.

Lambert, L. (2002). A framework for shared leadership. Educational Leadership, 8(37), 37-41.

Lawton, S., Bedard, G., Li, X., & MacLellan, D. (1999) *Teachers' unions in Canada.* Calgary, AB: Detselig.

Leithwood, K. A., Jantzi, D., & Steinbach, R. (1999). *Changing leadership for changing times.* Philadelphia, PA: Open University Press.

Moore, S., & Shaw, P. (2001). *The professional learning needs and perceptions of secondary school teachers: Implications for professional learning community.* New Orleans, LA. (ERIC Document Reproduction Service No. ED443793)

Mintzberg, H. (1979). *The structuring of organizations.* Engelwood Cliffs, NJ: Prentice Hall.

Musella, D. (1995). How CEOs influence school system culture. In Kenneth Leithwood (Ed.), *Effective school district leadership: Transforming politics into education* (pp. 223-244). Albany, NY: State University of New York Press.

Newmann, F. M., & Wehlage, G. G. (1995). *Successful school restructuring: A report to the public and educators.* Madison, WI: Center on Organization and Restructuring of Schools.

Parker, M. (2006). *How principals' beliefs about classroom assessment influence their leadership practices: An exploration.* Unpublished master's thesis, University of Lethbridge, Lethbridge, AB.

Silins, H., & Mulford, B. (2001, December). *Reframing schools: The case for system, teacher and student learning.* Australian Association for Research in Education (AARE) Conference Papers and Abstracts on the WWW, Perth, AU. Retrieved Nov. 28, 2003, from http://www.aare.edu.au/01pap/sil01398.htm

Sinden, J. E., Hoy, W. K., & Sweetland, S. R. (2004). An analysis of enabling school structure: Theoretical, empirical, and research considerations. *Journal of Educational Administration, 42*(4), 462-478.

Thiel, T. (2006). *Leadership and program evaluation practices influencing school improvement initiatives.* Unpublished master's thesis, University of Lethbridge, Lethbridge, AB.

Townsend, D., & Adams, P. (2003). *Exploring your learning community. Educational leadership, teacher empowerment, and action research through the Alberta Initiative for School Improvement.* Unpublished manuscript, University of Lethbridge, Lethbridge, AB.

Tyack, D., & Tobin, W. (1994). The grammar of schooling: Why has it been so hard to change? *American Educational Research Journal, 31*(3), 453-480.

University of Alberta. (2004, June). *Alberta Initiative for School Improvement: What we have learned.* Edmonton, AB: Author.

Wan, E. (2005). *Teacher empowerment: Concepts, strategies, and implications for schools in Hong Kong. Teachers College Record, 107*(4), pp. 842 861.

Appendix

Table 1: Staff Survey Scales and Questions

Scale	Items
Vision	In reference to the culture of our school: 1. We have a statement of shared beliefs with input/participation from stakeholders. 2. We have a mission statement to which we refer when developing our plan. 3. We have developed a current vision that clearly reflects the culture and context of our school. 4. Our school has processes and procedures to determine instruc tional and school wide effectiveness.
Goal Setting	In developing our 2000-2003 AISI projects our school: 5. Gathered data from various sources to determine desired results for student learning through the AISI project. 6. Used results of instructional data analysis to generate discussion and inform our AISI objectives. 7. Considered our school goals. 8. Created a timeline to guide our project. 9. Identified the necessary resources to reach our AISI goals. 10. Identified responsible parties for implementing action steps of the AISI project. 11. Developed a process for informing stakeholders of the goals and objectives listed in the AISI project.
Teacher Leadership	In conducting the 2000-2003 AISI projects our school: 12. Involved teachers in monitoring the progress towards the goals set forth in the AISI project. 13. Had teachers gather information and bring findings to the entire staff for consideration. 14. Collected data prior to and throughout the project.
Internal Support	The Principal and/or other members of the leadership team: 15. Monitored discussion during the project that included consider ing recommendations of action steps for change. 16. Monitored progress including checks on progress towards objectives. 17. Encouraged and supported attendance at conferences and work shops relevant to our AISI objectives. 18. Accessed and provided project-appropriate reading material. 19. Discussed new knowledge and pedagogy emanating from the AISI project. 20. Supported the AISI innovation through frequent classroom visits and follow up discussion. 21. Offered encouragement to AISI teachers. 22. Valued discussion and reflection about progress on the AISI projects.

A second part of the online survey consisted of open-ended questions to elicit the following perceptions of school administrators and teachers:

- I feel our AISI work has been productive because . . .
- I feel our success was limited because . . .
- Success in our next AISI project could be enhanced by . . .
- A successful AISI project may be defined by the following criteria . . .
- An unsuccessful project may be defined by the following criteria . . .
- I would like to add the following regarding the linkage between leadership practices and our AISI project . . .

Deviation between Teacher and Administrator Results

The mean ratings for all respondents completing the online survey were 3.3 (*SD* = 0.6), 3.2 (*SD* = 0.7), 3.1 (*SD* = 0.7), 3.2 (*SD* = 0.7), 3.2 (*SD* = 0.6) for the Vision, Goal Setting, Teacher Leadership, Internal Support and Overall Leadership Practice variables respectively.

For teachers, the mean ratings for Vision, Goal Setting, Teacher Leadership, Internal Support and Overall Leadership variables mean were 3.1 (*SD* = 0.7), 2.9 (*SD* = 0.8), 2.9 (*SD* = 0.8), 3.0 (*SD* = 0.8), and 3.0 (*SD* = 0.6) respectively. The mean ratings for administrators on these same variables were 3.4 (*SD* = 0.5), 3.4 (*SD* = 0.5), 3.3 (*SD* = 0.7), 3.3 (*SD* = 0.6) and 3.4 (*SD* = 0.5) respectively. Higher mean ratings suggest that leadership variables are more positively perceived. The mean ratings for teachers were lower than the mean ratings for administrators on all scale variables. The standard deviations of each scale suggest teacher scores were more variable or had greater dispersion than did administrator scale scores. So, from a statistical point of view, administrators and teachers emerged as two different populations in this study.

Chapter Four

Investing in Moral Literacy: Where are you now? A Manitoba Perspective

Carol Crippen, Ph.D.
University of Manitoba

Introduction

In recent years there has been a flurry of workshops, courses, professional development, books, (Fullan, 2003; Glickman, Gordon, & Ross Gordon, 2005; Goodlad, 2001; Pellicer, 2003; Power & Moore, 2004; Sergiovanni, 2005), and university courses related to democratic schools, healthy learning organizations, educational leadership, and the development of effective caring school cultures. All these topics, it seems to me, have a commonality; they centre on relationships and behavior, specifically, a moral way of being for the common good.

> Today, our schools are moving towards a more collegial, cooperative, transformative, service approach in the

> learning community. In these new postindustrial educational organizations, there are important shifts in roles, relationships, and responsibilities; traditional patterns of relationships are altered; authority flows are less hierarchical; role definitions are both more general and more flexible; leadership is connected to competence for needed tasks rather than to formal position; and independence and isolation are replaced by cooperative work (Murphy & Seashore Louis, 1999, p. xxii).

Herman (2007) explains moral literacy as "an ability to recognize and interpret moral facts that is a necessary condition for moral action and criticism, as well as the possibility of our together making reasoned moral progress" (p. ix). Starratt (2004) reinforces the importance of moral literacy in schools: "Those who lead schools need to have moral depth and a well-articulated platform for the moral work of learning in the school, as well as a clear sense of how to proactively engage teachers and students in an authentic process of learning" (p. 136). And, the importance of establishing moral values and ethical principles is echoed by Glickman, Gordon, and Ross-Gordon (2005) who state, "In a democratic society, it is vital that students learn to think reflectively, function at high stages of moral reasoning, and be autonomous decision makers" (p. 156). Ayers (2004) sums the value of moral literacy,

> The world of moral thinking and ethical action is as natural to children as any other. They are growing up in a physical world, true, but it is inseparable from a cultural domain and a moral universe. Moral thought and virtuous action in school begin with being cared for and accepted – teachers should demonstrate a fundamental belief in the unique vale of each human being, and recognition of our shared predicament (p. 23).

If administrators and teachers are models for students, then the responsibility falls upon teachers and school leaders to develop moral literacy in their classrooms among their students and colleagues in their schools. Herman (2007) explicates further: "Children need to be taught to recognize their duties (the content of obligations) and to understand the distinctive nature or moral action. Their recognitional abilities need to be honed and their character strengthened" (p. 131). Through such service and modeling it appears that both student and teacher benefit: "Teachers are best able to serve students when they themselves have been adequately served" (Sergiovanni, 2005, p. 101). The following chapter will discuss a university course, in Manitoba, focused on moral literacy and educational administration that was conceptualized within a framework of servant-leadership (Greenleaf, 1977).

Background

Demographics

Manitoba is a prairie province with a population of just over a million people. The population of Manitoba consists of a large Indigenous presence; European, South American, and Asian immigrants; clusters of French-speaking people; and a strong representation of Scots and British. The population is clustered into three main regions: 1) Winnipeg and surrounding towns including Melita, Selkirk, and Morden to the south; 2) Central Manitoba and the Parkland region which includes Brandon, Dauphin, and Ste. Rose du Lac; and 3) the cities and towns of the northern area: for example, Thompson, The Pas, Flin Flon, and many smaller communities and First Nation Reserves. Manitoba's population is grounded within a variety of cultural and strong religious beliefs. For example, Manitoba is home to a large population of Mennonites located in the southern portion of the province around the towns of Steinbach, Morden, Altona, and Carmen. The Mennonite communities are recognized for their strong moral character and community service agenda.

Links

As a result of forced school board amalgamations that took place in August 2002, fifty-four school districts were reduced to thirty-seven school divisions across the province (Manitoba Education, n.d.). The sensitive years following the compulsory amalgamation saw a reduction in school board trustees; fewer superintendents of schools; and a relocation of educational staff and students. I was invited in the fall of 2001 by the Manitoba Association of School Board Trustees (MAST) to deliver a keynote address on the topic of servant-leadership. The intent of this address was to recognize the efforts/service of the original trustee group before the impending reduction in their numbers and, hopefully, to initiate a healing process amongst them.

By early 2002, the superintendents of several Manitoba school divisions invited me to come to their school divisions and help chart *history walls* with their employees in the original school divisions, before they were reorganized and absorbed into a new configuration. These history walls were celebrations of past divisional accomplishments. Once again the focus was the aspects of servant-leadership that involved healing, building community, encouraging the growth of others, listening to colleagues, and becoming aware of the thoughts, feelings, and behaviors of each other. These presentations were followed by an invitation from the Manitoba Teachers' Society to speak on the topic of servant-leadership to a group of sixty-five educators from across the province. Over the last six years many other administrative area groups have included me in their team meetings to explain the servant-leader philosophy. Collectively, these circumstances provided the opportunity for the concept of servant-leadership to be introduced in Manitoba and, thus, the climate and timing seemed ripe to formalize and emphasize moral literacy within a servant-leadership framework into the educational community.

Rationale

The current awareness (Ayers, 2004; Herman, 2007; Keith, 2008) and need for moral literacy, plus many requests from the educational field in Manitoba, prompted me to design and deliver a course within the University of Manitoba's Faculty of Education titled *Servant-Leadership* beginning in the fall of 2007. The course is for school teachers and administrators to facilitate moral literacy within their school communities. Servant-leadership (Greenleaf, 1977) is a moral way of leading and serving provides a wide window of opportunity to investigate a means for introducing moral literacy into the school setting. Sergiovanni (2005) explains about the impact of this leadership form, "The virtues of serving, caring, respecting, empowering, and helping without asking for anything in return are far more powerful motivational devices than is the art for manipulation of motivational science that seeks to trade need fulfillment for compliance" (p. 74).

The course has now been delivered three times, on two university campuses, and once on site in a Manitoba school division. The following paper will briefly describe the course syllabus, content, guest speakers, readings, and literature resources for children, group activities, and the culminating course assignment. The closing comments will review student feedback related to readings, skills identified and developed, future revisions to the course, and general perceptions of usefulness of the servant-leadership course in building moral literacy in schools.

Course Description

Participants

The three-credit course spanned thirteen evening classes, each lasting three hours, usually on Wednesdays. Two class sizes reached thirty registrants and one class was capped at fifteen graduate students during a summer offering; two classes involved educators within the Manitoba school system and one class contained educators from other provinces. Every participant had at least two undergraduate degrees; the participants were split with approximately two-thirds comprised of classroom teachers and one-third comprised of administrators, superintendents, or educational specialists (special education resource teachers, counseling, and consultants). As well, there were twice as many elementary school educators as secondary school teachers within the class.

The Syllabus

The syllabus provided students with the course purpose; notice of required course textbooks; a list of suggested additional printed resources; a list of journal articles that were to be distributed in class for follow-up and discussion; a section outlining the four required class assignments; a detailed outline of each session; grading standards for the course as determined by the Faculty of Education; a reference to specific university policies and regulations; and a short section for additional study titled, *Take Your Work Deeper.* Classes were highly interactive and utilized two textbooks as the foundation for the theoretical framework. Readings from the texts were discussed each session. A *Table Talk* segment presented a school scenario for each table group to analyze and problem solve with the overarching rationale of a moral, ethical, servant-leadership approach. Each class included an opening segment of about fifteen minutes that provided an opportunity for discussion about a specific quote related to servant-leadership.

Purpose

The following purpose for the course was included in the syllabus:

> This is the beginning of a journey to understand a particular philosophy of leadership. As teachers we become leaders, first in our classrooms, and then in our schools. What is the purpose of our schools? And, how do we as educators contribute to that honorable purpose? We shall look briefly at the paradigm shift in school leadership today.
>
> Expressed somewhat formally, this course is an inquiry into the philosophy of servant-leadership as understood by Robert K. Greenleaf. This ethical, service form of leadership has recently become a fresh vehicle for working toward democratization and moral literacy in school communities. Greenleaf first wrote about the servant-leader concept in 1970 in a small 37-page essay, *The Servant as Leader.* Greenleaf was aware of the discomfort with the term servant-leader and wrote:
>
> Part of the problem is that serve and lead are overused words with a negative connotation. But they are also good words and I can find no others that carry as well the meaning I would like to convey. Not everything that is old and worn, or even corrupt, can be thrown away. Some of it has to be rebuilt and used again. So it is, it seems to me, with the words serve and lead (1991, p. i.)
>
> Through discussions, readings, and written reflections participants uncover the strong foundation of servant-leadership and come to understand the realities for build-

> ing democratic, caring, moral, inclusive learning communities. Servant-leadership is not a panacea; it is a consistent, deliberate investment toward the common good. Our schools are places to initiate that journey with students, staff, and parents.

Content

Each evening course session had several components:

Table Talk: Discussion related to their environment, i.e., Describe a time when you made the right decision for the benefit of your students or colleagues.

Topic for the evening: i.e., the paradigm shifts in educational leadership. This could be introduced by a PowerPoint presentation, a video, a DVD, overheads, or specific quotes on laminated cards.

Group Activity: The Puzzle, i.e., draw up a list at your table group that identifies the ways a puzzle and a well-functioning team are the same.

Readings: Specific sections of the required textbooks were discussed at length. Students were expected to have read the chapter or selection prior to coming to class that evening. Often the class was broken into a variety of table group configurations. This helped the large class of students interact with everyone at least five or six times over the duration of the course.

Guest speakers: During five evenings, members of the local Winnipeg community that exemplified servant-leadership came to speak to the class about their life stories and to answer questions were from the participants.

Story: Each class concluded with a piece of children's literature that had a moral message embedded in the story. There was a brief table group discussion followed by whole group sharing.

Sharing of food: Participants signed a roster to bring food for our learning community to share. Because of the timing of the classes, people already had put in a long day at work and came to sessions hungry and tired. The food encouraged people to share, talk, and interact in an informal and relaxed way. Usually two people were responsible for the food for each class.

During the first session we had a brief examination of the paradigm shift in school leadership and educational responsibilities today, particularly in response to societal pressures (i.e. family structure, poverty, cultural sensitivity, educational accountability). These topics curried considerable interest and lively discussion among the groups. Leaders in a school set the tone for the values and beliefs reflected in the school. The concept of moral leadership and moral literacy were examined, which segued into Greenleaf's servant-leadership philosophy. Greenleaf's ideas were not examined in detail until the evening of the third class. Considerable time was devoted to understanding and deconstructing the now famous quote by Greenleaf (1977) that defines a servant-leader:

> The difference manifests itself in the care taken by the servant- first to make sure that other people's highest priority needs are being served. The best test, and difficult to administer, is: do those served grow as persons; do they, while being served, become healthier, wiser, freer, more autonomous, more likely themselves to become servants? And, what is the least privileged in society; will he benefit, or, at least, will he not be further deprived? (p. 13-14)

I felt it was important for participants to understand the moral context and to see how their world fits into that framework. Issues of decision-making, listening/hearing, reflection, conflict/dissonance, and lateralization of leadership, modeling, and transference of philosophy, were integrated throughout the course. I wanted participants to answer the question, *Where are you now*, in their own moral literacy development. It was critical to identify their moral/ethical value system before trying to model it for a classroom of children or a school building of teachers and support staff. Identifying their personal values and beliefs established a starting point for them to move forward. Reflections directed their thoughts inward toward a personal analysis of where they stood and what they believed about their role in schools and society in general.

Readings

Readings included three types of sources noted below: 1) a variety of required course textbooks, 2) journal articles; and 3) a selection of children's literature embedded with a moral focus. Examples of the three categories are listed below.

Required Course Texts

Fullan, M. (2003). *The moral imperative of school leadership.*

Greenleaf, R. (2004). *The servant-leader within: A Transformative path.*

Pellicer, L. (2003). *Caring enough to lead: How reflective thought leads to moral Leadership, 2nd ed.*

Powers, J., & Moore, J. (2004). *Servant-leadership and the art of teaching.*

Sergiovanni, T. (1992). *Moral Leadership: Getting to the heart of school improvement.*

Journal Articles

Crippen, C. (2005). Inclusive education: A servant-leadership perspective. *Education Canada.*

Crippen, C. (Dec. 5, 2005). The democratic school: First to serve, then to lead. Canadian *Journal of Educational Administration and Policy.*

Crippen, C. (2006). Servant-Leadership. *Educators' Notebook.*

Polleys, M. (2002). One university's response to the anti-leadership vaccine: Developing servant leaders. *The Journal of Leadership Studies.*

Wheatley, M. (1999, June). *Servant-Leadership and community leadership in the 21st century.* Keynote address at the Annual Robert K. Greenleaf Center for Servant-Leadership Conference.

Children's Literature

Demi. (1990). *The empty pot.*

Madonna. (2003). *Mr. Peabody's apples.*

McPhail, D. (2002). *The teddy bear.*

Muth, J. J. (2002). *The three questions.*

Pfister, M. (1998). *How Leo learned to be king.*

Taylor, H. (2007). *Ruby's Hope.*

Upjohn, R. (2007). *Lily and the paper man.*

Waber, B. (2002). *Courage.*

Wild, M., & Brooks, R. (2000). *Fox.*

Wood, D. (2002). *A quiet place.*

Websites

I also suggested using The Robert K. Greenleaf Center's website as an additional resource: http://www.greenleaf.org.

Guest Speakers

In order to appreciate the concept of servant-leadership better, the participants could transfer classical examples of this particular moral leadership philosophy to people within their own context and local environment. Names such as Gandhi, Eleanor Roosevelt, Dali Llama, Mother Theresa, and Nelson Mandela were easily identified in class as ideal examples of servant-leadership, but holding up these ideal examples can sometimes obscure the practice of servant-leadership within the participant's context. Therefore, several guest speakers were invited from the local community "to tell their stories" and to engage in a dialogue with the students in order to provide a link to the present reality of the course participants. These guests included the founder of the local food bank, a pediatric oncologist, a school administrator, and an elementary school student. During follow-up to the presentations, the class analyzed the lives of each of the guest servant-leaders and identified the ways each helped create a caring community, kept growing personally, encouraged the growth in others. The students were then asked to reflect on the rationale behind the guest's service. Students identified concepts of strong listening skills, empathy, vision, persuasive action, stewardship, humility, and social conscience in each of the presenters.

Activities

It was imperative that students had an opportunity to share their ideas throughout the course. The class was divided into table groups of four to five people. These groups remained intact for the duration of the course, but many occasions arose whereby the students were rearranged and they eventually mixed with the entire class on at least ten occasions. By continually mixing the groups, the class was able to develop a strong social network for everyone and let everyone's voice be heard. I was intent on building an effective community of learners.

Delivery of the activities provided the chance for individual, pair/share, triads, table groups, and whole class scenarios. Each class required prescribed readings and time was spent at the beginning of that class discussing the material read for reflection. I observed a clear developmental shift as the classes progressed. Initially, the discussions were rather short (five to ten minutes) and confined to a few people. By the fourth class, everyone was giving their opinions freely and I *always* had to end their conversations (after twenty minutes) to move ahead with the course content.

During several classes we discussed the importance and practice of reflection. Together we "just sat" in silence. I also taught the class a simple procedure to totally relax while sitting in their chairs. Many people expressed satisfaction and surprise in this action. Quotes from the readings were often highlighted and analyzed for its relevance to their own school situation. Also, case studies were provided and table groups proposed possible actions that were reflective of moral leadership with justification for the actions. One consensus activity caused considerable dissonance for many. A coercive approach in the decision-making process from various table groups caused some people to shut down. Time became the variable; the table groups that were able to reach consensus took the longest, but members of these groups seemed content with the results. The concepts of *persuasion* and *coercion* where carefully analyzed after this activity and attention was paid to the effect each one had on participants; the class projected the outcomes for either administrative action (persuasion – coercion) would have on school staff and children.

Children's books by McPhail, Taylor, and Upjohn were used to carefully illustrate moral development. These books touch on the ideas of poverty and homelessness. Table groups reread the stories and discussed what transpired in the storyline and what the key factors of each were. What was the turning point? What moral behavior was reflected in the story? How as the behavior manifested? What difference did it make to the story? Were there mitigating factors that played a part in this behavior? The activity took nearly two hours to complete but the participants commented how worthwhile they found it and discussion was deep and very animated. We completed this exercise close to the end of the course so that everyone was knowledgeable about the topic of moral and servant-leadership and had accumulated a solid grounding in the general issue.

Assignments

In class: Independent, one-minute papers were completed at the end of five class sessions spaced throughout the entire course (as identified in the syllabus) and had to be completed on that particular evening. Topics included:

- What is the main thing you learned today?
- Why did you want to learn about servant-leadership?
- What one thing do you wish we would address in class?
- Describe a situation where you were a follower.
- How can servant-leadership help your school?

These one-minute papers kept a two-way written communication ongoing throughout the course between the participants and me. It kept me apprised of issues and concerns from the students and alerted me to topics that were problematic or needed further discussion.

Out of class: There were 4 external assignments.

1. The first assignment required the participants to analyze their own leadership style for strengths and areas that needed improvement. They were to explain how they have used their strengths and how their areas that needed improvement caused them problems. Students were to describe an incident where they believed they acted in a moral way and to explain why.
2. The second assignment was a group skit or brief dramatization that demonstrated some aspect of the course. Participants were creative and came with costumes, props, and a script. They also had questions for the observers at the end of their presentation. These skits provided a means of synthesizing their learning and generated considerable laughter and involvement.
3. Students were to read the biography of a leader – educational, political, business, or military. They were to prepare an 8-page paper which summarized the leadership style with examples from the book. This was not a book report or review; it was an analysis and evaluation of the particular leadership style and justifications for selection were required within the paper.
4. The fourth assignment and culminating activity was the design of an action plan to implement servant-leadership into their school or divisional setting. This plan was a positive step toward achieving moral literacy in their professional environment. Participants were to explain the rationale, time lines, key players, resources, costs, barriers, and outcomes/evaluation for success. I was pleased with the results.

The assignments provided the participants with opportunities to independently prepare a brief written reflection after several classes. The action plan and reading of the biography were also independent activities. The group skit involved each table group working together. These skits were highly creative and required considerable preparation and practice. A written submission was included with the skit that documented the rationale for the skit topic, the role of each player in the skit, and the contribution each member made to the overall presentation.

One outstanding plan was a collaborative effort from three novice teachers in a middle school. They prepared a plan which included a formal proposal to the local teachers' union for funding to purchase books and other materials. They also wished to conduct study groups with their school staff colleagues. Their paper was shared, with their permission, with their Superintendent who offered to fund the effort if funding did not come forward from the union. They did receive funding and eventually went on to attend the Values Conference in Victoria, British Columbia in October 2008.

Observations

All three courses were well attended. Participants commented that they were "sad to see the course end" and "sorry it was over" and "they would miss Wednesday nights." Five different table groups had set up strong networks and have been emailing each other throughout the courses. Two people said the course "was life changing"and many commented that they "would not see things the same way again in a school or elsewhere." Others had integrated a short period of quiet reflection into their daily activities. Listening to self and then listening to others became important to the class members. The concept of "being in the moment" or "being present "was introduced early, during the first class. Becoming aware of being *fully engaged* with people, of being completely present with them, was then stressed throughout the duration of the course. Starratt (2004) would identify such a self-reflection process as participating in a "presence audit" (p. 137). Several participants have sent me emails requesting an additional course in servant-leadership for deeper study.

Participants commented that they never stopped reading and rereading over the entire course. One woman said she was making a strong bond with Greenleaf's written words. This was my intention and hope, to immerse them in the related literature and to allow them time away from class to reflect. I wanted the students to challenge their own beliefs and values and to focus on their school environment as it fit into the concept of moral literacy. Starratt (2004) supports such an approach: "Leadership preparation programs have to more continually challenge candidates to probe the grounding of their ethical principles and moral values as human beings, as educators, and as a citizens" (p. 136). Beyond Greenleaf's work, they also enjoyed Sergiovanni and found Margaret Wheatley's article exciting and unique because of her application of chaos theory to leadership. Each class was amazed at the real school relationship to chaos theory. Fullan's (2003) *The Moral Imperative of School Leadership* generated comments of "good repetition of thought" and "a basic foundation" from students. They found Greenleaf's writing took several rereads. Many found them a challenge and said it "made them want to completely understand"; they kept reading it over and over slowly, absorbing the philosophy and pondering its impact.

It is interesting to note that after the course ran the first time, I received several invitations to speak about servant-leadership. I delivered a keynote address to a group of seventy school administrators; facilitated a two-day session on servant-leadership directed to the Winnipeg Roman Catholic Archdiocese school administrators; and spoke to divisional school administrators at their annual Gimli retreat in November 2008. Hopefully, the topics of moral literacy, values, ethics, and servant-leadership will have a lasting effect and not just become another passing trend in school leadership. The test of time will reveal its worth and effect in Manitoba schools.

My participation in and attendance at the *13th Annual Values and Leadership Conference*, organized by Dr. Paul Begley from Penn State University, inspired me to include one more assignment within the course. The concentration on moral literacy at this conference convinced me that servant-leaders need an in-depth understanding this topic, and I will now require the students to write a substantial research paper on moral literacy. Those themes identified in the conference's "Call for Papers" would work well in setting the scope of potential paper topics: (1) from theory to methodology; (2) pressure points for developing moral literacy, (3) culturally differentiated education, and (4) resources for moral literacy and ethical leadership.

Conclusion

I believe that the course on servant-leadership is a small start at formalizing the understanding and rationale for moral literacy. By identifying a form of moral leadership within a university course participants will recognize the significance of the topic. It is hoped that educators will ponder their own beliefs and actions about moral literacy and why they became educators. Often, it seems to me, teachers are drawn to the teaching vocation because of their love for people; this thought links to Sergiovanni (2005) who writes, "Servant leadership requires that one loves the purposes, goals and intents that define the leader's work and that of the school. Servant leadership requires that one loves those who are being served" (p. 100). Possibly, the issue of moral literacy will gain a higher profile in the educational community as a priority for effective and caring learning communities by school trustees, administrators, teachers, and faculties of education.

In conclusion, today's schools must instill a shared sense of mission and an inclusion of moral literacy that creates a culture of collaborative service toward strong, considerate communities. Tough questions must guide us. Where are we now? What is our legacy to our learning communities? Are our students being served effectively? What do we stand for? Servant-leadership is not a magic potion, but it does provide the basis for strong moral authority, an ethic of care, and service to students. Our schools need this moral highroad and we, as educators, need to proudly embrace our *raison d'être*.

Questions

1. What are the strengths and needs of this approach to teaching a course on servant-leadership?
2. What are the next steps in developing a this course?
3. Within your local context do you see evidence of servant-leadership?

References

Ayers, W. (2004). *Teaching toward freedom: Moral commitment and ethical action in the classroom.* Boston, MA: Beacon Press.

Crippen, C. (2005). Inclusive education: A servant-leadership perspective. *Education Canada, 45*(4), 19-22.

Crippen, C. (Dec. 5, 2005). The democratic school: First to serve, then to lead. *Canadian Journal of Educational Administration and Policy, 47.* Retrieved Jan. 3, 2009, from http://www.umanitoba.ca/publications/cjeap/articles/crippen.html.

Crippen, C. (2006). Servant-Leadership. *Educators' Notebook, 18*(2), 1-4.

Demi. (1990). *The empty pot.* New York: Henry Holt and Company

Fullan, M. (2003). *The moral imperative of school leadership.* Thousand Oaks, CA: Corwin Press.

Glickman, C., Gordon, S., & Ross Gordon, J. (2005). *The basic guide to supervision and instructional leadership.* Toronto: Pearson Education Ltd.

Goodlad, S. J., Ed. (2001). *The last best hope: A democracy reader.* San Francisco, CA: Jossey-Bass.

Greenleaf, R. (1977). *Servant leadership: A journey into the nature of legitimate power and greatness.* New York: Paulist Press,

Greenleaf, R. (2004). *The servant-leader within: A Transformative path.* Mahwah, NJ: Paulist Press.

Herman, B. (2007). *Moral literacy.* Cambridge, MA: Harvard University Press.

Keith, K. (2008). *The case for servant leadership.* Westfield, IN: The Greenleaf Center for Servant Leadership.

Madonna. (2003). *Mr. Peabody's apples.* New York: Callaway.

Manitoba Education, Citizenship and Youth. (n.d.). *Provincial Modernization of School Boundaries.* Retrieved Aug. 31, 2008, from http://www.edu.gov.mb.ca/k12/schools/amalgamation/index.html.

McPhail, D. (2002). *The teddy bear.* New York: Henry Holt and Company.

Murphy, J., & Seashore-Louis, K. (1999). Framing the project: Introduction. *Handbook of research on educational administration* (2nd ed.). San Francisco, CA: Jossey-Bass.

Muth, J. J. (2002). *The three questions.* New York: Scholastic Inc.

Pellicer, L. (2003). *Caring enough to lead: How reflective thought leads to moral Leadership* (2nd ed.). Thousand Oaks, CA: Corwin Press.

Pfister, M. (1998). *How Leo learned to be king.* New York: North-South Books.

Polleys, M. (2002). One university's response to the anti-leadership vaccine: Developing servant leaders. *The Journal of Leadership Studies, 8*(3), 117-130.

Powers, J., & Moore, J. (2004). *Servant-leadership and the art of teaching.* Indianapolis, IN: The Robert K. Greenleaf Center.

Sergiovanni, T. (1992). *Moral Leadership: Getting to the heart of school improvement.* San Francisco, CA: Jossey-Bass.

Sergiovanni, T. (2005). *Strengthening the heartbeat: Leading and learning together in schools.* San Francisco, CA: John Wiley & Sons.

Starratt, R. J. (2004). *Ethical leadership.* San Francisco, CA: John Wiley & Sons.

Taylor, H. (2007). *Ruby's Hope.* Winnipeg, MB: The Ladybug Foundation Education Program Inc.

Upjohn, R. (2007). *Lily and the paper man.* Toronto: Second Story Press.

Waber, B. (2002). *Courage.* New York: Houghton Mifflin.

Wheatley, M. (1999, June). *Servant-Leadership and community leadership in the 21st century.* Keynote address at the Annual Robert K. Greenleaf Center for Servant-Leadership Conference.

Wild, M., & Brooks, R. (2000). *Fox.* La Jolla, CA: Kane/Miller.

Wood, D. (2002). *A quiet place.* New York: Simon and Schuster.

Chapter Five

School Boards and Educational Leadership in Canada: The Changing Landscape

Duncan MacLellan, Ph.D.
Ryerson University

> Leadership is about creating, day to day, a domain in which we and those around us continually deepen our understanding of reality and are able to participate in shaping the future. This, then, is the deeper territory of leadership – collectively "listening" to what is wanting to emerge in the world, and then having the courage to do what is required. (Jaworski, as cited in Deans, Martens, & Gordezky, 2005)

In Canada, school boards are charged with powers to carry out duties associated with formulating and implementing elementary and secondary education policies within their respective provinces and territories. During the past decade, provincial education systems have undergone significant changes that reflect a systemic shift in how education is governed.[1] In particular, attention has focused on the following: school board reform, school curriculum, classroom enroll-

[1] Education systems were also being restructured in the United States, United Kingdom, and Australia. For a fuller explanation of these undertakings, see Manzer (2003).

ment capping, student achievement, social influences, school improvement and a range of other topics related to school effectiveness. In fact, school board restructuring has often topped the list of educational restructuring initiatives within Canada.

One reason school boards came under the restructuring knife is because they are composed of elected officials with varying sociopolitical agendas, and their leadership is often complicated by dynamic social, economic, and policy contexts within which their schools are situated. Added to this mix are central forces shaping the nature of school boards, which include critical changes in school demographics, shifting governance structures, stricter accountability frameworks, and the greater regulation of the teaching profession (Corbett, 2008; Dunning, 1997). Because of these factors and others, the changing role of school board leadership in relation to Departments/Ministries of Education and individual schools is an increasingly important issue in Canada's provincial and territorial education systems.

As society has become more global in its outlook, and our communities have witnessed significant population and financial shifts. Schools are viewed as the prism through which these shifts are transmitted. School boards are on the frontline of educational change, and their ability to respond effectively determines not only their success but also the schools they lead and that of the communities they serve. As such, school boards have become increasingly more complex organizations to lead and govern. In addition, the leadership capacity of school boards has shifted as a result of government restructuring and increasing demands from various stakeholder groups. The ability of school boards to respond to these demands can impinge their capacity to lead schools and initiate educational policies and programs (Henley & Young, 2008; Levin, 2005; Malcolmson, 2007; McAdams, 2006).

To bring these challenges into focus, I will begin with a brief but concise overview of the historic role and mandate of school boards. Then I will examine selected educational reforms introduced by provincial/territorial governments across Canada in the 1990s, specifically noting how these changes affected school boards. Finally, I will offer research that provides insight into how we can frame future school board leadership for the twenty-first century.

Evolution and Mandate of School Boards in Canada

Historical Overview

In Canada, many school boards can trace their roots prior to passage of the 1867 *British North America Act* (*BNA*). At this time, most citizens resided in rural communities and their children attended one-room school houses staffed by teachers who were hired and supervised by school boards. Local property and business owners comprised the membership of these local school boards (Corbett, 2008; MacLeod & Poutanen, 2004). Passage of the *BNA*, including section 93, gave provincial and territorial governments jurisdiction over education.[2]

During the twentieth century, as Canada industrialized, rural residents and new immigrants began to migrate and settle in urban centres. This led to demands for advanced educational services to match new skills required to work in these new urban-based industries. As a result, urban school boards, under the leadership of trustees, expanded their reach and became involved in new areas of educational programming (Gidney, 1999; Manzer, 2003). As Canada's population continued to increase, schools systems became larger and more complex in response the baby boom generation's entrance into public education.[3] In turn, school boards underwent significant organizational and structural changes to enable them to coordinate the ongoing curricular changes introduced by provincial educational officials across Canada (Fleming, 1997; Gidney, 1999).

As the population continued to shift from rural to urban centres, so too did this trend mirror the decline in rural school enrollment compared with increasing urban school enrollment. Across Canada, provincial officials began to look seriously at the need to consolidate or reduce the number of school boards, especially in rural communities. In many cases, this resulted in school boards being amalgamated into larger units as technology and improved modes of transportation enabled large geographic areas to be managed by a larger, single school board. This led to the following decreases in the number of school boards across Canada between 1950 and 1970: British Columbia from 700 to 77; Alberta from 774 to 50; Manitoba from 1,500 to 57; Ontario from 5 700 to 192; Quebec from 1 788 to 189; New Brunswick from 432 to 42; Nova Scotia from 85 to 22; Prince Edward Island from 432 to five; and Newfoundland from 270 to 20 (Dunning, 1997; Fleming, 1997; Manzer, 1994).

Beginning in the 1980s, attention was directed toward restructuring school governance in relation to decentralizing school control in terms of increasing accountability, enhancing parental and community involvement, and making schools more competitive to prepare students for the global economy. The shift can be attributed to discontent from parents, business leaders, and other stakeholder groups in relation to the quality of public schooling. In particular, these individuals and

[2] While jurisdiction for education does rest at the provincial/territorial level, the federal government has responsibility for educational services in relation to Aboriginal reserves, inmates in federal penitentiaries, and children of members of the armed forces. While territorial governments oversee their education, most of the funding originates from the federal government (Young, Levin, & Wallin, 2007).

[3] A study published by F. S. Rivers and R. W. B. Jackson noted that in Ontario from 1952 to 1966, school enrollment was estimated to increase by 417 000 pupils in the elementary panel and by 104 000 pupils in the secondary panel. This would require an additional 13 500 teachers at the elementary level and 4 430 at the secondary level (MacLellan, 2002).

groups were concerned that schools and school boards had grown too large and complex and were not meeting the growing needs of public schools. School boards were leading in a direction that did not recognize the variety of educational demands emerging within Canada's urban, suburban, and rural communities. Across Canada, a host of studies during the 1980s and early 1990s addressed educational topics related to financing, per pupil funding, parental and community involvement, large-scale curricular changes, methods of student assessment, introducing diversity programs, and restructuring schools to improve efficiency and effectiveness.[4] Many of these studies' recommendations formed the basis for the restructuring that occurred in the 1990s (Bedard & Lawton, 2000; Gidney, 1999; Howell, 2005; Manzer, 1994).

Some of these reports noted a tension between the need to govern education at the local level, where elected school board representatives familiar with community conditions could meet a range of needs with a variety of funded programs, versus the need to govern more centrally and use funds in a more efficient and equitable manner (Manzer, 2003). The concern over the role of school boards that arose in the late 1990s also brought the question of the mandate of school boards under close scrutiny by politician, concerned citizens, and other stakeholder groups. The opinion of some leaders within these groups was that the mandate of school boards needed to change radically if provincial/territorial educational systems expected to prepare students for an increasingly competitive workplace. To probe this assumption more fully, we will examine some of the key issues related to the mandate of school boards. This will then provide context for the wave of educational restructuring that swept across Canada during the 1990s.

Mandate

Most provinces delegate the operation of school systems to locally elected school boards of trustees or commissioners. The number of school boards, their size, and their district boundaries are defined in the various provincial/territorial legislation concerning education. School boards are generally responsible for the following: setting annual budgets; managing grants from provincial/territorial departments/ministries of education; delegating responsibility for the professional administration of schools; setting policies to be implemented by board staff; hiring, promoting, and dismissing teachers and

---

[4] Some of these studies included: British Columbia's (1988) *A Legacy for Learners: Report of the Royal Commission on Education;* the Economic Council of Canada's (1992) *A lot to Learn: Education and Training in Canada;* Newfoundland and Labrador's (1992) *Royal Commission of Inquiry into the Delivery of Programs and Services in Primary, Elementary, and Secondary Education;* Ontario Premier's Council's (1990) *People and Skills in the New Global Economy;* and Radwanski's (1988) *Ontario Study of the Relevance of Education and the Issue of Dropouts.*

school administrators; communicating with members of the public; building schools; and purchasing supplies (Young, Levin, & Wallin, 2007).

In certain provinces, boards are authorized to levy residential and commercial property tax. While trustees are generally under the jurisdiction of their provincial government, some provincial governments see the community as the most appropriate level to determine local education needs and, hence enable the communities to elect local trustees. Traditionally, most school boards have therefore enjoyed comprehensive taxing powers along with the ability to negotiate contracts and initiate management decisions within a local school district. (Dunning, 1997; Henley & Young, 2008).

In certain jurisdictions, school boards are also responsible for local programs such as daycare, breakfast, and adult education. School boards vary in size depending on the size of the community and the population being served. In rural areas, school boards oversee vast geographical locations with schools scattered across wide expanses (Ontario Public School Board Association, 1994).

Trustees fulfill the democratic principle of representation for taxation; they represent the local community, providing liaison between electors and their designated education system. The number of trustees per school board is generally based on student enrollment, although geographic area is sometimes included in the calculation of trustee numbers. Trustee elections may be held in conjunction with municipal elections and may also share three- or four-year terms. Depending on whether the province has both a public and Catholic (separate) system of trustees, citizens may determine which system they support financially as a precursor for casting votes (Dunning, 1997; Woolstencroft, 2002).

School boards normally select their own Director of Education or Superintendent of Schools, depending upon the province or territory involved. In some cases, the Minister of Education may need to approve the appointment of the Director/Superintendent before it can take effect. The Director/Superintendent is responsible for implementing board policies, administering the school system based on provincial laws and regulations, and delegating duties to senior administrators and principals. For all of the above, trustees are elected to work with board staff to accomplish these tasks and remain in close contact with their constituents (Corbett, 2008). In relation to municipal educational needs, a school board is given authority to represent all groups within its jurisdiction and be responsive to their needs. Board members exercise their authority as a group, consulting with school administrators who supervise the teaching staff in relation to board policies (Ontario Education Improvement Commission, 1997).

Summary

School boards employ teachers, administrators, specialist, and consultants on the human resource side of the ledger. On the physical plant side of the ledger, boards must operate and ensure schools and related services are maintained and meet provincial regulations. These two features are the foundation for most school board mandates, and their outcome is combined to provide students with a safe and positive learning environment that also reflects particular community needs. Examining the history and mandate of school boards across Canada has provided insights into significant changes that occurred since their inception. As the 1990s unfolded, we witnessed a degree of restructuring across many provinces that shifted the nature of the mandate of many school boards, particularly with respect to school governance, and this has had serious repercussion on school board leadership capacity.

Educational Restructuring: A Pan-Canadian Overview

The move to restructure and reform education across Canada, during the 1990s, involved a range of initiatives and system changes; common among many of these reforms was the reduction in the number and size of school boards. I will undertake a pan-Canadian examination of the restructuring of school boards, beginning in the mid-1990s and ending about a decade later. Table 1 provides an overview of board restructuring across Canada.

British Columbia

In November 1995, the British Columbia government announced its plan to reduce the number of school boards from seventy-five to thirty-seven; concerns were raised that this type of district consolidation would weaken community representation. As the provincial election drew closer, the BC government decided to reduce the number of school boards to fifty-seven. In response, the British Columbia School Trustees' Association (BCSTA) produced a discussion paper entitled *Our Children, Our Responsibility* (1997). This paper aimed to clarify the roles and responsibilities of school boards in relation to the British Columbia Ministry of Education. The BCSTA paper suggested that school boards be given greater independence in policy and administrative matters (Chan, Fisher, & Rubenson, 2007; Fleming & Hutton, 1997).

In March 2002, the Ministry of Education introduced *The School Board Flexibility Bill* (Bill 34), to give school boards flexibility and discretion over how funds could be allocated for supplementary board programs. As a follow up to Bill 34, the Ministry of Education developed a service plan to encourage school boards to seek new partnerships with other educational groups. In essence, these changes link accountability to the shifting nature of school board governance in British Columbia by promoting the following elements:

Table 1: Selected School Boards Across Canada: Pre and Post Restructuring*

Province	Number of Boards Pre-Restructuring	Present Number of Boards/Councils	When Restructuring Occurred
British Columbia	75	57	Implemented in 1996
Alberta	181	66	Implemented in 1994
Saskatchewan	119	28	Implemented in 1997
Manitoba	57	36	Partial implementation in 1995
Ontario	129	72	Implemented in 1998
Quebec	160	69	Implemented in 1998
New Brunswick	42	14 (district councils)	Boards eliminated in 1996
Nova Scotia	22	7	Implemented in 1996
Prince Edward Island	5	3	Implemented in 1994
Newfoundland	27	11	Implemented in 1997
Yukon		28 (school councils)	Implemented in early 1990s
Nunavut		10 (divisional councils)	Implemented in 1996

* Based on information from Owens' (1999) *Are School Boards Obsolete?* and from Chan, Fisher, and Rubenson's (2007) *The Evolution of Professionalism*. Information related to this table may have changed since it was first compiled.

- Reduce regulations and policies to make school boards more flexible.
- Have school boards begin to initiate accountability contracts with specific monitoring and public reporting processes.
- Encourage school boards to become more entrepreneurial in educational markets.
- Give parents a larger role as stakeholders with legitimate expertise and concerns in school board decision-making processes. (Chan, Fisher, & Rubenson, 2007, p. 21)

Alberta

Tough Choices (1993) was the first in a series of documents that examined the fiscal challenges in Alberta's education system. The report was the result of consultations with municipal leaders, school board administrators, business associations, and representatives of education groups in the year preceding the report's publication. The second major government report, *Meeting the Challenge: Three-Year Business Plan* (1994-1997), set in motion a number of educational changes. The plan included proposals to reduce the number of school boards, increase the role of parent councils, and transition to a school-based decision-making process. Additional attention was focused on school boards developing performance measures and creating partnerships with business interests (Chan, Fisher, & Rubenson, 2007; Fleming, 1997). By September 1994, the number of school boards had been reduced from 141 to 71 and in the same year, a five percent wage roll back was imposed on all public sector employees, including teachers (Chan, Fisher, & Rubenson, 2007).

One year later, *Accountability in Education* (1995) was released as a policy framework designed to direct the reporting and monitoring of schools and school boards towards improving accountability. All school boards were now required to prepare education plans and meet provincial requirements. In 2003, *Every Child Learns, Every Child Succeeds: Report and Recommendations*, was released and it suggested the provincial government exercise fewer controls over school boards' use of funds, provided that boards meet new accountability standards, and that teachers and parents play a role in how boards set their funding priorities. During the course of its restructuring of education, the Alberta government amalgamated 181 school boards into 66 with most of these occurring in suburban and rural boards where savings could be accomplished. Ministry of Education officials made few adjustments to Alberta's urban boards because they realized savings would be insignificant (Chan, Fisher, & Rubenson, 2007).

Saskatchewan

Established in 2003, the Boughen Commission on Financing Kindergarten was charged with studying and reporting on a variety of complex issues related to funding the province's education system. The general consensus was that the Commission would examine the issue of amalgamating school boards. In response to the final report of the Boughen Commission titled, *Finding the Balance*, the Saskatchewan government announced that the eighty-two public and separate school boards that existed as of spring 2004 will be reduced to approximately forty school districts comprised of no less than 5 000 students in each district. Over the next few years, this number was reduced to twenty-eight school divisions (Newton, Burgess, & Robinson, 2007).

Manitoba

Despite undergoing close scrutiny by members of the Manitoba School Divisions/ Districts Boundary Review Commission, which filed its findings in 1993, Manitoba's school division boundaries remained intact. The recommendations contained in the final report of the review commission strongly supported locally elected school boards as essential for promoting democracy and ensuring governance accountability (Sutherland, St. Hilaire, & Anderson, 2007). According to Henley and Young (2008), this endorsement was put forward along with a recommendation that the existing fifty-seven school divisions be consolidated into twenty-one divisions, which was later increased to thirty-six. The recommendation was met with strong opposition, particularly from rural divisions, where the effect would be most felt. In 1996, the Minister of Education bowed to public pressure and announced that school boundaries would not be changed, but added that the government would work with school divisions to promote voluntary amalgamation (Levin, 2005).

The Manitoba government followed in the footsteps of other provincial government and began to stress the need for greater accountability to help reduce increasing educational costs. In the 2003-04 school year government reports were released that stressed the need to improve educational accountability by focusing on outcomes-based education, implementing standardized testing regimes, and increasing community/parental involvement in schools. Partly in reaction to shrinking educational funding, school board amalgamation formed a key part of the government agenda from 1990-2004 (Levin, 2005: Sutherland, St. Hilaire, & Anderson, 2007; Young & Henley, 2008).

Ontario

When *The Fewer School Boards Act* (Bill 104) came into effect in early 1998, it reduced the number of Ontario school boards from 129 to 72, and renamed them district school boards.[5] Bill 104 cut the number of trustees per board and capped their salaries at $5 000 per year. Critics argued that these district boards would erode community participation in school governance, and reduce teacher and student access to significant district support services that had evolved under the previous system (Anderson & Jaafar, 2007; MacLellan, 2007).

Then, less than a year later, the *Education Quality Improvement Act* (Bill 160) became law and it centralized control over education funding and removed the power of school boards to manage the education portion of local property taxes. Bill 160 mandated greater restric-

[5] Elements of Bill 104 were based on the Ontario School Board Reduction Task Force's (1996) *Ontario School Board Reduction Task Force: Final Report* as well as Paroian's (1996) *Review of School Boards' and Teachers' Collective Negotiations Process in Ontario.*

tions on the use of special purpose grants (e.g., special education, transportation), and more financial accountability. In keeping with its emphasis on efficiency and fiscal restraint, the Ontario government legislated amendments to the Education Act, making it illegal for school boards to operate on deficit budgets (Anderson & Jaafar, 2007; MacLellan, 2007). In June 2002, three of the province's largest public school boards (Toronto, Ottawa, and Hamilton) defied the law, insisting that they could not maintain educational services under the existing funding formula without deficit spending. The government responded by appointing auditors to inspect the finances and operations in each of these boards. Trustees and parents critical of the government portrayed the takeovers as an assault on local democracy (MacLellan, 2007).

In 2002, the Ontario government commissioned a task force to review the following aspects of the province's education funding formula: distribution among school boards, cost benchmarks, local expenditure flexibility, school renewal, special education, and student transportation. The Commission's report, *Investing in Public Education: Advancing the Goal of Continuous Improvement in Student Learning and Achievement*, recommended the Ontario government inject an additional $1.8 billion over a three-year period into education and give school boards more autonomy to make expenditures to support at-risk students. After being elected in 2003 to govern Ontario, the Liberal Party embarked on an education policy platform that reversed several Conservative policy initiatives and restored local governance to elected trustees in the Toronto, Hamilton, and Ottawa District School Boards (Anderson & Jaafar, 2007).

Quebec

In June 1994, the Quebec government released *Preparing Young People for the 21st Century*, which subscribed to the idea of non-denominational schools, while continuing to recognize a religious and ethnic dimension to the human experience. In 1996, a report from the Commission for the Estates General on Education advocated abolition of both denominational school boards and schools. In March 1997, the Quebec government passed the following educational changes: creation of non-denominational school boards, maintenance of schools' denominational status until new linguistic schools boards were in place, and parents' right to choose the nature of moral and religious education given to their children. In June 1997, Bill 109 was adopted, creating French and English school boards while reducing the total number of boards from 160 to 69 (Lessard, Henripin, & Larochelle, 2007; MacLeod & Poutanen, 2004).

New Brunswick

In 1992, the New Brunswick government released, *Consultation Meetings on the Reorganization of School Districts*. The document noted that the New Brunswick Department of Education and its school boards agreed to the following proposals in relation to education:

- To create a provincial forum on public teaching that would emphasize collaboration and partnership so that the school boards, the Department of Education, and the different players could communicate among themselves.
- As a result of their [geographic] areas becoming larger, school boards would focus attention on questions of a more regional nature as well as the application directives and would move away from specifically local issues.
- Because they were now larger and there was a greater distance between the schools and the boards' administrative centres, school districts would delegate certain powers to the schools. To ensure good communication ...school advisory committees would be put into place. (Lessard & Verdy, 2007, p. 141)

Shortly after these modifications were implemented, the New Brunswick government reduced the number of school districts from forty-two to eighteen. Then in March 1996, school boards were dissolved and the Department of Education then established fourteen district councils to look after pedagogical questions related to education in New Brunswick (Lessard & Verdy, 2007).

Nova Scotia

In the mid-1990s, a report titled, *Restructuring Nova Scotia's Education System* was released. The report was based on the findings of a legislative committee that travelled across the province to gather information from its citizens. One year later, the Nova Scotia government released a response paper, *Education Horizons*, which outlined the government's intentions in relation to the *Restructuring* report. The response paper offered proposals to mandate school councils, harmonize French and English school curricula, restructure school boards, and focus on developing a more efficient and effective educational system for the province. To meet the goals of *Education Horizon*, Nova Scotia's twenty-two district school boards, which roughly paralleled the geography of individual counties were amalgamated into seven regional school boards as a cost saving measure. Government officials noted that larger boards would provide better economics of scale, reduce duplication and offer services that small board could not provide to the wider range of students currently in the province's school system (Corbett, Copp, Wright, & Monette, 2007).

Prince Edward Island

In 1994, the number of school boards in Prince Edward Island was reduced from five to three: two English-languages and one French-language. In 2001, the Prince Edward Island government declared that, even though provincial school enrollment was decreasing, the government was committed to a new staffing and funding model to ensure Prince Edward Island's pupil-teacher ratios remained among the highest in the country. The new funding model was also intended to reduce class size in the early grades and add teachers in key program areas. The Department of Education also attempted to address adequately the need for increased administrative and staffing resources at the school board level (Wright, Brunet, & Monette, 2007b).

Newfoundland and Labrador

The period from 1990 to 2004 was one of major change and reform in the Newfoundland and Labrador school system. At the beginning of this period, the K-12 school system in Newfoundland and Labrador featured a governance system shared between the Department of Education and the major Christian churches. The first referendum to restructure religious-based school system was held in 1995 and it received the support of fifty-five percent of those who voted; however, due to political pressure, changes were not implemented. Two years later, another referendum on the same topic was held and it received seventy-three percent of support from Newfoundland and Labrador citizens. Buoyed by these results, the Newfoundland and Labrador government implemented changes to reduce the number of religious school systems and this resulted in the establishment of an interdenominational educational system. An outgrowth of this policy was that the number of school boards was reduced from twenty-seven to eleven (Wright, Brunet, & Monette, 2007a).

Yukon, Nunavut, and the Northwest Territories

Together, the *Yukon Act* and the *Education Act* (1990) guide the authority for education in this region of Canada. The *Education Act* provides for the establishment of school councils, a French-school board, and provisions for special education. In addition, the *Education Act* mandates an emphasis on First Nations' culture, as well as jurisdiction over French-speaking residents living in the Yukon. The Commission scolaire francophone du Yukon (CSFY) was established as a Francophone school board in 1996, and it has five elected members; however, the school board does not have the authority to tax. School councils play an important role school operation and the education system in the Yukon. Each council has three to seven elected members that draw from members of the community. There are currently 28 school councils with 152 members and (Anderson et al., 2007).

In the Northwest Territories (NWT), the Department of Education, Culture, and Employment oversees public education. The focus in the NWT has been on decentralization and deregulation of government, and this has been the case in education as well. In 2001, the NWT Department of Education published the *Performance Indicators Reporting Manual* to assure parents that their children were receiving the best education possible (Anderson et al., 2007). The Nunavut Ministry of Education is charged with ensuring that education is based on language, the culture, tradition, and heritage of the people. The education system is decentralized and guided by district councils. In 1996, the new *School Act* converted school boards into Divisional Educational Councils (DECs), as in the Northwest Territories. Ten DECs, which consist of elected parents and community representatives, make decisions that guide and influence the functioning of the schools. The DECs are responsible for the coordination and promotion of educational programs and services in their administrative region (Anderson et al., 2007).

Summary

While school board restructuring is not a new phenomenon within Canada, many of the initiatives marking the 1990s wave, focused on saving money by reducing the number of school trustees and increasing the geographic size of school boards. The Alberta government established a template that was followed by other provincial governments in relation to stressing accountability as a priority while reducing costs (Lawton, Bedard, MacLellan, and Li, 1999). In Ontario, Bill 104 reduced the number of trustees per board and created the largest school district in Canada, the Toronto District School Board (MacLellan, 2007; Manzer, 2003. The Newfoundland and Labrador government created eleven interdenominational school boards to replace the denominational-based school boards. Perhaps the most dramatic change was in New Brunswick where school boards were dissolved in 1996 and replaced with fourteen district councils. The following four trends appear common in most of the 1990s educational restructuring initiatives across Canada's provinces and territories:

- Reduction in the number of school boards.
- Redefinition of school board powers and responsibilities.
- Centralization of power at the provincial/territorial level.
- Redirection of some responsibilities to school-board parents or community advisory councils. (Dunning, 1997, p. 4)

Many of these educational restructuring decisions either reduced the number and size of boards or amalgamated boards making them larger but less representative than previous structures. In both cases, administrative, financial, and personnel functions sometimes left these boards rudderless as they tried to deal with the drastic changes to their organizations. The rationale for school board amalgamations varied across provinces and territories. In some, restructuring was to save money and then direct these funds back into classrooms to improve the quality of education. For other provinces, restructuring rested on improving accountability, increasing parental and community involvement, giving students greater choice in school selection, greater rationalization in the use of teacher and administrative resources, less duplication of services, or to inject market-based ideas into schools (Chan, Fisher, & Rubenson, 2007; Levin, 2005; Malcolmson, 2007). One school board official called the educational restructuring process "conflicting discourses." Restructuring created a powerful potential for frustration for many board and school administrators as well as for teachers, who protested being expected to implement lofty ideals and wide-ranging change agendas with little or no new money and an inequitable funding formula (Corbett, Copp, Wright, & Monette, 2007). The next section will review selected literature in the field of school board leadership and offer observations to frame the challenges and opportunities that beset school boards in the twenty-first century.

School Board Leadership: Exploring the Literature

Research in the field Canadian school board leadership offers insightful scholarly work that increases our understanding of this field (Bezeau, 2007; Fleming, 1997; Henley & Young, 2008; MacLeod & Poutani, 2004; Manzer, 2003; Newton & Sackney, 2005;). A number of these authors have opined that the emergence of new demands and dwindling financial and human resources has often made it difficult for school boards to focus their attention on board leadership matters. In particular, current policy making in provincial/territorial school systems has become more complicated, in response to the decisions that emerged from the 1990s educational restructuring initiatives. In addition, many Canadian cities have expanded their population base rapidly during the past decade leading to a greater diversity within these cities. One major outcome of this situation is that urban and suburban schools are becoming more ethnocultural in their student population; therefore, building authentic school-community relations requires a greater degree of commitment and leadership from schools boards, at a time when they are being pulled in a variety of directions. Setting priorities and maintaining timelines for delivering educational programs and services have become more problematic as school boards struggle under the weight of being overloaded with greater demands from provincial educational officials, community groups, parents, and other interested educational stakeholders (Bezeau, 2007; Chhoun, Gilkey, Gonzalez, Daly, & Chrispeels, 2008; Columbia Institute, 2007).

School Boards and Provinces/Territories

One of the challenges school boards face in relation to leadership is the increasingly strict oversight exercised by many provincial governments that resulted, in part, from the restructuring initiatives introduced during the 1990s. While school boards exercise some degree of freedom in selected policy areas, increasingly these boards are finding that their autonomy in relation to education policy is become less flexible. In the constant climate of educational change, school boards find themselves spending large blocks of time responding to provincial government directives and statements. Due to increasing provincial oversight of their board budgets, school boards cannot be forward-thinking organizations and often are not able to plan ahead in times of financial uncertainty. Often boards feel overwhelmed in terms of excessive directives from the provincial government (Ontario Public School Boards Association, 1994; Storms & Gonzalez, 2006). Too often provincial governments focus on both the broad strategic directions and intervening directly in board policy making. When this happens, boards are often hobbled and their ability to act on behalf of community interests is weakened (Bezeau, 2007; Levin, 2005; Paquette, 1998).

School Boards and Teachers

Teachers have become more prominent and their voiced more articulated in terms of educational reforms and policies at the board level. Given that boards are their employers and boards are required to follow collective agreement reached with teacher unions, there are often barriers that prevent boards from recognizing and rewarding exceptional educational talent, performance, or special skills. Teacher decision making is key to promoting professionalism, and yet boards are often sensitive to allowing teachers this opportunity. Research shows that teachers want to be involved in decisions that affect their own work in terms of what to teach, texts to be used, and the nature of classroom activities. In essence, these features are what most connect teachers to their students; however, teachers feel powerless in many of these areas. Boards would benefit from increasing teacher participation in these and similar areas of decision making. In this way boards can show a strong leadership role by facilitating teachers and encourage school administrators not to fear greater teacher autonomy. This will lead to coordinated input into district goals while supporting a shared vision (New York State School Boards Association, 1988; Schweitz, Martens, & Aronson, 2005; Young, Levin, & Wallin, 2007).

Policy and Management

The tension between school board engagement in policy versus management is addressed in the educational leadership literature, and some recent scholarship has posited the idea of a more balanced role between school board policy making and management. In traditional terms, school boards have two main responsibilities: developing policies related to educational programs and services in their community and ensuring that their financial and personnel resources are used effi ciently and consistently with the board's strategic plan. In essence, policies need to reflect the board's goals and philosophy and offer standards to guide the local school system. In this sense, board policy invites an overall direction for the system, a framework for the implementation of procedures, and criteria to measure accountability (Fullan, 2001; Ontario Education Improvement Commission, 1997; Young, Levin, & Wallin, 2007).

As restructuring initiatives were being implemented in jurisdictions across Canada during the 1990s, the role and duties of trustees began shifting. As a result, trustees often lacked direction and support in relation to governance and administration. Given the complexity of some board operations, and the fact that many trustees fulfill this role on a part-time basis, boards may experience difficulty separating their policy role from the management role, which is normally under the purview of the director of education and his/her board staff. The director of education as the board's chief administrative officer is accountable to the board of trustees. Specifically, the director is responsible for administration and management of staff; individual trustees are not. Elected trustees are supposed to be accountable to the public and representative of community interests. Often the lines between director and trustee become blurry. This is even more complicated because staff responsibilities are not always clear in relation to governance and administration and this has sometimes resulted in poor staff/trustee relations. In some boards, senior staff members have moved into policy decision making, which is clearly a trustee function (Newton and Sackney, 2005; Ontario Education Improvement Commission, 1997; Ontario Public School Boards Association, 1994).

Trustees as board members have a representative role, a policy-making role, and as a member of the corporate board in setting policy for the local educational system. One of the challenges is finding the balance between board and director relations. The board has one employee, the director; nonetheless, many board policies are directed at the entire board staff and this can be confusing for staff. In reality, most boards do become involved in the administrative side of the enterprise and directors do play a role in the policy side. This is because some trustees may lack policy experience and the board operates on a part-time basis (American Association of School Administrators, 1992; Chhoun et al., 2008; Tracy, 2007).

While local control of public education appears to be a deceptively simple concept, in fact, it is not for the following reasons. First, the demarcation presented between board member as policy maker and director as policy implementer is ambiguous and often invisible; Second, board members are supposed to be trustees – that is, public officials acting on behalf of all residents in that district – but they are often viewed as advancing their own interests or those of powerful interest groups. Third, the process of public policymaking is more difficult and contentious than it has been in the past due to the complexity of schooling in the twenty-first century (Kowalski, 2005).

School boards, as district policy-making bodies, can influence the direction of the community's schools by setting the vision for the district, governing through board policies, and setting the framework within which learning occurs (California School Board Association, 1996). A board's leadership role only becomes real to the extent that it is exercised. The schools which boards lead express the values of the society that support them. With respect to goal setting, over the past decade, Canadian school boards have withstood a host of changes. In response, provincial officials have pressed for legislation that reduced the number and salary of trustees, altered funding models quite significantly, and mandated programs with little board consultation. The result of these changes has seen an avalanche of inconsistent goals and programs that have not often addressed the real needs of many school districts. Concurrent with these changes has been demands for greater parental and community involvement in how schools operate. As school populations have become more diverse, demands have grown for programs that reflect growing cultural diversity in school programs. What school boards can attempt to do is lead by using close personal knowledge of the needs of their local students to determine what initiatives to support. This type of leadership can enable a board to be strategic while reaching into the community for student educational opportunities (Dunning, 1997; Fleming, 1997; New York State School Board Association, 1988; Young, Levin, & Wallin, 2007).

Rethinking School Board Leadership

The field of leadership studies has advanced a range of models and approaches that relate to a number of fields within education. In particular, systems and environmental analyses scholarship posits that school boards are not static, closed systems; instead, they are subject to sustained flows of inputs from their environment, their boundaries are often permeable and shifting. Strategic planning literature advises us that change is the only constant in most organizations and that boards need to be flexible and nimble to respond accordingly. For this reason, the lines of authority are not always clear and they are often determined by the nature of the problem in conjunction with budget and operating constraints that, in the end, may limit the choices. In recent years, as organizational theorists have noted, team building and collaborative decision making have become dominant in many educational settings to ensure greater representation and community involvement. Lately, effective school leadership literature has promoted a *ground up* approach with greater attention given to the role of individual teachers, principals, and parents; however, insufficient attention has been directed toward the affect of these changes on the ability of school boards to provide consistent and steady leadership in times of great change (California School Boards Association, 1996; New York Board of Education, 1988; MacLeod & Poutanen, 2004; Malcolmson, 2007; Murphy, 2002).

Leadership is a primary factor in most discussions about successful, system-wide change. We normally view leadership as a top-down perspective with formal power structures and supportive infrastructure needed to ensure ends are met. As Fullan (2001) suggests, change requires both support and pressure and it is not enough to say you want change, a supportive infrastructure matters. The degree to which school boards exert leadership is reflected by their legislative authority and the environments within which they operate. Boards operate in the real world and they need realistic and useful models for dealing with the complex issues that confront them on a daily basis. Across Canada, the racial and ethnic distribution of students needs to be considered along with the growing income gaps that affect the ability of boards to affect change and deliver sustainable educational programs. Fullan also notes that effective leadership is about more than one individual; however, we expect our leaders to provide solutions and often place them in untenable situations because we require them to manage a multitude of tasks and responsibilities, often with inadequate support. Instead, what we should be focusing on are leaders who will challenge us to confront problems that require more than simple solutions (Fullan, 2001).

With this in mind, Fullan (2001) provides an innovative framework for thinking about leading change with effective outcomes based on the following five core capacities: moral purpose, understanding change, relationship building, knowledge creation and sharing, and coherence making. Surrounding these five components are more personal characteristics that all effective leaders possess, which Fullan labels as energy, enthusiasm, and hopefulness. These three personal characteristic work with the five components that interact with both tension and support depending on the issue. Leaders develop skills to utilize these five capacities and the three personal characteristics can achieve long-term commitment in those with whom they work, and this will result in good decisions and fewer problems within an organization. Figure 1 visually represents Fullan's leadership model.

Fullan's (2001) framework for leadership provides a solid basis for a further exploration of leadership in relation to school boards. The Canadian School Board Association (CSBA) has developed the Leadership Dimension Framework (see Figure 2 on p. 137). Combining the overarching elements of Fullan's framework and those of the Leadership Dimension Framework enables us to focus on factors that can contribute to effective school board leadership with the highest goal being improved student achievement. Elements of Fullan's framework for leadership and the CSBA's leadership dimension framework can be synthesized to bring forward an approach to school board leadership that will contribute to student achievement, which is key for effective leadership outcomes for school boards.

Figure 1: A Framework for Leadership (Reprinted from Fullan, 2001).

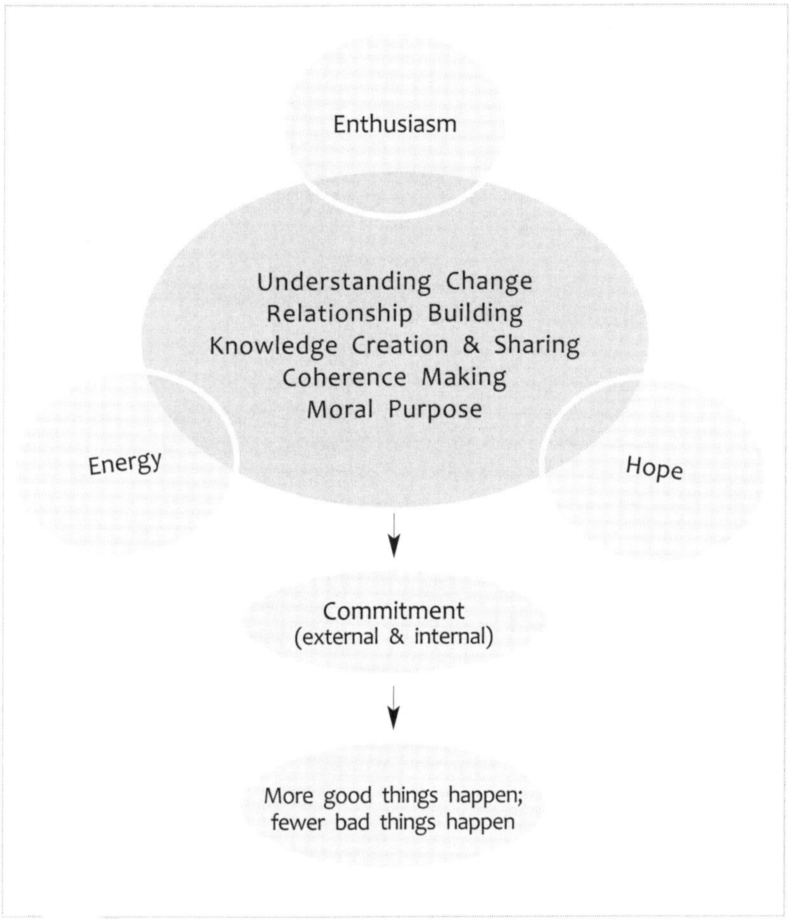

Vision

The development of a vision and strategic plan that involves school board and community members can articulate and reinforce core values in written and spoken communication, and it aligns organizational goals around the tenets of the vision. Central to this vision is for board members to have core beliefs and commitments because this is the conceptual starting point for a board's work. Board members should view themselves as integral to successful student achievement. In this way, boards can also focus on schools to help promote policies that will improve student achievement, while opening up new opportunities for other groups of students. Boards that do not share these beliefs and accept responsibility for these outcomes are not likely to succeed (CSBA, 2008; Fullan, 2001).

Communication Skills

Demonstrating the ability to present ideas and information in well-structure oral and written formation is imperative for school boards. Effectively addressing a range of audiences within the community, handling crisis communication, and defusing contentious situations are important communication tools for school boards to possess. Boards perform key communication roles with fellow board members, board staff, students, parents, community and business leaders, and elected officials at the municipal, provincial, and federal level. One role related to communication that often gets overlooked is with fellow board members. Leadership will be difficult to support unless board members work effectively with each other and with the Director of Education to establish a common language to assist in governance. Effective communication with the Director should avoid micromanaging into decisions related to personnel, facilities, and students that fall under the purview of the Director of Education. When good lines of communication are in place, board members can rely on the Director to manage without board members' participation beyond the advice given to help guide the Director's decisions in these areas (CSBA, 2008; Fullan, 2001, McAdams, 2006; Newton & Sackney, 2005).

Instructional Leadership

Recognizing and supporting effective research-based classroom practices can link school boards closer with teachers in relation to valuing pedagogy in a concrete manner. Boards would benefit from recognizing and funding a variety of supervisory models to improve active teaching and learning that reflects community needs. Technology for instructional purposes and current professional readings are important tools for teachers to have access to on an ongoing basis, and this can only be achieved if school board provide financial support for these resources to be available to school administrators and their teachers. Effective instructional leadership requires support on a range of levels in our education system and one of the key starting points is with school boards (CSBA, 2008; Chhoun et al., 2008; Fullan, 2001; Murphy, 2002).

Decision Making

Critical thinking and problem solving are essential so school boards can frame and prioritize issues effectively. Gathering data to use in the decision-making process can contribute to informed decisions that reflect an ethical foundation. Board meetings are the time and place at which decisions should be made to ensure transparency and to provide the public with an opportunity to have their voices heard. Therefore, the environment within which these decisions are discussed requires a high level of respect and strong leadership from the board to

Figure 2: Leadership Dimension Framework (Reprinted from CSBA, 2008).

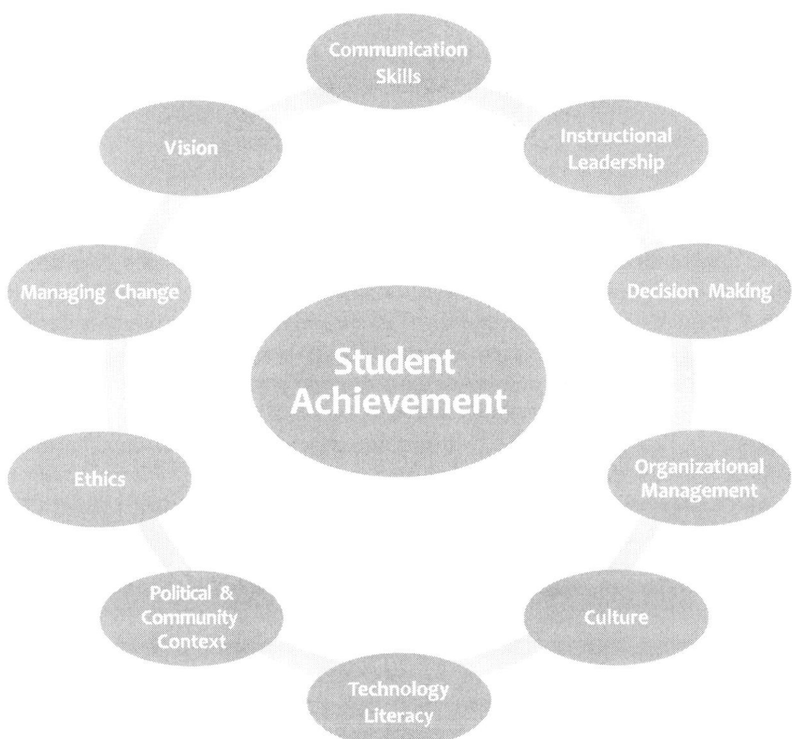

respond to internal questions from fellow board members but also from interested stakeholder groups attending meetings. Boards need to continue to exhibit fortitude, or "staying power" as is noted by Malcolmson (2007). This is important to ensure because after a decision has been reached, board staff will implement the policy, and later board members can follow up with the Director of Education for updates or to offer policy modifications, if necessary (CSBA, 2008, Davies, 2007; Fullan, 2001).

Organizational Management

Creating and fostering efficient learning environments that support resource allocation is important for school boards to consider. Establishing operational plans and processes that enable boards to analyze educational data and to interpret issues and trends will aid the policy making process. Coinciding with the importance of decision making is the need to foster a climate the supports learning at all levels of the board, from staff to trustee. Board members are often from variety of different educational and professional backgrounds and this may cause friction; however, by focusing on an open dialogue with the director and staff, board members can become knowledgeable about what areas they are responsible for without overstepping into areas that extend beyond their oversight. As noted earlier, given the closer alignment of policy and management decisions at many school boards, this can be a challenging situation; however, with good and open communication between the director and board members, differences can be accommodated (CSBA, 2008; Fullan, 2001; McAdams, 2006)

Political and Community Contexts

Facilitating organizational improvements by responding to community needs and interests within the larger political, social, economic, legal, and cultural context is an essential role for school boards. Creating and advocating for sustainable, meaningful partnerships with parents, community members, community organizations, and other levels of government can enhance school board effectiveness. No matter how much a board attempts to lead, its success is related directly to its degree of community support. Building civic capacity with citizens is crucial to enable a board to lead through both good and bad times. Schools have deep roots in their communities and boards need to understand this clearly. Reading the political landscape is important because it gives board members an opportunity to communicate with both well-established and issue-oriented organizations. Being unaware of the implication of board decisions on a community is political suicide for a board (CSBA, 2008; Fullan, 2001; Storms & Gonzalez, 2006; Tracy, 2007).

Managing Change

Effectively managing and evaluating change is a crucial skill for school boards to develop because it demonstrates an understanding of the change process. In addition, nurturing relationships within the organization can create clearer understandings when dealing with complex change situations, and this can help build deeper organizational capacity and greater knowledge around these issues. As noted earlier, boards are not static organizations because the schools they lead are ever changing in response to shifting societal, economic, and political forces. Some trustees view their board time as an opportunity to gain experience and then seek election to another order of government and so this leads to a high level of turnover in school boards that must be managed. In other cases, school boards may select Directors of Education for short-term appointments to give the board greater flexibility. Even with all of these changes swirling around, the public still expects school boards to manage policy and management issues in a timely and efficient manner (Newton & Sackney, 2005; Schweitz, Martens, & Aronson, 2005). Fullan (2001) has written extensively on the complexities of organizational change, especially within educational setting. He notes that traditional organizations, such as school boards, operating in a twenty-first-century world, are often ill-equipped financially and administratively to dig deep into the question of how to manage change. Managing change can be made easier with succession planning. Succession planning also relates to supporting individuals who may want to seek election for a trustee position to help "grow the board" and connect with community members (McAdams, 2001).

Culture

Creating and promoting an organizational culture that is a healthy, sustainable learning community is an important task for school boards. Celebrating educational successes can help board members, teachers, students, and administrative staff members feel valued. Monitoring instructional programs and then recognizing and celebrating educational leaders who achieve wonderful accomplishments can help to improve teaching and learning across school boards. Boards are instruments of democracy and large-scale reform requires significant changes in board culture; this cannot be overlooked because it is an essential ingredient to successful leadership. Each board is unique and a one-size-fits-all approach may be politically and financially expedient but it ignore the unique features of each board. These same features are what contribute to a board gaining and maintaining broad public support for deep and ongoing reform. Recognizing and supporting a vibrant culture that connects to schools will enable a school board to prepare and lead changes that will have the strong community support (Fullan, 2001; McAdams, 2006).

Ethics

Promoting integrity and fairness are key ingredients for successful boards. Effectively demonstrating integrity through respecting the rights of others and acting fairly can build board collegiality. Ethical behavior has become a key ingredient for determining successful leadership, especially in response to some of the financial and political issues that have confronted school boards recently. Citizens give school boards a significant amount of their trust in the hope that trustees will make decisions that reflect the best interests of the community. For a trustee to gain privately at the expense of the board is a violation of this trusted relationship and it weakens the board's leadership. A key ingredient for a successful board is ethical leadership. The ethical culture of an organization is the set of values that frames board decisions, the stronger the values exercised by individuals within the decision-making process, the more you ensure people make the correct choice and for the right reasons. All those who work in school boards, whether as staff members or volunteers, are representing the board in their actions to the public (CSBA, 2008; Fullan, 2001;

McAdams, 2006; Young, Levin, & Wallin, 2007). Justice Bellamy's comment, in the *Toronto Computer Leasing Inquiry Report*, regarding the importance of ethical leadership is worth noting:

> The history of political offices reinforces the value of leadership. The legacy of political actors revealed as corrupt has been, invariably corrosion of respect for the offices in which they served. Equally, political leaders widely admired for their integrity have enhanced the status of the offices they occupied. It follows that a continuing exploration of how best to ensure ethical behaviour by leaders is good for democratic institutions and for those that govern. (City of Toronto, 2005, p, 28)

Technological Literacy

School boards are complex organizations. Using technology effectively is key in improving work performance and communication with fellow board members, staff members, and schools. Boards should want to keep the power of information technology current to assist with citizen inquiries. Ever changing information technology continues to update the work world of all those involved in educational decision making, regardless of level. Currently, most school boards manage information, with a focus on curriculum, professional development, formative assessment, and student information systems; therefore, trustees have a wealth of information and knowledge to access to assist with policy making decisions. Technological literacy and knowledge capacity for effective leadership can be enhanced when trustees lead, supported by staff, in ways that use data to formulate policies and programs that support school board leadership and build better learning communities for students (McAdams, 2006).

Conclusions

Historically, school systems evolved with trustees occupying a lead role in many policy and administrative areas that helped build provincial educational systems. In the decades that followed, provincial school systems in Canada experienced major changes that, beginning in the 1950s, led to both a rapid expansion of the education system and waves of educational restructuring. In particular, as this chapter has noted, during the 1990s, education restructuring has included: major restructuring of school boards; reorganization of school district; focus on accountability; standardized testing; promotion of educational partnerships with private interests; national and international achievement testing; interprovincial curriculum development; introduction of site-based management; educational services for children with special needs; promotion of non-denominational schools and boards; and minority language education agreements with the government of Canada. These restructuring initiatives have led many school trustees to confront profound changes related to the financial, governance, and policy capacities of their school boards (Chan, Fisher, & Rubenson, 2007; Gidney, 1999; Manzer, 2003). Yet, despite the rapid pace of educational restructuring during the 1990s, many school boards continued to remain engaged in a wide array of educational programs including after-school recreation and day care programs; setting up evening instruction for students who are employed or single parents; designing recruitment and incentive plans for staff; and participating in school/business partnerships of various kinds (Canadian School Board Association, 2008; Chan, Fisher, & Rubenson, 2007; Deans, Martens, & Gordezky, 2005).

Currently many schools face major demographic transitions, a vast expansion of technologies, and increasing demands for greater levels of involvement and accountability from public and private interests (Howell, 2005; Storms & Gonzalez, 2006). Regardless of these challenges, school boards work to provide effective school leadership, which is vital to the maintenance and continued growth of schools across Canada (Chhoun et al.; Columbia Institute, 2007; Howell, 2005). One key ingredient that can support decision making based on both the work of Michael Fullan and the Canadian School Board Association is to ensure community participation in education, equity in access to services, and local implementation of programs and policies that are responsive both to social and economic goals and to community needs (Canadian School Board Association, 2008). Trustees can connect to community needs while building leadership capacity at the board level by bringing a positive approach to all board engagements, making governance a priority, and focusing on the human dimension of board-director relations because school boards today are being called upon to play a greater role in school leadership (Fist & Walberg, 1992).

One of the most important aspects of being a trustee is the role of community leader. As elected members, representing the educational interest of students, the board's role is to inform the community, business, and government leaders about the conditions and needs of students in the community and what the district is doing to respond to student needs. Effective board and community relations are important because the community is not only the chief source of support for the school but its main client. Constant reaching out to various communities within the district is needed, especially in districts where there are many ethnocultural communities that may not be knowledgeable about the school board's role and mandate. In this era of educational partnerships, boards often see value in linking with business or non-profit groups to help facilitate programs or services for students that the board may not be able to offer. In this way, communities can play a role in shaping the goals and vision of the educational system (Fullan, 2001; Storm & Gonzalez, 2006).

In recent decades, the growing pressure and restrictions on school boards have so burdened and constrained their operations that functioning as the district's educational leader have become more difficult. By recognizing the diversity of local needs and goals, school boards can adopt leadership approaches that will offer greater flexibility in response to community needs. Boards can strengthen their leadership in constructive and meaningful ways by collecting appropriate information to assess local needs, promoting an ethical culture, focusing on school boards best practices, consulting with stakeholder groups, establishing educational goals and policies, and communicating them to local constituents and provincial officials. In addition, what is important from a leadership perspective is that school boards and Directors of Education work out their areas of responsibility, respectfully (Deans, Martens, & Gordezky, 2005; McAdams, 2006; Schweitz, Martens, & Aronson, 2005).

School board leadership is a massive responsibility, especially in this era of large school districts that are expected to respond to a host of local and provincial demands. School boards are required to bring together students from many different cultural, economic, social and geographic locations, and then to develop policies that will be delivered equitably across a district; therefore, fulfilling this leadership requirement is a challenging undertaking (CSBA, 2008; Corbett, 2008; Davies, 2007; Fullan, 2001). As we progress through the twenty-first century, profound changes are occurring around the world that will continue to influence what is taught in our public schools. Therefore, those who govern and administer our public schools must share a vision, clear expectations, and the ability and courage to lead in accordance with the sentiments expressed by Jaworski at this chapter's beginning (CSBA, 2008). In terms of relating to groups, boards should consider carefully relations with school administrators, school educators, board staff members, parents, employee associations, and the community at large. Doing so will help to ensure that school board structures exist that involve sharing with key groups when it comes to sharing the board's vision and in implementing curriculum policy. In addition, the more clearly a school board can articulate to parents and the community why changes are occurring and then offer community members a chance to ask questions, the closer that board comes to reflecting the leadership approaches advocated by Fullan and the CSBA (Davies, 2007; Fullan, 2001).

School boards are critical to help create environments that foster and support learning within Canada's provincial and territorial educational systems. Developing board policies that facilitate student learning, promote knowledge creation, and build ethical and moral relationships will deepen a board's place within its community. As policy makers, school board members influence the direction of school curriculum by establishing frameworks within which educators work. Therefore, school boards hold the critical leverage points for bringing about and leading system-wide educational changes that benefit student achievement (Davies, 2007; Fullan, 2001; Howell, 2005; McAdams, 2006).

Questions

1. What can we learn from studying the history of school boards across Canada?
2. To what degree has school board leadership changed and what are some of the features that have led to this shift?
3. What are some of the current leadership challenges and opportunities that are before school boards?
4. In what ways can school board connect more closely with teachers, parents, community groups, and other key stakeholders in education?
5. What features can you suggest that would contribute to school boards becoming more effective in your community?

References

Anderson, S., & Jaafar, S. (2007). Policy narrative for Ontario. In A. Chan, D. Fisher, and K. Rubenson (Eds.), *The evolution of professionalism: Education policy in the provinces and territories of Canada* (pp. 79-97). Vancouver, BC: University of British Columbia, Centre for Policy Studies in Higher Education and Training.

Anderson, S., Chan, A., Corteau, R., Fisher, D., Gaydos, S., Lessard, C., & Rubenson, K. (2007). Policy narrative for the Yukon, Nunavut, and the North West Territories. In A. Chan, D. Fisher, & K. Rubenson (Eds.), *The evolution of professionalism: Education policy in the provinces and territories of Canada* (pp. 203-218). Vancouver, BC: University of British Columbia, Centre for Policy Studies in Higher Education and Training.

Bedard, G., & Lawton, S. (2000). The struggle for power and control: Shifting policy-making models and the Harris agenda for education in Ontario. Canadian Public Administration, 43(3), 241-269.

Bezeau, L. (2007). *Educational administration for Canadian teachers.* Retrieved on Aug. 1, 2008 from http://www.unb.ca/education/bezeau/eact/eacttoc.html

British Columbia. (1988). *A legacy for learners: Report of the Royal Commission on education.* Vancouver, BC: Queen's Printer for British Columbia

British Columbia School Trustees Association (1997) *Our children - our responsibility: A framework for clarifying the roles and responsibilities of the Ministry of Education, and school boards.* Retrieved Feb. 12, 2009, from http://www.bcsta.org/pub/Reports-Briefs/Roles-Response.htm

California School Board Association. (1996). *Increasing rigour and relevance: The school board connection.* West Sacramento, CA: Author.

Canadian School Boards' Association. (2008). *Leadership dimension framework.* Ottawa, ON: Author. Retrieved on July 15, 2008 from www.cdnsba.org

Carlson, D. (1993). The politics of educational policy: Urban school reform in unsettling times. *Educational Policy, 7*(4), 149-165.

Chan, A., Fisher, D., & Rubenson, K. (2007). Policy narrative for British Columbia. In A. Chan, D. Fisher, & K. Rubenson (Eds.), *The evolution of professionalism: Education policy in the provinces and territories of Canada* (pp. 11-30). Vancouver, BC: University of British Columbia, Centre for Policy Studies in Higher Education and Training.

Chan, A., Fisher, D., & Rubenson, K. (2007). Policy narrative for Alberta. In A. Chan, D. Fisher, & K. Rubenson (Eds.), The evolution of professionalism: Education policy in the provinces and territories of Canada (pp. 31-47). Vancouver, BC: University of British Columbia, Centre for Policy Studies in Higher Education and Training.

Chhoun, V., Gilkey, E., Gonzalez, M., Daly, A., and Chrispeels, J. (2008). The little district that could: The process of building district-school trust. *Educational Administration Quarterly 44*(2), pp. 227-281.

City of Toronto. (2005). *Toronto computer leasing inquiry and Toronto external contracts inquiry. Volume two, Good governance.* Report by the Honourable Madam Justice Denise Bellamy Commissioner. Toronto: City of Toronto.

Columbia Institute. (2007). Protecting democracy: Governing issues and local democracy. Vancouver, BC: Author.

Corbett, M., Copp., D., Wright, A., & Monette, M. (2007). Policy narrative for Nova Scotia. In A. Chan, D. Fisher, & K. Rubenson (Eds.), The evolution of professionalism: Education policy in the provinces and territories of Canada (pp. 149-167). Vancouver, BC: University of British Columbia, Centre for Policy Studies in Higher Education and Training.

Corbett, M. (2008). Democracy, neo-liberalism, and the dismissal of the Halifax Regional School Board. *Our Schools, Our Selves, 17*(2), 33-42.

Deans, P., Martens, K., & Gordezky, R. (2005). Success and system readiness: Lester B. Pearson school board and its commitment to educational excellence, Montreal, Quebec, Canada. In R. Schweitz, K. Martens, & N. Arson (Eds.), *Future search in school district change: Connection, community, and results* (pp. 192-207). Toronto: Rowman and Littlefield.

Davies, B. (Ed.). (2007). *Developing sustainable leadership.* Thousand Oaks, CA: Paul hChapman Publishing/SAGE Publications Ltd.

Dunning, P. (1997). *Education in Canada: An overview.* Toronto: Canadian Education Association.

Economic Council of Canada. (1992). *A lot to learn: Education and training in Canada.* Ottawa, ON: Minister of Supply and Services.

Education Improvement Commission. (1997). *The road ahead: A report on learning time, class size, and staffing. The first report of the Education Improvement Commission.* Toronto: Author.

Fist, P., & Walberg, H. (1992). *School boards: Changing local control.* Berkeley, CA: McCutchan.

Fleming, T. (1997). Provincial initiatives to restructure Canadian school governance in the 1990s. *Canadian Journal of Educational Administration and Policy, 11,* 1-20.

Fleming, T & Hutton, B. (1997). School boards, district consolidation, and educational governance in British Columbia, 1872-1995. *Canadian Journal of Educational Administration and Policy, 10,* 1-16.

Fullan, M. (2001). *Leading in a culture of change.* San Francisco, CA: Jossey-Bass.

Gidney, R. (1999). *From hope to Harris: The reshaping of Ontario's schools.* Toronto: University of Toronto Press.

Henley, D., & Young, J. (2008). School boards and education finance in Manitoba: The politics of equity, access, and local autonomy. *Canadian Journal of Educational Administration and Policy, 72,* 1-12.

Howell, G. (Ed.). (2005). Besieged: School boards and the future of educational politics. Washington, DC: Brookings Institute.

Kowalski, T. (2005). Foreword. In G. Petersen & L. Fusarelli (Eds.), *The politics of leadership: Superintendents and the school boards in changing times.* Greenwich, CT: Information Age Publishing.

Lawton, S., Bedard, G., MacLellan, D., & Li, X. (1999). *Teachers' unions in Canada.* Calgary, AB: Detselig Enterprises Ltd.

Lessard, C., & Verdy, J. (2007). Policy narrative for New Brunswick. In A. Chan, D. Fisher, & K. Rubenson (Eds.), *The evolution of professionalism: Education policy in the provinces and territories of Canada* (pp. 133-148). Vancouver, BC: University of British Columbia, Centre for Policy Studies in Higher Education and Training.

Lessard, C., Henripin, M., & Larochelle, M. (2007). Policy narrative for Quebec. In A. Chan, D. Fisher, & K. Rubenson (Eds.), *The evolution of professionalism: Education policy in the provinces and territories of Canada* (pp. 99-114). Vancouver, BC: University of British Columbia, Centre for Policy Studies in Higher Education and Training.

Levin, B. (2005). *Governing education.* Toronto, ON: The Institute of Public Administration of Canada and the University of Toronto.

MacLellan, D. (2002). *Two teachers' associations and the Ontario college of teachers: A study of teacher and state relations.* Unpublished doctoral dissertation, University of Toronto, Toronto, ON.

MacLellan, D. (2007, June). *The fewer school boards act and the Toronto District School Board: Educational restructuring 1997-2003.* Paper presented at the annual meeting of the Canadian Political Science Association, Saskatoon, SK.

MacLeod, R., & Poutanen, M. (2004). *A meeting of the people: School boards and protestant communities in Quebec 1801-1998.* London, ON: McGill-Queen's Press.

Malcolmson, J. (2007). School district governance: Recent changes. In *Protecting democracy: Governance issues and local democracy* (pp. 7-12). Vancouver, BC: Columbia Institute Centre for Civic Governance.

Manzer, R. (1994). *Public schools and political ideas: Canadian educational policy in historical perspective.* Toronto, ON: University of Toronto Press.

Manzer, R. (2003). *Education regimes and Anglo-american democracy.* Toronto: University of Toronto Press.

McAdams, D. (2006). *What school boards can do: Reform governance for school boards.* New York: Teachers College Press.

Murphy, J. (Ed.). (2002). *The educational leadership challenge: Redefining leadership for the 21st century.* Chicago: University of Chicago Press.

Newfoundland and Labrador (1992). *Royal Commission of inquiry into the delivery of programs and services in primary, elementary, and secondary education.* St. John's, Newfoundland and Labrador: Queen's Printer for Newfoundland and Labrador.

Newton, P., Burgess, D., & Robinson, S. (2007). Policy narrative for Saskatchewan. In A. Chan, D. Fisher, & K. Rubenson (Eds.), *The evolution of professionalism: Education policy in the provinces and territories of Canada* (pp. 49-64). Vancouver, BC: University of British Columbia, Centre for Policy Studies in Higher Education and Training.

Newton, P., & Sackney, L. (2005). Group knowledge and group knowledge processes in school board decision making. *Canadian Journal of Education 28*(3), pp. 434-457.

New York State School Boards Association. (1988). *Essential leadership: School boards in New York State.* Albany, NY: Author.

Owens, D. (1999). *Are school boards obsolete?.* Winnipeg, MB: Frontier Centre for Public Policy. Retrieved June 10, 2008 from www.fcpp.org/main/publication_detail.php?PubID=426

Ontario Education Improvement Commission. (1997). *The road ahead-II: A report on the role of school boards and trustees.* Toronto: Author.

Ontario Premier's Council. (1990). *People and skills in the new global economy.* Toronto: Queen's Printer for Ontario.

Ontario Public School Boards Association. (1994). *Ontario's public school boards: Investing in hour communities.* Toronto: Author.

Ontario School Board Reduction Task Force. (1996). *Ontario school board reduction task force: Final report.* Toronto: Queen's Printer for Ontario.

Paquette, J. (1998). Re-engineering Ontario education: The process and substance of the Harris reforms in education in Ontario. *Education and Law, 9*(1), 1-43.

Paroian, L. (1996). *Review of the school boards' and teachers collective negotiations process in Ontario.* Toronto: Queen's Printer for Ontario.

Radwanski, G. (1988). *Ontario study of the relevance of education and the issue of dropouts.* Toronto: Queen's Printer for Ontario.

Royal Commission on Learning. (1994). *For the love of learning: Report of the Royal Commission on Learning. Mandate, context, issues. Volume one.* Toronto: Queen's Printer for Ontario.

Schweitz, R., Martens, K., & Aronson, N. (2005). *Future search in school district change: Connection, community, and results.* Toronto: Rowman & Littlefield Education.

Storms, B., & Gonzalez, S. (2006). A model for successful district-based leadership development partnerships. *Educational Leadership and Administration, 18*(1), 15-35.

Sutherland, S., St. Hillaire, B., & Anderson, S. (2007). Policy narrative for Manitoba. In A. Chan, D. Fisher, & K. Rubenson (Eds.), *The evolution of professionalism: Education policy in the provinces and territories of Canada* (pp. 65-77). Vancouver, BC: University of British Columbia, Centre for Policy Studies in Higher Education and Training.

Tracy, K. (2007). The discourse of crisis in public meetings: Case study of a school district's multimillion dollar error. *Journal of Applied Communication Research, 35*(4), 418-441.

Woolstencroft, P. (2002). Education policies: Challenges and controversies. In E. Fowler & D. Siegel (Eds.), *Urban policy issues: Canadian perspectives* (pp. 276-297). Toronto. Oxford University Press.

Wright, A. Brunet, V., & Monette, M. (2007a). Policy narrative for Newfoundland and Labrador. In A. Chan, D. Fisher, & K. Rubenson (Eds.), *The evolution of professionalism: Education policy in the provinces and territories of Canada* (pp. 169-185). Vancouver, BC: University of British Columbia, Centre for Policy Studies in Higher Education and Training.

Wright, A., Brunet, V., & Monette, M. (2007b). Policy narrative for Prince Edward Island. In A. Chan, D. Fisher, & K. Rubenson (Eds.), *The evolution of professionalism: Education policy in the provinces and territories of Canada* (pp. 187-202). Vancouver, BC: University of British Columbia, Centre for Policy Studies in Higher Education and Training.

Young, J., Levin, B., & Wallin, D. (2007). *Understanding Canadian schools: An introduction to educational administration* (4th ed.). Toronto: Thomson Nelson.

Chapter Six

Developing School Administrators Who Lead with the Emotions in Mind: Making the Commitment to Connectedness

Brenda Beatty, Ed.D.
Monash University

Introduction

This chapter presents the case for the importance of emotions in educational leadership. The argument maintains that the success and wellbeing of school leaders are enhanced by the explicit integration of emotional meaning making as part of a reconceptualization of leader professionalism. The chapter begins by reviewing several key factors in the current context of education and then outlines several theoretical underpinnings for repositioning emotion's place in conceptions of mind and considerations of workplace relations. These theories are then applied to various situations encountered within schools where the significance of the emotions must come to the forefront: different kinds of emotional understanding (Denzin, 1984), working conditions that require emotional labor (Hochschild, 1983), the inevitability of leader wounding (Ackerman & Maslin-Ostrowski, 2002), and the obstacles presented by a predominant culture that maintains a professional silence on matters of emotion.

In schools, the norms for establishing, maintaining, and repairing trust (Tschannen-Moran & Hoy, 2000) have come to light as a critical factor in predicting the success of leaders, teachers, and students (Bryk & Schneider, 2002). Trust, in turn, is profoundly affected by the emotional valence of relational experiences. Left unconsidered and hidden below the surface, inferred emotional understandings about self, others, and organizations remain powerfully influential. The knowledge embodied within our emotions is experienced as a visceral signal system that feeds back to the individual insight gleaned from continuously scanning the environment for danger, safety and opportunity, even as it provides access to the ethical fabric of the self (Margolis, 1998). Correspondingly, knowledge received from the emotions, shapes and reflects behavior choices. In a reinforcing spiral of cause and effect, emotional *knowings* affect and are affected by communication, perceptions of individual and organizational trustworthiness, perceptions about vulnerability and risk, and thus the openness to collaborate with peers, superordinates, and subordinates as well as the inclination to make discretionary contributions.

A brief review of exemplars from prominent models of educational leadership, positions inner leadership and emotional meaning making capabilities as inherent in operationalizing these models' idealizations. The final section considers research results from studies conducted in Canada to explore the emotions of teachers as well as principals and head teachers across six different countries. This research led to the design and implementation of leadership preparation and development protocols, trialed in the US and Australia, involving both deductive and inductive approaches to deepening emotional epistemological perspectives (Beatty, 2002a, 2005; Beatty & Brew, 2004). This work centred on the efficacy of incorporating exchanges among peers. These exchanges were derived from a practice of sustained reflective writing that involves the deliberate integration of personal, professional, organizational, and scholarly dimensions. The responses from participants in these programs highlight the utility of promoting emotional meaning making as a foundational element in professional leadership practice.

Current Context

With the foreseeable and unforeseeable complexities of the future hanging over all of our heads, educators and those who prepare them are engaged in a desperate global struggle to get schooling right. A renewed and reconceptualized view of the role of school leaders, that includes the responsibility of creating optimal conditions for teaching and learning at all levels, puts principals squarely in the middle of a maelstrom. Echoes of earlier UK and US desperation to make schools accountable for improving student performance can be heard in current policy imperatives like the Australian national threat to sack principals and fire teachers in failing schools. As my colleagues Williams and Brien (2009) argue, both the notion that academic standards can be achieved by edict and the belief that the professional collaboration necessary for school improvement can be produced through hierarchical control was, at that time, a new leadership mentality that grew out of experiments in the UK and US. The pitfalls of this kind of new leadership mentality are quite well documented. In the UK, attempts to use super-principals to turn schools around led to burnout and loss of momentum when those leaders left. Inspections by the Office for Standards in Education (OFSTED) brought public humiliation, parent uproar, and teacher disillusionment as league tables ranked schools against each other – in a process seemingly designed to negate the value of teachers' daily efforts. As the stress on the health and wellbeing among principals and teachers alike increased, so to did the urgency of addressing the importance of emotions to teaching, learning, and leading within the scholarly discourse (Jeffrey & Woods,1996).

Despite these critiques, I still agree with Robert Evans (1996) and Michael Fullan (1999) that we do need an impetus for change and accountability pressures bring with them the energy of urgency. Indeed, a new focus on student results has definitely resulted from these regimes. However, the fear and resentment associated with labeling and blaming entire schools, has done a tremendous amount of damage

In the current context of many western nations, accountability pressures continue to mount and correspondingly, the appeal of a career in education, especially in school leadership, continues to dwindle, just as the retiring baby boomer generation is leaving the scene. Succession planning as well as teacher and leader preparation and development have never been more important. These need to go hand in hand with the reigning imperatives that are challenging schools to change.

Visions and Realities

The ideal learning environment is regularly envisioned to have secure students who enjoy a strong sense of belonging and connectedness with their school (Osterman, 2000; Beatty & Brew, 2005). Such students engage eagerly in their learning and achieve well on standardized tests. Within this ideal community, the students and their parents are supported by and collaborate with educators who actively participate in dynamic professional learning communities within which they continually investigate and refine their practices. Such communities are fostered by transformational leaders who attend to individual needs, provide intellectual stimulation, promote a shared vision, and share decision-making authority (Leithwood, Jantzi, & Steinbach,1999). They exemplify the ways of seeing and being that they wish to promote among all members of their school communities. These characterizations have long been envisioned in scholarly, professional, and policy discourses alike.

Yet, collaborative cultures are far easier to put into policy than into practice. We might wisely ask ourselves the following questions:

- Why is it so hard for leaders and teachers to communicate openly and freely with each other?
- What could explain leader resistance to sharing decision-making authority?
- What is it about teacher-leader, teacher-student, and teacher-parent relationships that we need to understand and address?
- Do we need more carefully articulated leadership models?
- Are stronger penalties for poor student results likely to motivate change?
- Should we just close the schools whose means on standardized performance measures suggest they are not making the grade?

In answer to the last two points I think not. The fear factor as a motivator for professional learning and collaborative culture building isn't working, and there is an emotional reason for this. The fear factor erodes the conditions that foster trust.

Macro- and Micro-Reforms

Policy decisions in Ontario have made a significant turnaround in recent times. Whereas in the 1990s standardized test results were used for shaming and blaming, now those same results are being applied as evidence of the need for improved funding and better support. This illustrates the importance of the macro-level of influence upon conditions for learning.

At the micro-level, there are further personal, interpersonal, and relational complexities that do not readily respond to dictates and directives. Leaders, teachers, students, and parents are being asked to work together in new ways, to rethink and reconfigure their mental models of schooling. Many students, perhaps the most technologically comfortable with our increasingly wireless world, still find that trust remains a rare commodity. Relational issues persist within digital environments, witnessed by the ubiquitous phenomenon of cyber-bullying. The emotional demands of developing respectful, caring, connected and socially responsible relationships are as real for adults as they are for children. When fear surfaces, anger, shame, and blame are often right around the corner. Left unexamined, emotional pressures can lead to betrayal and damaged relationships that quickly become a liability to learning.

The Emotional Challenge of Change

Being pressured to change is upsetting. It threatens one's attachment to the status quo; it invades and disturbs comfort zones. The pressure to change can feel downright dangerous and therefore frightening. What follows is some of the emotional implications of the expectations for change in the current context.

Leaders are expected to change from being hierarchical – withholding of information and inclined toward authoritarianism – to becoming empowering, transparent, and unleashing, as they share and widely distribute their leadership authority. They are expected to create collaborative cultures in their schools and their communities, even as the pressures for performativity mount (Ball, 2000). To respond to the call for moral leadership, principals need to address the pressures for performativity, without losing their integrity. However, in the US, leaders were driven by fear for their jobs, which was intensified by their isolation from and competition with each other. This pressure to be seen to be performing well led many leaders to lean on and alienate teachers and manipulate student performance results to satisfy their communities' hunger for evidence of their school's success. Just scratch the surface of the "Texas Miracle" to find out more about this slippery slope (Amrein & Berliner, 2002; Winerip, 2003).

Under such threatening conditions, it can feel downright counter-intuitive to reach out, relax, let go, and trust. Furthermore, there is a long standing tradition in educational leadership of doing anything but trusting others. Inherent in the mental models of the past is the danger of dysfunctionality. *School leader* has traditionally meant someone particularly proficient at command-and-control tactics, the all powerful all knowing, larger than life, heroic commander-in-chief. These qualities have been well respected and rewarded in days gone by. Yet what is needed is openness and humility in leaders: leaders who understand that they are learning too and are given space by those they lead to make mistakes as they learn. Under current pressures, it is a perfectly natural tendency to clench one's fists and harden one's resolve, while keeping an even firmer grip on the wheel. And yet in the process, there is a tendency to lose sensitivity – to self and others' needs. It is difficult under such internal conditions, to achieve the kind of truly *new leadership mentality* that is desperately needed.

I love the cartoon of the principal with the army helmet on, who is sitting behind his desk as his advisor suggests, "Staff feel that calling your office 'the bunker' sends the wrong message" (Moore, 2005). It is time for new metaphors!

Teachers are expected to change, too. But often change seems to mean more work piled on teachers who are already stressed and on the verge of burnout. Yet they are being asked to shift from comfortably private, solo work to vulnerable, relatively public, collaborative, data-driven practices: from teacher-centred to student-centred learning processes and back again, with the resurgence in popularity of *direct instruction*. For teachers to learn new practices, and rework old ones for new applications, they need support from each other, support that can come from collaborative learning leaders who can model a different way.

Consciousness raising *is* essential and practitioners *do* need to come out of the privacy of their own classrooms and publicly engage in meaningful collaborative considerations with their colleagues about what is best for children's learning. Yet this is a very threatening mandate for teachers. If teachers are to have collaborative, data-based dialogues with each other, they need to feel safe enough to have those conversations or they simply won't occur. We have known for a long time that collaborative learning communities flourish in emotionally comfortable spaces (Nias, Southworth, & Yeomans, 1989). The call for interactive professionalism and the creation of professional learning communities is pervasive (e.g., Fullan, 2008; Hord & Sommers, 2008). Yet there persists a professional silence on emotion that can make the building of trusting relationships hard to achieve. On the other hand, when they are emotionally prepared for the challenge, leaders can skillfully demonstrate the courage to acknowledge vulnerability and create safe spaces for genuine inquiry. They can insist upon and model an ethic of mutual respect, care, and professional support (Beatty, 2002b). Such leaders can make a commitment to restorative practices that work through emotional meaning making to create the kind of cultures where bold self-critique and deep change can occur. To do so, however, requires leaders to redefine their mental models of leadership.

Theoretical Basis for Leading with Emotions in Mind

Emotion in Mind and at Work

Contemporary neuroscience shows us that Descartes erred (Damasio, 1997) in attempting to wall off reason from emotion in his model of the mind. It simply can't be done. Emotions are not optional. Intellectual activity wouldn't happen at all without emotion's motivating powers. So it is time that we got on with the work of deliberately reconnecting with the whole of our consciousness, our embodied minds and the seamless blend of thinking and feeling.

Norman Denzin (1984) provides us with some insights into various kinds of emotional understanding. He cautions that spurious or mistaken emotional interpretations of others, are the most common to occur, especially in workplaces. He suggests that emotional embracement that occurs through the experience of a shared field of emotionality is the ideal. To overcome spurious emotionality, and avoid settling for imagined experiences of the other, there needs to occur a cross checking and connecting to discover what people are actually feeling and what those feelings mean to them. In a culture of silence on emotions, emotional embracement is likely to remain a long way off.

When in the line of duty, one must make a constant effort to mask real feelings and feign feelings one is not having, such as exuding enthusiasm and disgust, or attempting to seem unemotional so as to appear purely rational; this involves emotional labor (Hochschild, 1983). In her research with airline attendants and bill collectors, Hochschild found that perpetual emotional labor can lead to a divided self and emotional numbness. Educators are no strangers to emotional labor. It is essential to the work that we do. But it takes a toll. The *feeling rules* (Hochschild) of our schools need to be challenged and changed.

A study of 100 Ontario teachers' stories of emotionally positive and emotionally negative experiences with school principals (Beatty, 2002a, 2007a), yielded some insights into their emotional meaning-making processes. The findings exposed a Maslovian-like hierarchical pyramid where respect formed the foundation, caring was built on respect, and professional support formed an apex requiring both care and respect. Unfortunately, the study also showed that anything more than respect was considered by teachers to be a wonderful bonus, when you could get it. The lack of respect teachers perceived from leaders undermined professional confidence, creativity, and any expectation of receiving care or professional support; moreover, teachers who felt disrespected tended to retreat and retract in their practices.

Explorations into the power of emotion in teachers' lives can inform leadership practices. Matters of teacher motivation, morale, burnout, satisfaction, commitment, and self-efficacy can all be viewed through the lens of emotion, as Ken Leithwood and I try to illustrate in our book *Leading with Teacher Emotions in Mind* (Leithwood & Beatty, 2008a). We note that leaders cannot be expected to magically manufacture an emotionally attuned orientation. It takes focused practice of a particular kind, which is the focus of the next section.

Challenging the Normative Professional Culture of Emotional Silence

It is not that leaders or teachers can afford to indulge in rampant emotional display. This is not my message. Emotional control, which involves the ability to make good decisions about managing the display of emotion, is tantamount to leadership itself, and so it should be. Leading change means deliberately disturbing the status quo. If a leader is making a difference, she or he is likely to get "splattered" (Hollowell as cited in Maslin-Ostrowski, 2007).

But when leaders, who are inevitably going to get wounded, remain isolated from each other, they are more likely to suffer from withdrawal, protectionism, defensiveness, detachment, and loss of the *feeling function* (Ackerman & Maslin-Ostrowski, 2002). From over 250 stories of principal woundings in these authors' study, conducted through a series of interviews taking place over more than a decade, one third of the leaders became lost and dispirited and so did those in their care. Many left the job. Another third had become altered, increasingly cautious and protective, and more inclined to the command and control tactics noted above. Yet a final third had discovered that the wound was an opening, an opportunity for new learning and even transcendence. The processing of the wounding experience was the catalyst in these cases. The healing occurred because these leaders worked through their emotions and recounted their stories with trusted others. In so doing they reclaimed their feeling function, reintegrated their whole, fully dimensional selves, and *re-storied* (Beattie, 1995) their subsequent life chapters, as they reconnected with their secret selves, their personal and professional principles, and their moral purposes.

We have long known that in the initial stages of change, peoples' concerns are largely oriented around personal impacts. The Concerns Based Adoption Model (CBAM) (Hord, Rutherford, Huling-Austin, & Hall, 1987; Hall & Sommers, 2008) tells us that this is a natural part of the change process. Yet if, in the line of duty, we are systematically marginalizing matters of emotion, how can we ever work through such personal, emotionally charged concerns? Given this, it is easy to explain why so many change initiatives falter. When the professional culture constrains the ability of people to work through their emotions, even those initiatives that seem to succeed initially will often fail to last.

Inner Leadership

There is a paradox of emotion and educational leadership: the dichotomy between the way leaders and teachers believe they must seem – in control and emotionally detached – and the ways they need to be as fully integrated, highly functioning people. Emotional control is one thing. Emotional numbness and relational disconnectedness are quite another (Beatty, 2000a).

In order to embrace the challenge for change, the genuine concerns of teachers and leaders, students and parents, need to be respectfully aired, acknowledged with care, and worked through with support. Doing this creates an exchange of meaningful narratives that emerge from the lived experiences of the self and others. From this exchange, people can story and re-story the self (Beattie, 1995) and renew a sense of wholeness. Educators, therefore, need the opportunity to engage in focused reflection and shared experiences of inner self-leadership if they are to reclaim their emotional integrity within the workplace. This can occur in carefully planned programmatic approaches that deliberately break the professional silence on matters of emotion.

We need new metaphors because we need deep transformation. The surface stuff just isn't doing the trick. And the starting place for transforming leadership lies within leaders:

> As leaders change their own lives they are better equipped to appreciate what it means to help create the conditions for others to change their lives. (Ackerman & Maslin-Ostrowski, 2002, p. 69)

To change our own lives, however, we need to stay connected or become reconnected with our inner experiences, which involves becoming reflexive. We need to get beyond the numbing dis-integration of self that is associated with leader isolation. Doing so means creating safe spaces for acknowledging and working through the health-threatening fear of reprisal and humiliation, loss of control, and shame. These are understandable feelings, and they deserve to be addressed. Most critically, we need conditions that foster respect care and professional support for leaders too.

In a mid-air crisis, we are reminded by the attendants to put on our own oxygen mask first. Now *that* is a metaphor for educational leaders. To help others thrive, leaders need first to look after themselves. This means ensuring their integrated selves are healthy and, thus, likely to survive. This is fundamental to leader wellbeing and sustainability.

So why is this so hard? The traditional professional silence on emotions makes a point of ignoring the elephant in the room. The culture both deliberately and inadvertently promotes disconnection from the emotions. Perhaps there is a clue in some earlier research on enculturation to educational administration (Marshall, 1992; Marshall & Greenfield, 1987). These authors discovered just how commonplace it was for aspirants to be required to leave their ethical convictions and emotional integrity at the door in order to gain entry into the club of school leadership. Such an initiation was requiring leaders to undergo a deliberate detachment from their emotions, even though the emotional dimension is the self's relationship to itself (Greenberg & Paivio, 1999) and a key to health and wellbeing. Leadership preparation and development needs to address and confront the contrivance of a de-emotionalized educational administration culture.

The Trust Factor

One important factor emerges from this research that cannot be addressed with a superficial approach; the change needs to go deeper. One of the most critical conditions for learning is trust. Trust, while arguably the result of cognitive attributions one makes to conditions perceived, is also deeply embedded with matters of emotion, as is all cognition. In major studies largely coming out of the Chicago school system, it has become well established that trust among adults in schools is predictive of student performance (Bryk & Schneider, 2002; Tschannen-Moran & Hoy, 2000). But even ideal leadership behaviors can only create the necessary conditions – necessary but not sufficient – to foster teacher learning and success. Additionally, schools need dynamic learning communities that engage in data based, clearly focused, collaborative reflective learning among leaders, teachers, students, and parents.

Wisely, we are now beginning to acknowledge that constructive engagement with the *emotional complexities* of schools, schooling, and school leadership can help to promote the relational connectedness that is necessary for schools to succeed. With a firm footing in resilient relationships, people can afford to make themselves vulnerable to bold self-critique and get on with the important business of improving their practices together, especially in such trying times.

All people in schools need to celebrate their interdependence and cooperate in their learning to be effective. This requires the co-construction and co-maintenance of a culture of respect, care, and support; in short, teachers and leaders must develop trust so that the dynamic learning potential across all members of the entire educational community can begin to manifest.

Kinds of Trust

Reina and Reina (1999) propose three kinds of trust: communication, contractual, and capability trust. Trusted others communicate openly and honestly and keep us informed of the things we need to know. We trust people who do what they say they will do and what they know they should do. We can afford to trust colleagues when we know they are capable of their professional obligations. These are necessary elements of trust, but again, not sufficient, as there is more to trust than this. We also look to those we trust to care, and to take care not to betray us, damage us, or wound us. If they do, we need to be able to trust that we will both honor the importance of our relationship and take the necessary steps to repair the damage and heal the wounds. The commitment to developing this kind of relational trust is core business if we are to create the collaborative cultures that we need in our schools. In times of mounting pressures and accompanying fears and frustrations, the maintenance of healthy relationships with one's colleagues is an emotionally demanding and even counterintuitive proposition. But it is where we need to go.

A multi-disciplinary review of the literature on trust by Tschannen-Moran and Hoy (2000) explored the dynamics of trust, including initiating, sustaining, breaking and repairing it. As well, they synthesized the research as it pertains to organizational processes and examined trust in schools in terms of communication, collaboration, climate, organizational citizenship, efficacy, and effectiveness. These authors noted that leaders are expected to trust those to whom they grant decision-making discretion. In schools, this includes teachers who work with relative autonomy in their classrooms and parents who need to work for the common good and not solely the interests of their own child. In order to get teachers to question beliefs and challenge each other about their practices, leaders must foster trust among teachers. Teachers can then extend this trust to their students as they give them opportunities for "greater voice in their lives at school" (Tschannen-Moran & Hoy, p. 549). Tschannen-Moran and Hoy further outline the dire importance of developing trust within schools:

> To be effective and productive, schools, like other organizations, must be cooperative, cohesive, efficient, and well managed. Trust is pivotal in efforts to improve education. And yet, trust seems ever more difficult to achieve and maintain. . . . Distrust tends to provoke feelings of anxiety and insecurity, causing people to feel uncomfortable and ill at ease and to expend energy on monitoring the behaviour and possible motives of others. When students feel unsafe, energy that could be devoted to learning is diverted to self-protection . . . to minimize vulnerability. (p. 550)

These researchers go on to describe the situation within schools under conditions of distrust:

> Subordinates may withhold information and use pretense or even deception to protect their interests. . . . [O]nce it is established, . . . [distrust] has a strong tendency to be self-perpetuating. When one is interacting with a distrusted person, even normally benign actions are regarded with suspicion. . . . Distrust impedes the communication which could overcome it. (p. 550).

Part of the reason that distrust impedes the communication which could overcome it is the fact that it is not only initially emotionally uncomfortable to experience distrust, but it is also emotionally counterintuitive to move toward the danger (Maurer, 1996) associated with persons who have perpetrated betrayal and inflicted pain from a wounding. What is damaged is not only the trust of the individual and the trust of the organization and sense of safety at work, but also the trust in one's own judgment about the trustworthiness of others. Betrayal of trust can damage the victim for life. Left unresolved and unrepaired, woundings from betrayal of trust can lead to a predisposition to doubt, within which it is often seen as better to be safe than sorry. The over-caution that can result from a lack of trust in a school culture can dull the edge of inquiry and compromise the openness to new ideas.

Given the distance and disconnection in traditional teacher-leader relationships, it is often difficult for teachers to determine what leaders feel about them and, subsequently, how leaders will treat them. Unless there is confidence that respect, care, and professional support (Beatty, 2002a, 2002b) are to be expected, applications of new teaching approaches are far less likely to occur at all.

The Teacher-Leader Relationship

The relationship between teachers and leaders is essential in fostering change within schools: "A principal who wants to change the culture of a school needs to unleash creativity as teachers and administrators alike find new solutions to old problems" (Tschannen-Moran, 2007, p. 106). However, the teacher-leader relationship regularly remains problematic (Starratt, 1991), stimying the potential for change. This problem remains in part because it is difficult to develop trust without having made a personal connection to develop confidence in the expectations of goodwill in another. Yet, the lack of relationship between teachers and leaders can lead to spurious emotionality and the tendency to experience a heightened sense of vulnerability and self-surveillance, which may or may not be warranted. Unless the emotional substrate, that is inherent in building and maintaining relationships of trust, is on the radar for both leaders and teachers, they will continue to find it very difficult to reform their school culture together. Even with shared emotional meaning-making processes embedded in daily practice, reculturing is never easy. It is hard going, but well worth the effort.

Starratt (1991) characterizes the traditional teacher-principal relationship as one of antagonism. By contrast, he describes a constructive teacher-principal relationship as open and trusting. The gap between the normative pattern and that described below represents a gap in emotional understanding:

> The administrator who is concerned with nurturing the growth of teachers will have to ensure that teachers experience the relationship with the administrator as one of regard, mutual respect, and honest contact between two persons. Even though their traditional organizational roles have conditioned administrators and teachers to an antagonistic relationship, in a school intentionally restructuring itself and concerned about issues of empowerment, it is possible to move toward a relationship based on caring. For relationships of caring to develop, administrators will initially explore with their teachers those conditions necessary to initiate and maintain trust, honesty, and open communication. (Starratt, p. 196)

The capacity for organizational change is defined by the extent to which emotionally significant matters can be openly addressed (Fineman, 1996). With current pressures for educational change, Starratt's (1991) statements are loaded with emotional implications for leaders and teachers. If they are to change the nature of their relationship from antagonistic to collaborative, trust – so hard won and easily lost – will be the deciding factor.

Starratt (1991) suggests a number of specific and emotionally demanding efforts that would be required of such a leader of educational change. These include reorienting one's concerns toward nurturing the growth of teachers; ensuring that there is a relationship with the administrator; developing mutual respect, regard, empowerment, and caring; ensuring honest contact between two persons; intentionally restructuring the school; and exploring solutions *with* teachers. There is no room for antagonism in one who would be nurturing and open, respectful, and trustworthy, honest and caring. All of these actions and qualities on the part of an educational leader involve shifts into a praxis that is philosophically and emotionally different from the status quo in many schools.

To reculture our schools for the future, we need to understand the patterns of the past. The silencing of individual emotion happens in the midst of an insidious social emotional phenomenon: the adherence to organizational feeling rules where "the altruist is more susceptible to being used – not because her sense of self is weaker but because her 'true self' is bonded more securely to the group and its welfare" (Hochschild, 1983, p. 196). This has a disturbingly familiar ring to it for teachers and school leaders, who are professional altruists in the end, using their inner resources for professional service. The more that emotions are treated as organizational assets, such that "the company offers the worker's true self for sale, [then] the more that self risks seeming false to the individual worker, and the more difficult it becomes for him or her to know which territory of self to claim" (Hochschild, 1983, p. 196). The cultural norms that drive emotions underground by exchanging silence for membership can, ironically, rob the entire organization of any chance at authenticity.

However, for leaders and teachers to engage meaningfully with each other, they need to be trustworthy (Tschannen-Moran, 2007, pp. 99-113). To be trustworthy they need to be credible (Kouzes & Posner, 1993), which stems from being genuine and authentic. This is easier said than done:

> Just as genuineness can't be artificially manufactured – it simply is – neither can authenticity: it can't be generated; it can only be discovered. . . . leadership begins at one's centre: *authentic leaders build their practice outward from their core commitments rather than inward from a management text.* (Evans, 2007, p. 143).

The importance of collaborative relationships is not a new idea within the educational context. Most educators appreciate the power of social interaction in children's learning (Vygotsky, 1978) and the importance of the "gift of confidence" when they provide support and guidance for young learners who are entering the zone of their proximal development (Mahn & John-Steiner, 2002, p. 46). We also have learned about the impact of interactive learning among adults with peers upon cognitive epistemological perspectives (e.g., Baxter Magolda, 1992; Belenky, Clinchy, Goldberger, & Tarule, 1997; Perry, 1970), which supports a shift in the locus of a learner's sense of knowledge authority from external to internal. A focus on the learning relationships among adults in schools needs to feature among the most important leadership concerns. The ethic of mutualism can be a catalyst:

> Mutualism, in the form of mutual trust and respect between administrator leaders and teacher leaders . . . [results in] the creation of an environment conducive to the generation of new ideas, reflective of a willingness to acknowledge and support each others' ideas, and supportive of the application of others' proficiency. (Crowther, Kaagan, Ferguson & Hann 2002, p. 39)

It should not surprise us that among the most important conditions for school success are the qualities of relationships; that is, whether these relationships create or fail to create a sense of safety and belonging that fosters collaborative inquiry (Little, 1982).

Trust and Student Performance

Empirical evidence by Goddard, Tschannen-Moran and Hoy (2001) has revealed a strong correspondence between trust and school effectiveness. Relational trust among adults in schools is also predictive of student academic performance (Bryk & Schneider, 2002). The connections between the relationships among adults and the learning conditions experienced by children deserve careful attention (Beatty & Brew, 2005).

Research with young people demonstrates that the greatest risk factor for developing a life of crime is the detachment from school altogether. The presence or absence of social protective factors is well known to be predictive of pro- or anti-social behaviors and learning outcomes (Dean, Beatty, & Brew, 2007). However, we are just beginning to explore how intertwined are the relationships among adults in schools with the social emotional conditions for student learning. In a study that developed and validated an instrument to measure student sense of connectedness with school (Beatty & Brew, 2005), structural equation modeling provided evidence of plausible connections among student trust in leaders, trust in teachers, sense of belonging with peers, academic engagement, confidence in self at school, and academic performance. The suggestion of a shadow effect – from perceived leader trustworthiness through teacher trust by students to student engagement – underscores the importance the role of the principal in setting the tone and creating a culture that will provide optimal conditions for student learning.

The principal is a deciding factor in the culture of schools. Teacher openness to new learning and creativity in the classroom are connected to the sense of social emotional and professional safety that engenders the willingness to trust. Understanding trust involves an appreciation of emotional risk. Hence. trust in general may be defined as an individual's or group's willingness to be vulnerable to another party based on the confidence that the latter party is benevolent, reliable, competent, honest, and open" (Hoy & Tschannen-Moran 1999, p. 189).

The leader trust factor is critical for teacher learning and confidence in the classroom: "Quality school administrators lead their schools by transforming their culture into one that emphasizes cooperation, trust, openness, and continuous improvement" (Hoy & Miskel, 1996, p. 237). The trustworthy principal makes a commitment to relationship.

> In a disposable society known for revolving door relationships, trustworthy principals stand for something different. They let all their constituencies know that conflict and even betrayal are not necessarily the last word. They hold out the hope of reconciliation and the repair of trust. But it's not enough to just lift up a vision; trustworthy leaders must also play the role of mediator when trust breaks down. (Tschannen-Moran, 2007, p. 107)

The teacher leader relationship (Beatty, 2002a) and the leader's influence upon the overall working conditions of teachers (Leithwood & Beatty, 2008a) are among the most important keys to school success.

The need for a secure foundation from which to reach out and grow by experimenting and taking learning risks is as important for adults as it is for children. Leaders influence the sense of safety and cooperation experienced by adults in the cultures of their schools and thereby influence learning conditions of their students (Silins & Mulford, 2002) and teachers (Leithwood & Beatty, 2008b). When leaders demonstrate respect, they model and teach trustworthiness. In such schools, all adults can have a positive impact upon each other, children, and parents through flow-on effects that are most accurately envisioned in exponential terms. Correspondingly, the all too common distance and disconnection among adults, among children, and between adults and children in schools can create conditions far from ideal for learning, with proportionally similar ramifications.

Sounds great, doesn't it? Yet, when we listen for signs of relational connectedness – the sharing of inner experiences, the things about which teachers feel most strongly – we are lucky if we hear anything at all, unless we happen to be standing in the parking lot. Far less likely are acknowledgments of fear, embarrassment, anger, and vulnerability. Indeed in the traditional professional discourse, the silence on matters of emotion is deafening.

Particularly pressing then for today's leaders, and those who would prepare them, is the paradox of emotion and educational leadership: the dichotomy between the ways leaders (and teachers) believe they must seem – in control and emotionally detached – and the ways as fully integrated, highly functioning people, they need to be. Emotional control is one thing. Emotional numbness and relational disconnection are quite another.

Envisioning a New Leadership Mentality in Preparation for Leadership Development

As Sergiovanni (1992) reminds us, educators acquire over years of experience, "bundles of beliefs and assumptions about how schools and school systems work, authority, leadership, the purposes of schooling, the role of competition, the nature of human nature, and other issues and concerns"; these "mindscapes" shape their practice (pp. 10-12).

The research theory and practice of leadership preparation and development have emerged in recent years as the next place to put the onus for the fulfillment of society's needs. However, Leithwood and Levin (2008) argue convincingly that

> formal development experiences are just one of many influences on leaders' actual behaviors and they are less powerful than others such as leaders' internal states, existing skills, beliefs, values and dispositions. Internal states constitute the perceptual filters and meaning-making "tools" through which all other potential influences must pass if they are to change leaders' behaviors. In order to change leaders' behaviors, other types of influences must actually change some aspect of a leader's internal states. (p. 289)

Additionally, they note the powerful influences on leadership development, of social, cultural and historical contexts of leaders' work. They appreciate that power, respect, hierarchy, and diversity may play very differently in different parts of the world and, for that matter, in different school regions. This internal state domain, Leithwood and Levin argue further, composes an enormous storehouse of tacit knowledge which they consider to be by definition, inaccessible. However, Polanyi (1962) who coined the expression tacit knowledge was more interested in tacit knowing processes, a more dynamic image if you will.

After a few years in the job, teachers come to do what they do, without consciously thinking about it. When it works, that's great! But if success is to spread, the private practice of intuitive teaching has to become the public sharing and active reflection and meta-reflection about what teachers do and why they do it. Let us imagine these pools of tacit knowledge and consider the renewing generative powers that lie beneath the surface of these waters. The same is true for leaders. Importantly, exploration into our tacit ways of knowing can be very successful, but it requires inner work and personal contact with peers in a context of trust. We *can* make the tacit explicit, by engaging in focused reflection, alone and with others.

As Roland Barth (1993) recommends, and I too have found, focused reflection works well for transformation when it is written and shared. To enliven our reflective powers, we may tell our stories and listen deeply to each other, using various frames for listening: for instance, the facts, the emotions, the values, the implications, and so. As we do this, we begin to re-story ourselves together, as we rediscover and reframe with new understandings, that which we have always *known* implicity but could not explicitly express. In preparation programs, the deliberate exploration of leaders' tacit ways of knowing can support them in making new discoveries about themselves and each other, even as they begin to create new knowledge together.

Yet, this notion of sharing one's inner leadership experiences is counter to the dominant educational administration culture. A tall order to be sure, especially when tradition has it that leaders leave their integrated selves at the door in order to gain entry to the leadership league. However, to be prepared for the challenges facing today's school leaders, we need nothing less than emotionally grounded and connected leaders. Leaders need safe spaces to discover and rebuild their confidence on new fully dimensional foundations. There are other ways of discovering and coming to know that involve access to a broader spectrum of emotional frequencies, greater attunement to multiple dimensions of self and others, and an increased awareness and appreciation of the origins of diverse perspectives. Engagement in the relearning of perceptual processes helps leaders ensure their own and others' entitlement to be who they really are so that they can be truly invitational, extending a hand to their fellow travelers from their actual point of entry into a shared learning journey.

An abiding sense of well-grounded emotional security emanates from a mature and sensitive sense of self and genuine respect and care for the other. The philosopher Martin Buber (1974) refers to this as reverence for the I and Thou. It is in such leaders' non-anxious presence (Friedman, 1985) that educators can embrace vulnerability and risk offering their trust so that they can thrive in the act of learning together. Think about the most positively influential leaders in your life, and consider how their presence affected you. Leaders who instill confidence in ourselves encourage us to acknowledge our vulnerability and admit to our needs to know. This is the learning readiness moment that all teachers look for. The learning leader lives for these moments too, and knows how to create them.

Finding Emotion's Place in Models of Leadership

There are many models of leadership. Fullan's (2008) *Six Secrets for Change* and Hargreaves and Fink's (2006) seven principles for

Sustainable Leadership are prominent currently. They represent distillations of many years of these scholars' work. Starratt (2004), another wise prophet, offers his invocation to ethical leadership.

In Fullan's (2008) *Six Secrets of Change*, he has distilled the essence from a working lifetime of studying leadership. In his commentary on the book during a recent conference in Australia (Fullan, 2007),[1] we find the role of emotion at the heart of his six secrets. He tells leaders to (1) love your employees; (2) connect peers with purpose; (3) resist bullying because it will backfire; (4) learn with others, as this is the work; (5) be transparent, the ultimate in vulnerability; and (6) help systems learn, which happens when leaders use the wisdom of their knowledge by doubting what they know, retaining their humility, and, thereby, retaining their confidence for making progress happen.

Hargreaves and Fink's (2006) seven principles of *Sustainable Leadership* are no less emotionally demanding. They propose that all educators value and take action to achieve these principles:

1. Depth
2. Endurance
3. Breadth
4. Justice
5. Diversity
6. Energy
7. Conservation

Depth grants educators a clear view of learning. This requires teachers and leaders to re-examine, explore, and question their beliefs about learning and teaching. To accomplish this, they have to feel socially and emotionally safe enough to be candid with each other. It helps to reconnect with one's actual feelings of incompleteness to reclaim one's entitlement to be respectfully considered a work in progress. *Endurance* means taking a long-term perspective rather than short term focus. Such calm and measured security, contrasts with the panic that leads to performativity and overly test-focused teaching and leading behaviors. *Breadth* in action demands shared leadership, broad consultation, and collaboratively grounded staff development. Sharing leadership authority can be an anxiety inducing endeavor for leaders, who are being asked to loosen their grip on control so that teachers can develop confidence and become prepared for new roles. *Justice* in Hargreaves' model means caring for others: the strong helping the weak, teachers helping each other, students helping each other, and schools who are doing well helping those who are not. Such an ethic of care is grounded in social and emotional connectedness and healthy trusting relationships. *Diversity* involves the embrace of multiple perspectives,

[1] Although the podcasts produced from Fullan's and Hargreaves' speeches at the 2007 Australian Council for Educational Leaders annual International Conference are only available to those who attended the conference, valuable print material can be found at http://www.acelconference2007.com/papers.php

a counterintuitive endeavor for one who is emotionally threatened by opposing views. The inner work required to become open to opposition, is grounded in emotional meaning making first, so that a leader's inclination to marginalize dissent can be confronted and overcome. *Energy* is essential since "dead, sick, burned-out leaders won't work" (Hargreaves, 2007). Restraint from allowing themselves to be spread too thinly and commitment to renewal provide leaders with access to energy. Yet as we know from Ackerman & Maslin-Ostrowski (2002), leaders who lead change will be wounded. The emotional work involved in addressing this phenomenon and retaining the feeling function is critical to keeping the energy flowing. *Conservation* on individual, group, and whole school community levels makes sense. By going through the emotions, people can become reconnected with their past experiences, affirmed in their present personhood, as they become reoriented to connect with new possibilities for a better future.

Starratt (2004) provides leaders with an inspiring invocation to embrace the challenges of ethical leadership. *Becoming Moral: The Test of Leadership* describes inner leadership of the most personally and emotionally challenging variety. To *become* moral requires one to become re-integrated, reunited with one's integrity, which involves facing into the fear that one's integrity may have been compromised or lost. *Taking responsibility* for self and others and the success of school and society is inherent in the role of the principal. The weight of the world is quite literally upon their shoulders. To retain consciousness of the extent of their realm of responsibility, leaders need to retain a sense of connectedness, something which does not occur when emotions remain walled off and discounted. Starratt's model, also calls for *discovering authenticity*. The access to one's authentic self cannot occur without going through the emotions so as to connect the emotional with other meaning-making systems of the embodied mind. From the reintegration of personal, professional and organizational dimensionalities of one's identity, authenticity can be rediscovered, which makes the opportunity for *offering presence* possible. Furthermore, a leader can offer a non-anxious presence (Friedman,1985) when she or he has come to terms with her or his moral, responsible, authentic self. The first four precepts in Starratt's model give rise to the fifth, *giving birth to virtue*. Virtue emanates from the exquisite connectedness between self and others. Emotionally divided dis-integrated leaders, who have become emotionally numb from emotional labor and unaddressed woundings, lose connection with their emotions and their emotional meaning-making processes, which are the ethical fabric of the self (Margolis, 1998). By becoming moral, taking responsibility, rediscovering authenticity and offering presence, leaders can in a sense rebirth their virtuous selves, even as they provide the generative conditions for the renewal and regeneration of others and their whole school cultures.

In all of these models, the secrets, principles, and moral imperatives rely on relationships. As Fullan (2007) said, "There are three Rs in leadership: Relationships, Relationships, and Relationships, or maybe four and the fourth one is Relationships too!" To maintain relationships, one must understand and work through the emotions that endanger them, especially in times when betrayal and wounding have damaged trust. We all need to learn to engage in reflective emotional meaning making to be able to enact our commitment to connectedness. This is how we sustain the relationships upon which our very survival depends. By looking beneath the outcomes implicit in these models' various imperatives, and by appreciating the emotional work required to get there from here, this review should help to make clear emotion's place in school leadership. It is by doing the hard emotional work of reflection upon and enactment of these leadership secrets, principles, and moral imperatives that deep transformation can occur. The question that arise is how do we provide leaders with appropriate preparation and development opportunities so that these possibilities may become reality.

Canadian Research Results Leading to Programmatic Approaches.

It is one thing to call for the reculturing of schools (Hargreaves & Fullan, 1996) and the repositioning of priorities in leader praxis; it is quite another to provide workable ways of helping leaders to redefine their professional selves and begin to practice with new priorities. What would it take? And how might it be applied in leadership preparation programme designs? These questions have formed the impetus for a research agenda that has held me in its grip for over a decade.

To understand the existing patterns in teacher-leader relationships, it has been helpful to explore the lived experiences of teachers and leaders to learn more about the spaces they occupy together, in schools and in each other's minds. Given that emotional silence is regularly taken to be synonymous with professionalism, the first step was to break the silence by creating opportunities for teachers and leaders to provide access to their inner worlds. This research agenda has assisted me in discovering the role of emotional understanding in healthy relationships and those characterized by disconnection and antagonism.

Embracing the Pedagogy of Discomfort[2]

It is true that emotions are messy and unpredictable. They can make us feel decidedly uncomfortable. Yet as Starratt (2004) reminds us, the ethical moral imperative is tantamount to leadership itself. This is inner work. Therefore, we need to recognize that part of this work is

[2] Megan Boler's (1999, p. x) reference to this expression occurred in the context of conducting her tertiary social issues class, in which she noticed that the textbook was emotionally safer as a point of reference than the rich resources within the lived experiences of the people who were present in the class. She advocated for the value of learning from the immediacy of this experience, even if it is uncomfortable to do so, and coined the expression a pedagogy of discomfort.

to stay connected with the emotions. They are threaded into our warp and weft, or in Margolis' (1998) metaphor, the ethical fabric of the self.

The deliberate reintegration of personal/emotional dimensions of lived experiences with public dimensions of one's organizational and professional identity, can be powerfully transformational, engendering healing, renewal, and even an increased sense of the potential for flow at work (Csikszentmihalyi, 1990; Sergiovanni, 1992). These themes emerged in a study of teachers leading their own professional growth through collaborative reflection. Shared leadership and self-directed learning, changes in perceptions of self and work were significant in their directionality across the entire group: for instance, self-directed learning readiness, motivation, self-efficacy, and sense of potential for flow at work (Beatty, 2000b).

Through my studies of teacher emotions and research with an international group of school principals and head teachers (Beatty, 2002b, 2007a, 2007b) it became evident that through the practice of emotional meaning making, emotional epistemological perspectives shift. That is, a shift occurs in perceptions about where emotional knowledge authority resides and how one may engage alone and with others to explore emotional ways of knowing. Engagement in emotional meaning making helps to shift perceptions of self, others, and relationships. This occurs through changes in the mental model of emotional knowledge authority, which moves from a locus that is relatively external to one that is relatively internal. Four stances in this theoretical framework help to characterize emotional epistemological perspectives which were conceptualized from the grounded theory analysis of all of the teacher and leader data in that study: (1) emotional silence which literally and/or figuratively relegates emotions to the sidelines; (2) emotional absolutism, which operates when there is acceptance of norms or feeling rules whereby emotions are rewarded and punished to ensure compliance and assure continued membership in the organizational entity; (3) transitional emotional relativism, within which explorations into shared emotional meaning making occur inadvertently or deliberately; (4) resilient emotional relativity, within which emotional meaning making becomes foundational to perception forming, communication, action, and decision making. (Beatty, 2002a, 2002b, 2005; Beatty & Brew, 2004).

I am delighted to have had the opportunity to integrate the essence of these and others' theories of emotion into the design and implementation of several programmatic approaches for supporting leader learning.

Programmatic approaches

More and more, leadership development is embracing collaborative reflective practices. An excellent example is the workshop *Leaders Lead*, directed by Jeremy Hurley and provided by representatives of the

Australian Principals Association Professional Development Council. This workshop addresses the issues of leader wellbeing in part, by inviting participants to take the time to reflect and explicitly share their inner emotional lived experiences as leaders.

Over the past ten years of working with incumbent and aspirant leaders in various programs and award courses, both in the US (see Beatty & Brew, 2004) and Australia, I have found that the most effective way to foster personal and professional growth – transformation if you will – is by *going through the emotions* rather than stepping around them, denying them, silencing them, rationalizing them, and even shunning them as pesky interlopers (Beatty, 2000b). I reject the proposition that we should feel shame that we have emotions. This is nonsense! Emotions are simply not optional. While it may feel counter-intuitive to acknowledge them and even countercultural to speak of them, our new mental models for leadership wisely include emotions and the continuous process of emotional meaning making. To address the serious issues of wellbeing – that is, to survive *and thrive* – our leaders and all of the people in our schools cannot afford to settle for anything less:

> The nonnegotiable that I come back to most often is being true to myself – heeding the call of my heart, my core, for better or worse. Sooner or later a true leader is going to stir the pot and, if great things happen as a result, is going to get splattered and slopped on. Spillage is inevitable. (Hollowell as cited in Maslin-Ostrowski, 2007)

The messing reality Hollowell describes calls for inner leadership – the deliberate adoption of practices that keep leaders whole and help them heal when they are wounded. When your job is to disturb the status quo and change peoples' boundaries as you intrude on their comfort zones, leadership involves learning to expect the unexpected. It's part of the job. I take evocative title of Ackerman and Maslin-Ostrowski's (2002) *The Wounded Leader* literally and consider woundings explicitly in my programs as moments that are loaded with potential for learning.

> Understanding the meaning of wounding through the prism of the educational leader's experience offers a path, not only to real leadership but to being a real person in one's leadership. The leadership wound, itself, represents an extraordinary source of learning and a critical opening to what may be most at stake in the practical exercise of leadership; namely, one's self. (Maslin-Ostrowski, 2007, p. x)

Leaders need to be emotionally prepared for this. When leaders enter into processes that deepen these support systems within themselves their emotional epistemological perspective, they develop new neural pathways. They can do this by connecting candidly and regularly with their colleagues, thereby becoming stronger and better prepared emotionally to take each new experience – even and especially the painful ones – as an opening for new learning. As they develop this newfound confidence and centredness, they can help others acquire mental models that will sustain them to do the same.

This requires leaders to embrace willingly and knowingly a pedagogy of discomfort (Boler, 1999). It takes practice, but it can be learned. However, leaders need support to counterintuitively move toward the danger as it were (Maurer, 1996). By developing an intra- and inter-connectedness, they come to insist upon a professional entitlement to their own humanness. The fact is that good leaders are learners too; they are works in progress. We all are. This mental model of leaders who suffer and recover, connect and reconnect, and who commit to learning through maintaining a healthy relationship with themselves and others can help to establish the kind of *new leadership mentality* that we need. Eckhart Tolle (2005, p. 20) expresses quite elegantly, the enormity the situation:

> When faced with a radical crisis, when the old way of being in the world, of interacting with each other and with the realm of nature doesn't work any more, when survival is threatened by seemingly insurmountable problems, an individual human – or a species – will either die or become extinct or rise above the limitations of their condition through an evolutionary leap. This is the state of humanity now, and this is its challenge.

We need nothing short of a transformation of consciousness. This is the new metaphor for our age. And I believe we can achieve this together, by reconnecting deeply and wholly with ourselves and each other. Intellectual argument is not enough. The many models of leadership have described the conditions which we know we need to create. We can imagine them, but how do we accomplish them when they feel so foreign and threatening within the normative culture? The answer lies in emotional meaning making.

Emotional Meaning Making

Past emotional patterns exert an enormous influence over our ability to address our current situations. Perhaps this is due in part to the emotional power of nostalgia (I confess to having a particular penchant of classic movies). But replaying old patterns is only going to get us right back where we started from. We are emotionally stuck in our ways and, although intellectually aware of what needs to be, we are still needful of support and different patterns of practice in order to recreate ourselves and redefine our mental models of the way we work.

Part of this work in formal programs as well as informal exchanges is enhanced by appreciating that some of the very behavior that was heralded as exemplary in the past is likely to doom present day principals and teachers to failure. Old mental models of leadership need to be challenged and changed. Emotionally speaking, under such personally and professionally threatening conditions, these suggestions may seem unduly frightening and demanding, even strange. Reflective practice in writing and exchanging deeply held feelings and beliefs does not come naturally to many. It is tough going. It is confronting and uncomfortable at first, to say the least. But these are challenging times which call for different measures.

Emotional meaning making involves remembering experiences and the feelings and meanings we have associated with them, then reconsidering these in focused reflection. Emotional meaning making helps leaders challenge assumptions about themselves and others. When we explore the ways we experience emotions, how and what we believe about them, and what they have been telling us about ourselves and our world, we come to value, respect, and understand them. We also can begin to challenge ourselves to change. Leaders come to appreciate that by acknowledging and talking about the ways they have interpreted their world through their feelings, they can reconnect with their past, affirm their present, and reinvent themselves for a better future. This is the synergy of constructivism and transformational consciousness.

Programmatic approaches to leadership support and development need to help leaders story and re-story themselves. I have successfully trialed this approach with hundreds of leaders in programs both in the US and Australia. We start by identifying and recounting stories of facing our fears, ultimately matching them with conscious courage. Leaders who exemplify personal courage inspire. They are secure enough to take the risk of unleashing others so that they too can achieve their potential. The real secret of developing collaborative cultures is to enliven the trust factor. We need to do this systematically and deliberately. The following section outlines how these theories are put into practice in The Monash Master in School Leadership and Human Leadership: Developing People programs.

Progamme Design Principles

Key Design Elements

- **Working from the inside out**
  - A Fixed Sequence of units for a cumulative effect
    - Self
    - Other
    - Learning Community
    - Environments
    - Leading Change through action research
    - Sustained collaborative reflection
- **Collaborative learning processes and challenges for leaning into fears**
  - Mentors: learning to ask for help
  - Sharing stories of leaning into fears, learning from wounds

  - Networking – initiating
  - Job shadowing – reaching out
  - Immersion in learning with each other
    - Face to face
    - Online asynchronous forums
    - Real time distance learning with WEBEX
    - Website creation
    - Sustained collaborative reflection
- **Experiential learning**
  - Learning community immersion
  - Networking
  - Expanding perspectives – other sectors: the Melbourne zoo and ecological leadership
  - Relationships, relationships, relationships
  - Living Leadership
  - Team preparation and presentation
  - Sustained collaborative reflection and meta-reflection
- **Leading change in professional settings**
  - Becoming an Action researcher over two years, through the study and application of of research methods, and the creation of a publishable journal article to document the learning journey and research progress.

Figure 1: An Intervention, The Monash Master in School Leadership

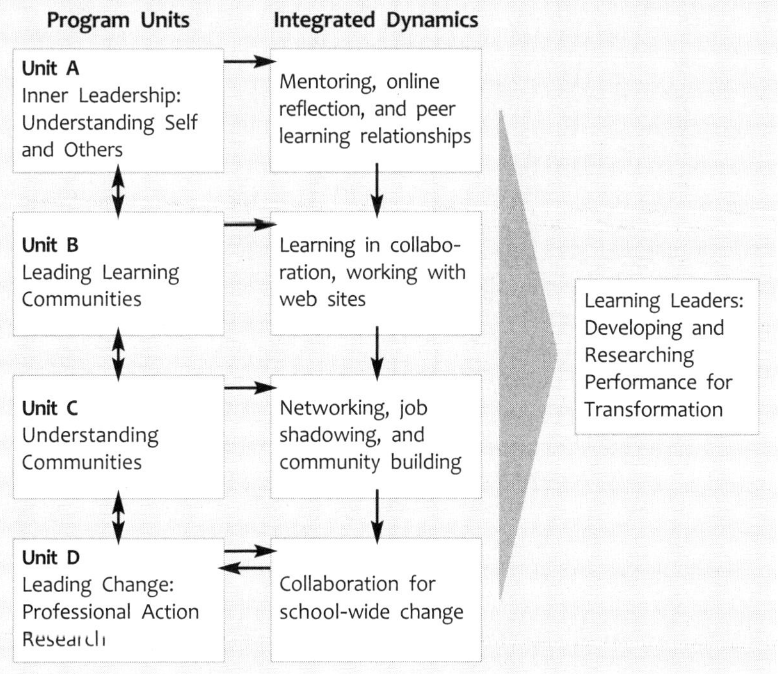

Remembering the Impact of Emotional Meaning Making

Findings from audit tools and interviews immediately upon course completion suggest a range of associated changes in Monash MSL participants' perceptions and behaviors associated with self and work in school leadership:

- increased sense of wellbeing, self-efficacy, reflective powers, courage, confidence to lead, and commitment to collaboration.
- Patterns of promotions across the cohorts suggest a strong and successful uptake of leadership positions (DEECD reports over 60% have since joined principal class).
- Findings from follow-up interviews over a year later reveal that transformational changes are resilient and persistent as they continue to contribute to leader wellbeing and effectiveness. Several new leaders have received state level awards.

The following section offers a sampling of typical Monash MSL graduate comments which help to illustrate some of the inner leadership learning experienced by going through the emotions.

Acknowledging vulnerability transforms it into a strength:

- When we got started on the course, with the emotions, that started to unpack my feelings of inadequacy and my protective walls around that so that I could better recognize the protective walls, and how to reach across to other people.

Making emotions explicit creates inner change:

- You can give lip service to emotions but until you're forced into reflecting and working with people in that way you don't actually change. And I think that's what's happened for me over the last two years is that [with emphasis and deep conviction] *I've changed.*

Learning to go through the emotions to lead:

- When people are really angry, . . . you've stepped into their personal space and inadequacies, so you step out, do something different and then work along side them. . . . it sort of gives you that mental space to think okay, it's not what I'm saying, . . . they've got their emotions engaged in that defensive way. How can we diffuse this?

Staying connected to help people who need to leave the job:

- I said [to her], you just seem really unhappy here aren't you? And it was like she just physically . . . she just kind of took a physical deep breath and relaxed and I said do you need to talk to me? And so we went to my office and she talked about why she was unhappy and it wasn't about her grade . . . it was about her personal life and she had come to a point in her life where she didn't want to teach any more. So then we talked about well, how? You need to get out of here. How can I help you move on?

Facing fear of seeming uncertain:

- Underneath I saw myself, . . . like a phony . . . Someone's going to find out that I don't know everything. I'm going to make mistakes and I shouldn't be making mistakes at this stage in my career. I knew that was wrong and yet other people expected me to be fully formed as a leader.

Redefining leadership as the entitlement to imperfection:

- I think I'm more confident in being allowed not to know everything. And I'm more confident in that I'm a work in progress, that I'm not complete yet and that's okay.

The emergence of the authentic self with confidence, courage, and commitment to connectedness:

- Well inside at the beginning there was nothing there. I hadn't explored what I truly was on about, what motivated me, why I was still wanting to be a leader, what was leadership about. It was all surface stuff? . . . And I think through being constantly reflective, finding out where we're coming from, finding out what's wounded us and the undiscussibles and being able to connect with others and know it's not a sign of weakness. Actually it's a sign of strength!

By going through the emotions to acquire self-knowledge and acceptance, connecting with others comes naturally

- So in terms of now, there's this inner core and that I know who I actually am, deep down, you know, values and those sorts of things . . . . I'm not inwards trying to protect myself outwards. I've got a solid core inwards and I'm connectable to other people. That's how I see myself now.
- It's very hard to be a good technical leader without having strong relationships with the people you're working with. A good technical leader without the relationships would be more likely the efficient tyrant, rather than someone who is able to get the best out of their people. Because people want to do their best.
- I think my whole understanding of my emotions and those around me has been a huge sort of shift.
- Before I do anything now, I stop and think about what emotions are driving me and how is that going to impact on the people that I'm looking to implement some sort of change or do some sort of program with.

With an emotionally grounded sense of oneself, there comes a non-anxious presence

- And if you think about Hamlet and "To thine own self be true," it is true. It is very true. When you're not being true to yourself, when you're not being your authentic self, that's when emotion or stress can consume you. But when you are your essential self, your real self and you feel that you can be that, then, even when

there's contention, problems, there's still a certain peace, a calm, a joy in that. You know, you're being true to yourself.
- I think that's certainly made me more resilient.

From controlling to collaborating (the trust factor):
- What I've noticed with emotions is that if you . . . [introduce change] in a confrontational way what you get is resistance, anger and frustration. [So] . . . before I would have run away from people [who were] feeling upset. I would have thought that they needed to recover themselves, and . . . not mention it again, rather than, tackle it as a way of building trust.

Human Leadership: Developing People

The Victoria Department of Education and Early Childhood adopted human leadership from Sergiovanni's (1992) leadership models and, hence, created provisions for a range of developmental learning programs for leaders. The invitation from the government department to design and deliver a shorter program entitled Human Leadership: Developing People (HLDP) provided another opportunity to try to engineer some inner leadership and collaborative learning opportunities that could catalyze and help to sustain cultural transformation of school leadership in Victoria's state school system.

The following objectives are indicative of the goals of the HLDP program:

- Increase participants' ability to develop strong and purposeful relationships in order to achieve school goals;
- Enhance participants' ability to address behaviors that impact on the maintenance of a cooperative environment;
- Develop participants' ability to create the organizational conditions that are conducive to the learning and growth of all members of the school community;
- Strengthen participants' ability to develop the capacity of others.

Its design elements, not surprisingly consider the integration of Inner, Relational, Scholarly, and Organizational dimensions.

I have had the valuable help of international keynote speakers including Pat Maslin-Ostrowski, Jeremy Hurley, Andy Hargreaves, Ken Leithwood, Carl Glickman, and a range of Monash faculty members and other local talent that varies from year to year.

In the HLDP, we try to broaden awareness and invite depth of thinking, feeling, reflecting, and responding. Processes of face to face and online learning collaborations, involving the study of a core text and learning group book discussions provide content, structure, and vehicles for professional learning and networking. Participants develop HLDP projects that they implement in their schools, connect with each other online throughout the intervening months between intensives, and at the end of the program provide summary reports on their progress. They also write case stories, framing human leadership dilemmas, thus providing others with openings for further consideration of human leadership (Beatty & Riley, 2008).

Like the Monash Master in School Leadership, it is through the impact of synergies among the content, sequencing, collaborative process, and experiential learning that participants find they are experiencing change. They report changes in themselves and their leadership practices. They are pleased to note that their human leadership work is having a recognizable impact in their settings. Some typical comments follow:

- I would label it as the best professional development that I have ever attended.
- Gems/Nuggets appeared through the entire program. I found my ability to draw parallels with aspects of the program and my work place circumstances provided many worthwhile opportunities to improve aspects of my school's operation.
- My understanding of leadership models and capabilities and my ability to apply them on a day-to-day basis have grown enormously. The corresponding effect is that I am operating at a more senior leadership level than I was previously
- I have since had the opportunity to develop and expand a Professional Learning Team Activity that will be the focus of our P-4 team. I was surprised at how easily it came together from idea into plan using many of the tools and ideas that had been presented to us over the three days
- Dialogue, reflection, and debriefing. I have gained a greater appreciation for the power of these tools for supporting and encouraging staff.
- We have made great progress as a result of this program. As far as PD programs go this has been one of the more enjoyable and relevant that I have attended.

In Summary

Leaders who change the feeling rules and break the silence on emotion

- Help to create new neural pathways for improved emotional meaning-making powers.
- Deepen understanding and respect for self and others
- Make better decisions
- Stay connected and better informed
- Build and maintain professional relationships, teams, and collaborative professional learning communities
- Enact the secrets, principles, and moral purposes of their leadership through collaborative reflection with peers and applications in their schools.

It is not an easy road, but the embrace of a pedagogy of discomfort (Boler, 1999), is a powerful catalyst and a great way to begin. When we learn to lean into our fears and share them with each other, we build trust in ourselves and confidence for connecting with others. With trust, we can face anything together.

Although our unexamined emotional patterns are tied up with egoism, when we become consciousness of them, and their meaning to us in the past and in the moment, we engage in a process that releases and unfetters us, freeing us to experience deeper awareness and profound connectedness with a deeper consciousness. Limitless possibilities emerge in these moments. Going through the emotions is not for the faint of heart. It is hard work. It is courageous, inspiring, unleashing leadership in action.

Questions

1. Do you believe that some of the emotional implications of the expectations for change in your current context can cause teachers/peers to decline leadership opportunities? Why or why not?
2. When in the line of duty one must make a constant effort to mask real feelings and feign feelings one is not having, such as exuding enthusiasm and disgust, or attempting to seem unemotional so as to appear purely rational, which involves emotional labor. Do you believe this is true? What purpose does it serve?
3. On the issue of trust, is the following statement a true or false one? Why?

   > We trust people who do what they say they will do and what they know they should do. We can afford to trust colleagues when we know they are capable of their professional obligations.

4. Consider the statement below. How can this help us to lead? Relate your response to your local context.

   > Emotional meaning making involves remembering experiences and the feelings and meanings we have associated with them, then reconsidering these in focused reflection.

5. Do leaders who change the feeling rules and break the silence on emotion actually

   - Help to create new neural pathways for improved emotional meaning-making powers.
   - Deepen understanding and respect for self and others
   - Make better decisions
   - Stay connected and better informed
   - Build and maintain professional relationships, teams, and collaborative professional learning communities
   - Enact the secrets, principles, and moral purposes of their leadership through collaborative reflection with peers and applications in their schools.

   Assume a position and argue why it is true, half-true, and/or untrue.

References

Ackerman, R., & Maslin-Ostrowski, P. (2002). *The wounded leader: How real leadership emerges in times of crisis.* San Francisco, CA: Jossey-Bass.

Amrein, A. L., & Berliner, D. C. (2002, March 28). High-stakes testing, uncertainty, and student learning. *Education Policy Analysis Archives, 10*(18). Retrieved Oct. 14, 2008 from http://epaa.asu.edu/epaa/v10n18/.

Ball, S. (2000). Performativities and fabrications in the education economy: Towards the performative society. *Australian Educational Researcher 27*(2), 1-25.

Barth, R. S. (1993). Coming to a vision. *Journal of Staff Development, 14*(1), 6-11

Baxter Magolda, M. (1992). Knowing and reasoning in College. Gender-related patterns in students' intellectual development. San Francisco, CA: Jossey-Bass.

Beattie, M. (1995). *Constructing professional knowledge in teaching: A narrative of change in professional development.* New York: Teachers College Press, Columbia University, and Toronto: Ontario Institute for Studies in Education Press.

Boler, M. (1999). *Feeling power: Emotions in education.* New York: Routledge.

Beatty, B. (2000a). The emotions of educational leadership: Breaking the silence. *International Journal of Leadership in Education, 3*(4), 331-358.

Beatty, B (2000b). Teachers leading their own professional growth: Self-directed reflection and collaboration and changes in perception of self and work in secondary school teachers. *International Journal of In-Service Education, 26*(1), 73-97.

Beatty, B. (2002a). *Emotional epistemologies and educational Leadership: A conceptual framework.* Paper presented at the Annual Meeting of the American Educational Research Association (New Orleans, LA, April 1-5, 2002). Eric Document. ED468293

Beatty, B. (2002b). *Emotion matters in educational leadership: Examining the unexamined.* An unpublished doctoral dissertation, Ontario Institute for Studies in Education, University of Toronto. (Canadian National Award Winner CASEA Thomas B. Greenfield Dissertation of the Year 2002 in Canada)

Beatty, B. (2005). Emotional leadership. In B. Davies (Ed.), *The essentials of leadership.* Thousand Oaks, CA: Corwin Press.

Beatty, B. (2007a). Feeling the future of school leadership: Learning to lead with the emotions in mind. *Leading and Managing, 13*(2), 44-65.

Beatty, B. (2007b). Going through the emotions: Leadership that gets to the heart of school renewal. *Australian Journal of Education, 51*(3), 328-340.

Beatty, B. (2008). *Theories of Learning.* In Gary Crow, Jacky Lumby, &Petros Pashiardis (Eds), *International handbook on the preparation and development of school leaders.* New York: Routledge.

Beatty, B., & Brew, C. (2004). Trusting relationships and emotional epistemologies: a foundational leadership issue. *School Leadership and Management, 24* (2), 329-356.

Beatty, B., & Brew, C. (2005). Measuring student sense of connectedness with school: The development of an instrument for use in secondary schools. *Leading and Managing, 11*, (2), 103-118.

Beatty, B., & Riley, P. (Eds.). (2008). *Human leadership: Cases of professional dilemmas.* Melbourne, AU: Victoria State School Department of Education and Early Childhood Development.

Belenky, M. F., Clinchy, B. M., Goldberger, N. R., & Tarule, J. M. (1997). *Women's ways of knowing: The development of self, voice and mind* (2nd ed.). New York: Basic Books.

Bryk, A. S., & Schneider, B. (2002). *Trust in schools: A core resource for improvement.* New York: Russell Sage Foundation.

Buber, M. (1974). *I, Thou.* (W. Kaufman & S. G. Smith, Trans.). New York: Scribner.

Crowther, F., Kaagan, S., Ferguson, M., & Hann, L. (2002). *Developing teacher leaders. How teacher leadership enhances school success.* Thousand Oaks. CA: Corwin Press.

Csikszentmihalyi, M. (1990). *Flow: The psychology of optimal experience.* New York: Harper & Row.

Damasio, A. (1997). *Descartes' error: Emotion, reason and the human brain* (2nd ed.). New York: Harper Collins.

Dean, S., Beatty, B., & Brew, C. (2007). "Creating safe and caring learning communities": Understanding school based development of social capital. *ACEL 2007 Yearbook.*

Denzin, N. (1984). *On understanding emotion.* San Francisco, CA: Jossey-Bass.

Evans, R. (1996). *The human side of school change.* San Francisco, CA: Jossey-Bass.

Evans, R. (2007). The authentic leader. In *The Jossey-Bass reader on educational leadership* (2nd ed., pp. 135-158). New York: Wiley.

Fineman, S. (1996). *Emotion in organizations* (2nd ed.). London: Sage Publications.

Friedman, E. H. (1985). *Generation to generation.* New York: The Guilford Press.

Fullan, M. G. (1999). *Change forces: the sequel.* Bristol, PA: Falmer Press.

Fullan, M. (1991). *The new meaning of educational change.* New York: Teachers College Press.

Fullan, M. (2007, October). The six secrets of change. Speach delivered at the 2007 *Australian Council for Educational Leaders Annual International Conference.* [podcast]. Retrieved Oct. 14, 2008 from http://www.acel conference2007.com/podcasts/index.php

Fullan, M. (2008). *Six Secrets of change: What the best leaders do to help their organizations survive and thrive.* San Francisco, CA: Jossey-Bass.

Goddard, R. D., Tschannen-Moran, M., & Hoy, W. K. (2001). A multilevel examination of the distribution and effects of teacher trust in students and parents in urban elementary schools. *Elementary School Journal, 102*(1), 3-17.

Greenberg, L., & Paivio, S. (1997). *Working with emotions in psychotherapy.* London: Guilford Press.

Hargreaves, A., & Fink, D. (2006). *Sustainable leadership.* San Francisco, CA: Jossey-Bass.

Hargreaves, A. (2007, October). The long and short of educational change. Speach delivered at the 2007 *Australian Council for Educational Leaders Annual International Conference*. [podcast]. Retrieved Oct. 14, 2008 from http://www.acelconference2007.com/podcasts/index.php

Hargreaves, A., & Fullan, M. (1996). *What's worth fighting for out there?* Toronto: Ontario Public School Teachers' Federation

Hochschild, A. R. (1983). *The managed heart: The commercialization of human feeling*. Berkeley: University of California Press.

Hord, S. Rutherford, W., Huling-Austin, L., & Hall, G. (1987). *Taking charge of change*. Alexandria, VA: Association for Supervision and Curriculum Development.

Hord, S., & Sommers, W. (2008). Leading professional learning communities. Thousand Oaks, CA: Corwin Press.

Hoy, W. K., & Miskel, C. J. (1996). *Educational administration: Theory, research, and practice* (5th ed.). New York: McGraw-Hill.

Hoy, W.K., & Tschannen-Moran, M. (1999). The five faces of trust: An empirical confirmation in urban elementary schools. Journal of School Leadership, 9, 184-208.

Jeffrey, B., & Woods, P. (1996). Feeling deprofessionalised: The social construction of emotions during an OFSTED inspection. *Cambridge Journal of Education, 26*(3), 325-343.

Kouzes, J., & Posner, B. (1993). *Credibility: How leaders gain and lose it, why people demand it*. San Francisco, CA: Jossey-Bass.

Leithwood, K., & Beatty, B. (2008a). *Leading with teachers' emotions in mind*. Thousand Oaks, CA:Corwin Sage.

Leithwood, K., & Beatty, B. (2008b). Leadership for 'hot' climates. *International Studies in Educational Administration*.

Leithwood, K., & Levin, B. (2008). Understanding and assessing the impact of leadership development. In J. Lumby & N. Foskett (Eds.), *International handbook on the preparation and development of school leaders*. Mahwah, NJ: Lawrence Erlbaum.

Leithwood, K., Jantzi, D., & Steinbach, R. (1999). *Changing leadership for changing times*. Philadelphia, PA: Open University Press.

Little, J. W. (1982). Norms of collegiality and experimentation: Workplace conditions of school success. *American Educational Research Journal, 19*(3), 325-40.

Mahn, H., & John-Steiner, V. (2002). The gift of confidence: A Vygotskian view of emotions. In G. Wells & G. Claxton (Eds.), *Learning for life in the twenty-first century: Sociocultural perspectives on the future of education* (pp. 46-58). Oxford, UK: Blackwell.

Margolis, D. R. (1998). *The fabric of self: A theory of ethics and emotions*. New Haven: Yale.

Marshall, C. (1992). *The assistant principal: Leadership choices and challenges*. Newbury Park, CA: Corwin Press.

Marshall, C., & Greenfield, W. (1987). The dynamics in the enculturation and the work in the assistant principalship. *Urban Education, 22*(11), 36-52.

Maurer, R. (1996). *Beyond the wall of resistance.* Austin, TX: Bard Books.

Maslin-Ostrowski, P. (2007, May). *Leading with integrity: The promise of creating space for the inner work of leadership.* Keynote address at the Monash University Human Leadership Program, Melbourne, AU.

Moore, M. (2005). *The staff feels . . .* [Editorial cartoon]. Retrieved Jan. 3, 2009, from http://www.motivationalplus.com/laugh.html

Nias, J., Southworth, G., & Yeomans, R. (1989). Staff relationships in the primary school. London: Cassell Education.

Osterman, K. F. (2000). Students' need for belonging in the school community. *Review of Educational Research, 70*(3), 323-367.

Perry, W. G. (1970). *Forms of intellectual and ethical development in the college years: A scheme.* New York: Holt, Rinehart, & Winston.

Polanyi, M. (1962). *Personal knowledge.* Chicago: The University of Chicago Press.

Reina, D. S., & Reina, M. L. (1999). *Trust and betrayal in the workplace: Building effective relationships in your organization.* Stowe, VT: Berrett-Koehler Publishers.

Silins, H., & Mulford, W. (2002) Leadership and school results. In K. Leithwood & P. Hallinger (Eds.), *Second international handbook of educational leadership and administration* (pp. 561-612). Dordrecht, NL: Kluwer Academic Press.

Starratt, R. J. (1991). Building an ethical school: A theory for practice in educational leadership. *Educational Administration Quarterly, 27*(2), 185-202.

Starratt, R. J. (2004). *Ethical Leadership.* San Francisco, CA: Jossey-Bass.

Sergiovanni, T. (1992). *Moral leadership.* San Francisco, CA: Jossey-Bass.

Tschannen-Moran, M. (2007). *Trust matters: Leadership for successful schools.* San Francisco, CA: Jossey- Bass

Tschannen-Moran, M., & Hoy, W. (2000). A multidisclinary analysis of the nature, meaning and measurement of trust. *Review of Educational Research, 70*(4), 547-593.

Tolle, E. (2005). A New Earth. New York: Penguin Group.

Vygotsky, L. (1978). *Mind in society.* Cambridge, MA: Harvard University Press.

Williams, R., & Brien, K. (2009). Redefining educational leadership for the twenty-first century. In T. Ryan (Ed.), *Canadian educational leadership.* Calgary, AB: Detselig Enterprises Ltd.

Winerip, M. (2003). *The 'zero dropout' miracle: Alas! alack! a Texas tall tale.* The New York Times, Aug. 13, 2003.

Chapter Seven

Multicultural Educational Leadership in Canada

Verna L. McDonald, Ed.D.
University of Northern British Columbia

"Let us put our minds together and see what life we can make for our children."

Sitting Bull, Hunkpapa Sioux, 1877

Introduction: Sitting Bull's Request

This chapter begins with Sitting Bull's request for cross-cultural education – a joint effort of adults coming together across different cultural backgrounds for educational leadership. His request assumes principles are leading the adults involved; principles such as integrity, mutual trust, and responsible stewardship. Whether in Sioux and European communities in 1877, or in the global cultural blends of school districts of the twenty-first century, cross-cultural education is the backbone of peaceful and sustainable human development. Blended lifeways evolving in peace can replace colonial fears and violence, industrial pollution and resource mismanagement, monocultural superiority and elitist politics, and technology and science without ethics.

The most problematic of these destructive dynamics are all evident in current global corporatization patterns and the increasingly dysfunctional systems they represent. Neither marginalized populations or the elite, post-colonial global networks can sustain any quality of life for future generations in the shadow of those problematic dynamics. Sitting Bull was fully aware of the collaborative re-education needed for the future. He was calling for vision and engagement in building an equitable and healthy future. Currently, his call is repeated with increasing urgency from indigenous, marginalized, and poor people all over the world today.

In this chapter, I will examine how we might answer Sitting Bull's call within our context by establishing multicultural educational leadership. Multicultural leadership is described by Banks (2002) as mentoring a growth process with many dimensions: a growth process from monocultural or bicultural perspectives into multicultural worldviews. New academic knowledge, different pedagogical strategies across disciplines, multiple perspectives, and action on important social issues are some factors involved. Banks names four stages of teacher development in teaching cultural content: contributive, additive, transformative, and socially active. (p. 30). These stages are then described as follows: (1) teaching about holidays and celebrations, or "heroes and holidays" from other cultures; (2) teaching with additions from the cultural experience of those compatible with the dominant views of history or current events, without changing curriculum content, structures or approaches; (3) teaching in ways that make clear the gaps in dominant views, change "the canon, paradigms, and basic assumptions of the curriculum" (p. 31), and include the experiences of those missing in monocultural curriculum in order to open minds and hearts; and (4) social action teaching on significant and meaningful change efforts that extend "the transformative curriculum by enabling students to pursue projects and activities that allow them to take personal, social, and civic actions related" (p. 32) to their studies.

Fullan (2001) describes the impetus for education reform in the sixties as connected to the idea that education could be "one of the major societal vehicles for reducing social inequality" (p. 6): an impetus intensifying with the increasing complexity and inequity of a global society "requiring educated citizens who can learn continuously, and who can work with diversity, locally and internationally" (p. 6).

In Canada, the international immigration tapestry is hung on top of a cedar wall 40 000 years thick, carved by indigenous peoples. The colonial efforts to appropriate the wall, export it, or remove parts of it to a distant reserve, have all impacted indigenous lifeways tremendously (Helin, 2006). Recently, residential schools, removal of indigenous children from homes and reserves, and the continuum of profiteering from alcohol, drugs, gambling, and reserve resources, have all altered the carving. Yet, the inner cedar core remains. However, "the forces reinforcing the status quo are systemic" (Fullan, 2001, p. 7) in schools, in communities and in the social fabric of Canada as a nation. Educational leaders are finding "the spectacular lack of success of most social reforms" in the face of archetypal cultural patterns brought to "the new world." In spite of fifty years of effort towards more inclusive and progressive educational outcomes, the achievement, property ownership, criminal prosecution, gender violence, and wage gaps all remain. Holding to the status quo of Western culture will not address these issues. What is needed instead is "an educational approach that analyzes the increasing destruction of the world's diverse ecosystems, languages and cultures by the globalizing, and ethnocentric forces of Western consumer culture" (Smale & Young, 2007, p. 13).

Multicultural educational leaders in Canada work to address the dynamics of a global immigration history that interacts on campuses in locally specific ways. The European formal education system and later public school efforts here have created a blend. French immersion, English immersion, and combined language and culture schools all exist in Canada. The blend of First Nations languages and culture in private and public schools has been much slower to be developed. Residential schools were a mix of English immersion, military barracks discipline, industrial training, and religious catechism. Within these schools, racism, sexism, and classist discrimination, religious intolerance, cultural destruction, and all manners of abuse were experienced by First Nations children. In today's efforts to heal those abuses, successes have been created for indigenous students based on indigenous education models, mixed indigenous and progressive student-centred education, and locally developed autonomous community schools.

Classroom and campus change is a dynamic, relational process of responding to specific contexts. There are many examples of inclusive leadership with indigenous peoples: (1) on-reserve community education centres (toddler to adult as in Morristown, British Columbia); (2) high school First Nations English classes with British Columbia credit approval (English 12, First Peoples); (3) culturally congruent kindergarten beside the forest on Vancouver Island; (4) white identity studies, combined with First Nations epistemologies in teacher education; (5) indigenous support centres in urban areas; and (6) First Nations University of Canada, in Regina, Saskatchewan. All of these schooling models are teaching against the cultural grain. In these efforts they have struggled and are struggling to disentangle their vision and actions from *deculturalization* (Spring, 2003) into healthy alternatives. Culturally responsible educational leaders in rural and urban settings across the country are working towards healthy integration of cultural identity and language, ecological stewardship, and full human rights.

The twenty-four-hour schools in urban Toronto, home schooling support centres in Vancouver, and French Catholic schools of Edmonton all seek to address some part of both the individual cultural identities of families and the fact that Canadians are all living in an increasingly global cultural context.

These few examples keep alive the promise Canada represents to other countries. The Canadian ideal of multiculturalism contains a promise of equity and social justice support, and this promise of justice extends to stewardship of nature and our children for sustainable futures. Will Canada create leadership capacity in taking human potential beyond poverty/wealth polarities and into a global human consciousness centred on ecological stewardship and sustainable communities?

As an educational leader, Sitting Bull sought the promise of equitable indigenous and European leadership in sharing traditional lands, resources, and the education of children. For Michael Fullan, educational leadership has meant decades of academic and national leadership in teacher education. For James Banks, educational leadership has meant a progression from social studies teacher and curriculum leadership to university and academic leadership, and then to national and international systems leadership for equity across all groups. All of these diverse educational leaders continue to influence children, teachers, and school leaders today.

In the following pages, I wish to present some challenges, some successes, and several possibilities for what's next within the current context of educational leadership, as it is exercised at all levels of schooling. My views and those of some authors and activists in multicultural education are included. I invite you to make local, provincial or national additions from your context.

Educational Leadership in Multicultural Contexts

An Ill-defined Assignment

Educational leaders of the twenty-first century face a number of pressures:

- Locally and globally mobile corporations and workforce populations that produce rapidly increasing or decreasing school enrollments.
- Shifting commitments to education funding and tax-base priorities with increased privatization of tax revenues going to corporations in bailouts, financial restructuring, and alternative financing schemes.
- New cultural intersections related to gender, ethnicity, language, socioeconomic status, and religion.
- Environmental, social and international diseases increasing in children, including asthma, AIDS, and cancer.
- Increasing addiction issues – in younger and younger students and in care-givers – from huffing substances to selling prescrip-

tions, and from street drugs to cooking up over-the-counter modifications. Problem gambling, internet overuse, and sexual hook-ups are also increasingly affecting students.

- Parental engagement in efforts towards stabilizing family income, involving longer hours, multiple jobs, double shifts, commuting longer distances for work, and so on.
- Increasing peer participation in the time and activity structuring of other children, which limits the influences of adults and deminishes their guidance: "When a child becomes peer-oriented the transmission lines of civilization are downed. The new models to emulate are other children or peer groups or the latest pop icons" (Neufeld, 2005, p. 88).

Educational leaders may have their own roots in the "naivete of the 1960s, the cynicism of the 1970s, the partial successes of the 1980s, and the more informed large-scale reforms of the 1990s" (Fullan, 2001, p. 15). The kinds of complex intertwined factors affecting their campus employees and instructional teams may not be consciously accessible in their own experiences. For example, a professor who has not used text messaging may not realize her students are not looking down to read their textbooks, but are busy texting peers across the classroom instead. Examining the differences of experience requires making visible to students the complex relationships, and then allowing for creative responses to those differences. However, this is a skill that requires context specific training and experience across many aspects of current events, social trends, site policy, technology, child development, cultural behaviors, and many more factors.

How do public school teachers and leaders sort out priorities? Should time be spent on ecological concerns when teaching students with crack cocaine or crystal meth heart fibrillations? Should absentee parents be pursued for conferences or counselors engaged in the issues? Should information on career choices get school and teacher resources or information on fatal STDs? Do concerns for an academic future outweigh mentoring pregnancy choices or collaborative abuse reporting?

The tensions involved in the decisions educators are now making on a daily basis are extremely stressful, in constant motion, and have no certain outcomes. These stressors are sometimes new issues, yet often these stressors are combinations of old issues that have morphed in this century: For example, (1) mobile phone parenting as the new form of commuter parenting that began with multiple care givers, post-war single parent households, or industrial absentee parenting; (2) text message peer language acquisition as the current variant of *media cool* language that is propagated by multiple cell phones, and increasingly shorter sound bytes of media; or (3) increasing exposure to extreme media available in children's rooms on satellite channels 24/7 that was preceded by one local black and white TV channel in the living room.

These fuzzy zones of adult behaviors, engaged in by younger and younger children, create ill-defined parenting, teacher, and school administrator roles as children act out the dynamics they are immersed in.

Multicultural Educational Leadership Attributes and Skills

What kinds of *capacity building* and *reculturing* would be needed for academic equity when these behavioral pressures are amplified by the socioeconomically and racially charged conditions found in many multicultural school settings? Fullan (2001) acknowledges the central importance of addressing "the core of school capacity" (p. 238). Capacity building is defined as "a system of guiding and directing people's work, which is carried out in a highly interactive professional learning setting" (p. 236). Professional communities of learning are a reculturation process in themselves. The competitive, elitist colonial foundations for formal schooling need to be repeatedly torn down in order to discover the freedom, lightness, and creativity in equitable environments. Educators must first cross the intimidating hierarchies of gender privilege, class dominance, racism, and religious intolerance. The footsteps on that drawbridge of exclusion trigger behaviors and attitudes formed in centuries of reactive violence.

Sexual orientation is another important concern for cross-cultural leadership. Grace (2007) describes some of the attributes needed for transactional or transformational leadership in school communities inclusive of GLBT members: "To be a transactional leader, they need to know Canadian and provincial/territorial legislation and laws that frame an inclusive and accommodating Canadian culture and society (Grace, p. 19). Having gained this knowledge, educational leaders then need to be put this knowledge into effect through the implementation of policies and practices. Doing this may mean changing ones disposition, for in order "to be a transformational leader, school administrators have to believe . . . that change needed to make better schools and a better world is difficult but possible" (Grace, p. 19). Grace provides a clear example of such a change in the case of sexual minorities, "if school administrators are to be ethically and professionally responsible, then they need to separate exclusionary private *morals* form public *ethics* in dealing with sexual-minority students and teachers" (p. 20).

An extensive list by Grace (2007), briefly summarized below, outlines the basis for operationalizing of an inclusive culture. He describes some of the attributes and skills needed from campus leaders in regards to GLBT students. These skills could by adapted for marginalized groups in various settings:

- Interact everyday with students and teachers with minority differences
- Create caring and an ethic of respect
- Use inclusive language

- Educate yourself
- Learn the history and legislation around rights and citizenship
- Learn about the lived realities of GLBT students
- Get information from specific organizations like Egale Canada (Equality for Gays And Lesbians Everywhere).
- Build in teacher professional development
- Create a resource base on campus
- Work with the teachers association and the school district, or the school organization if private, on policy and climate
- Become an advocate
- Help students find teacher facilitators for support groups or clubs
- Intervene on teacher's behalf and learn the collective agreement or association policies
- Explore websites

In addition, being aware of current events can be a bridge and a learning tool for educational leaders working for inclusive climates. For example, the recent assault in Vancouver would likely send a ripple of tension through the gay community. The list of ways to operationalize inclusivity could be adapted for gender inclusion, religious respect, classism, and racial/ethnic differences as well. Some examples of operationalizing these areas of cross-cultural inclusion include:

- Creating a resource base for teachers in various content areas that supports the identities, histories, current concerns and contributions of races and ethnicities represented in the school.
- Examining personal prejudices through reflection or further education. Daniel (2007) states "We cannot continue to live with the notions of color-blindness or deficit thinking if school leaders, as public intellectuals, are going to transform schools" (p. 42).
- Working with teacher's association and school district leaders to reduce institutional sexism like differential salaries and promotions, professional networking differences, laddering into nurturing versus leadership roles, differential representation in the curriculum, pedagogical strategies that magnify gender imbalances, differential hiring practices, and so on.
- Critically examining images of hyper-masculinization (superheroes, war heroes, global profiteering heroes, and sports heroes) and decreasing the presence of these image. The same is true for sexualization and domestication of female representations, which increasingly occur in the media within violence situations (female characters in video games, wrestling, television law enforcement, and movie roles). These images are equally destructive to identity development for both girls and boys in schools. These images are increasingly present in advertising, book and magazine choices, computer programs, posters, event ads, clothing items, promotional items, sports mascots, food packaging, notebooks, lunchboxes, and so on.

- Building an inclusive calendar around major religious events and holidays, as well as non-denominational event representation at major ceremonies like graduations, and funerals, extreme weather events, or other traumatic stress.
- Including the interests and concerns of poor, working poor, and working class families in curriculum, in extra-curricular activities (transportation, materials fees, and uniforms), and required homework (particularly technology support and resource availability for projects).

Addressing the "isms" Effectively

Most mature educators possess an experience base that provides clarity in their actions and a refined networks of social justice resources They are aware of the history of broad institutional and "ism"-saturated policies, events, and reform movements. These experiences and resources are missing for many teachers immersed in the intense, detailed personal dynamics of a single classroom. New teachers may see leadership as simply employing a technique or following a chain of command to the arrive at the *correct* course of action in each specific dilemma. Either way, someone else is making the decision for them. Actually, the skills needed in leadership involve using what the new teacher knows, including how to learn more about specifics, applying this knowledge to the setting where the teacher works, and responding to the students in that particular classroom. When teachers discount their specific knowledge, their ways to access more information, and the details in their classroom – often in hopes of an expert or leader solving the situation – they leave the parents, guest speakers, or children on the margins (with even less information on the situation) forcing them to act as the authority or knower when they are not. For example, when a new teacher invites a cross-cultural speakers into the classroom without preparing the students with background, context, and meaning, the guests may find themselves bridging prior events or conflicts specific to that context that they are unfamiliar with, engaging students with biased views that have not been previously challenged, or becoming the spokesperson for their whole group concerning complex tensions – all in a very limited time. The teacher's effort in bringing community members into curriculum development and, thus, fostering cross-cultural innovation then results in more issues, not to mention a frustrated teacher who fears that their innovation did not work. For a teacher in this situation, consulting with a successful mentor and drawing from her or his experience base could have changed the single event into a learning theme over time and created different results.

Sustained involvement in cultural learning is a key skill in every level of educational leadership, from the classroom to legislature. Broad community partnerships in innovation can change student life outcomes as well as their academic outcomes.

However, for these innovations to produce such changes, they must not be of the type that Fullan (2001) describes: "The main problem is not the absence of innovation in schools, but rather the presence of too many disconnected, episodic, fragmented, superficially adorned projects" (p. 21). These types of projects may exist at the national level or occur in a single classroom where tacos are made to mark Cinco de Mayo. The life decisions and developing identities students are forming can be left in the background as the foreground is filled by staff, faculty, and parents with accommodating more of the superficially adorned projects.

A recent teen murder in our Northern British Columbia community highlights this very painful breakdown of life decisions and school decisions. The young man had been, in the words of one of his teachers, "lost in the gaps" of the education, social support, and health systems. She had intervened for him many times, but the pressures kept building for him as he progressed towards and into high school. Expelled for fighting for most of the past year, he had been left at home largely alone until a recent reinstatement. Disconnected, fragmented, and superficially part of the school again, he returned to an escalated pattern of using violence to cope with his experiences. From this local example of one student to the greater sense of violence creeping northward, the evidence that our school projects are not helping students in making good life decisions cannot be ignored. The need to aid these adolescence in developing their cultural and personal identity and their meaning-making capacity, which is so crucial as they enter adulthood and their careers, too easily gets lost in an academic milieu focused on compliance via assignments, behavior, and attendance. For educators, the task of developing these students is further obscured by dealing with the tensions of funding, contracts, schedule changes, shifting numbers of students, new curriculum standards, performance reviews, and so on.

Caracciolo (2007) expresses the importance of partnering as an effort at bridging cultural differences; the same holds true in bridging education achievement differences. The work of allies within the dominant culture in such partnerships for educational justice is important to reaching critical mass – where awareness becomes compassion deep enough to translate into action for change. The effort of culturally responsive planning of curriculum, activities, strategies, parent conferences, school projects, and so on is linked to educational integrity and student success. From the micro-level of visual aids and texts that represent students and their families positively, to the macro-level of working with provincial organization towards the goal of increasing the rate of completion in professional degree programs by First Nations people, allies from all community groups are essential to the success of Indigenous students.

Without this work to bridge the difference, the frustrations of First Nations will continue to escalate as representation within politics and communities remains marginal and their voice goes unacknowledged. Instead they see gatekeepers at every level of education: registration, instruction, financial aid, testing, and graduation requirements. Canadians can take a lesson from the racial tensions in US cities and act before the tools of confrontation become the only path First Nations children see as effective for being noticed, heard, or responded to by media and educators. This distorted path towards changes seems viable for marginalized people when decades of peaceful approaches have only seen minimal changes while their exposure to suicide, gang violence, substance use, violence against women, and more has increased during the same period.

Respect for diversity must move beyond hollow abstractions. Darder (1995) makes it clear that "teacher education programs must move beyond diversity in the abstract and recognize that in order to live diversity in the concrete there must exist diversity in the population to enact such an environment" (p. 344). What if it were your children dying? Living with diversity in the concrete makes the suffering of another's child as personal as the suffering of one's own. Likewise, living diversity in the concrete makes the plight of the community part of one's own experience. Educational leaders need to be able to read the community and respond. A principle I was working with recently wrote a community newsletter full of messages for the family of a recently ill elder who had died on the way to the hospital. A voluntary ceremony of respect was set up on the lawn for the next day.

Multicultural educational leaders need to keep taking the pulse of not only young people, but also their teachers, families, cultural and political dynamics, funding realities, and their school boards and districts. More than just another task to be taken on, educational leaders who keep close to these groups add a network for regeneration and resources that can aid their efforts. Leaders then direct this knowledge towards effective change for the lifeways of the individual students and on the institutional culture, change that is cohesive and produces positive long-term outcomes. This, however, is an ill-defined assignment, one critical to evaluating and sustaining effective innovation over time.

In a recent conference on learning in higher education settings held at UNBC in August 2008, the term *ill-defined assignments* was used to describe open-ended, higher-order thinking tasks that are being shown to increase student engagement, achievement, and collaborative learning. Some of the professors who were conference participants were making an effort to think of cross-generational teaching as a potential for engagement and collaboration. One way of doing this was through what the students saw as ill-defined assignments (open-ended assignments that involved complex thinking), and what the professors saw as higher-order thinking assignments, well designed to show the students abilities and attitudes. There was room for cross-generational cultures as students chose ways of communicating ideas and knowledge – from blogs to video and from GPS satellite images to conventional essays. This leadership skill in crossing generations and frames of reference is essential to meaning making for the future.

Shields (2004) writes about leadership for social justice and describes how leadership immersed in status quo frames of reference participate in marginalizing large numbers of students and their families. The dominant discourse can prevent marginalized families from having their voice heard or even acknowledged, and their investment in the proceedings are often dismissed. Leadership for social justice requires educators to engage "in moral dialogue that facilitates the development of strong relationships, supplants pathologizing silences, challenges existing beliefs and practices, and grounds educational leadership in some criteria for social justice" (p. 1). Doing this is a transformative practice aimed towards the success of all children.

Boxes of Evidence: Some Challenges

A graduate student in education administration once asked me what the pay-off was for taking on the institutionalized racism at his school and doing a *real* Master's project. His frustration was directed towards some surveys other graduate students were working with, while he faced a deeply troubling situation at his school concerning differential discipline. He wanted to address the data he had inherited. He had boxes of evidence that pointed towards racial discrimination. Each box contained several referral slips he had sorted into piles where the same offense was listed but the consequences were very different. He said he was haunted by the differential in punitive consequences given to the African-American and Hispanic students in his school. In response to his frustration, I asked him what would be the outcome for these students if he did not take on status quo inequities.

He developed his idea and ended up with a strong literature review and data set that formed the basis for a professional development plan for the next two years at his middle school. The need to take on sexism, heterosexism, and particularly racism and classism emerged from the data analysis. He did not feel confident in dealing with the human dynamics between students and teachers in those areas. He learned many more and less effective strategies in the process of the professional development planning and evaluation that followed the analysis of his data. He then documented the changes in teacher behavior.

In Joshee and Johnson's (2008) volume on multicultural education policies in both Canada and the US, historical context and ideological struggles are examined regarding the veneer of globalism. Globalism could be viewed as a thin layer of international profit and privilege – networks overlaying a foundation of colonial privilege and violence against indigenous peoples. Some of the aspects of globalism and colonialism that are found in twenty-first-century education include both racist and anti-racist policy making, backlash against affirmative action, multi-lingual education conflicts, and the social status privilege shaping immigration. Progressive leadership in building capacity for change, autonomy, and community activism are also discussed within Joshee and Johnson's work. Educational leaders choose daily what their contribution will be in these areas – status quo or progressive activism. White allies for educational justice are increasingly taking leadership and partnership roles in implementing less-colonial policies. The story of the principal looking at hundreds of suspension and expulsion referrals is a story of alliance with students and parents who feel that profiling is going on in disciplinary actions.

Shields and Sayani (2005) suggest that "an undue focus on conflict results in perceptions of diversity as a problem, as needing resolution and solution" (p. 384). The conflict resolution, peer mediation, and peace builders era of the 1990s grew out of efforts to work with diversity, rather than problematize it to the point where children rationalized reactive violence in the "us and them" dynamics adults modeled. These efforts pushed for a recognition that "diversity is simply a fact of life, a social reality; it is dangerous and damaging to equate it with difficulties" (Shields & Sayani, p. 384). The early playground territoriality often learned in communities with segregated housing divided by race, class, and gender roles can grow into the territoriality of urban gangs. Polarities around issues of difference deepened the educational-intervention mindset from programs for peace or conflict resolution, resulting in efforts to deal with deficit and deficiency in institutional perpetuation of social boundaries and privilege.

Is the growing diversity of Canadian classrooms an opportunity for human growth and development for everyone? Or is it a phenomenon requiring extreme measures of differential discipline and militarization of schools, as in the US? I examined this question one day while returning to my car at a southern California high school. I had been sent back to the car in order to get the two picture ID cards required to enter the school grounds. My photo ID granted me access past the security guard. He was a very large and imposing man in uniform who monitored the metal detector that covered the gate in the eight-foot, barbed-wired, chain-link fence positioned in front of the campus office. The ID cards remained in the office while I went to class to observe an intern teacher.

These increasingly military- and prison-like security measures were one of many reasons for my decision to return to Canada. The racial, ethnic, language, and socioeconomic tensions being acted out on high school campuses were described by one local prison guard as directly related to the activities and tensions of local, regional, and national gangs. He talked about authorities being trained to look for signs of criminal behavior in younger and younger students through profiled patterns that included increasingly innocuous signs such as tattoos, dress, and haircuts. Some school districts have their own police forces, like Fontana, California. Canadians have the opportunity to watch the results of increasing police presence and militarization of schools and observe the results. One California school I was working with went from two alternative classes to six in one year. More officers on campus meant more students out of the mainstream, mores students being watched constantly, and more students looking for ways to regain identity status with peer groups meaningful to them – ones often found on the streets.

Social development, equity, and social justice goals are often pushed into the background under a relentless message from politicians polarizing "us and them"; from corporations lobbying for profit from schooling; from future workers seeking to use and advance technology applications; and from managers seeking the social and collaborative skills to develop innovations in business. Educators working towards social justice are pushed farther into the margins as economic themes take the media spotlight. The direction toward increased emphasis on standardized test score, curriculum publishers leading instructional content, school privatization under the label of *accountability*, and expanded roles for technology in classrooms are often occurring simultaneously, reducing the ability of educators to enact social justice. The local school leadership is faced with responding to these factors concurrently with the human stressors and pressures listed previously. Students may react to increased stress with increased entertainment and peer interactions, reducing adult influence to the minimum. The shifts in the US, and increasingly in Canada, to economic policy, entertainment and media agendas, and political expedience as significant drivers of educational policy are evident. These economic development and profit interests are at odds with children's healthy development needs.

The good news is that encouragement of parent participation, diversification of teachers, culturally creative curriculum, research on learning styles, developmentally based instruction, and student-centred learning are simultaneously and continuously being developed. Educational leaders who understand these contexts can facilitate teacher and parent involvement, with the best of current knowledge bases, in learning together how to meet the needs of local students.

The challenges of cross-cultural educational leadership can be noted in leading the direction of both our learners and our society, which is examined by Shields and Sayani (2005). The descriptors "intercultural or intracultural" are mentioned as better ways to describe "the myriad of competing individual and group needs" (p. 37) that are involved in school community building. Placing the entire campus in a context of diversity that includes students, staff, faculty, administration, and community – locally and globally – is essential for both the vision and the practice of socially progressive education in the twenty-first century. Local dynamics are no longer the only, or even the leading, influences in schools. An entertainment, technology, or sports phenomenon may have more impact on students than their upcoming tests or math project. In many families these influences compete with the cultural values, goals, and roles of traditional lifeways that are centuries old. Immigrant, indigenous, and corporate or urban culture backgrounds may all be learned together, yet remain worlds apart. How do educational leaders ameliorate the political push towards further social stratification from one-size-fits-all rankings of standardized test scores? Will the arc of moral and equitable educational leadership move a nation towards social justice and out of the entitlements, privilege, and superiority patterns of colonialism?

Multicultural Equity or Monocultural Privilege: Some Successes

Shields and Sayani (2005) point out some of the successes of multicultural educational leadership in creating anti-racist curriculum, building critical multiculturalism, expanding nuanced cultural understandings, welcoming authentic encounters, creating communities of difference, facilitating on-going learning dialogue, rejecting deficit thinking and redesigning institutional deficit policies, deepening campus cultural experiences beyond cultural tourism, incorporating the lived experiences of students and adults and rejecting colorblindness or spiritual indifference in favor of including those experiences most meaningful to students and their families (p. 385-393).

In Canada a major success won through decades of persistent effort by First Nations leaders and their allies is the legislation for education jurisdiction by Indigenous peoples across the nation. The First Nations Education Steering Committee (FNESC), has been instrumental in building educational leadership capacity across British Columbia and throughout Canada. Some successes include: legislation for educational jurisdiction by First Nations (Matthew & Williams, 2006), annual conferences highlighting indigenous leadership and innovations in education; English 12, First Peoples; and a network of annual regional meetings to maintain connection with communities and their needs (FNESC, 2008).

Nisga'a First Nation, in the Nass Valley of British Columbia, has navigated the formal education jurisdiction to build a K-12 and a post-secondary education system locally. In June of 2008, a variety of certificate and degree candidates graduated in a joint convocation with Northwest Community College, the Ministry of Justice, and the University of Northern British Columbia on traditional territory in the community of Gitwinksihlkw.

The twenty-four-hour schools in urban Toronto created a tremendous stir at one school administrator graduate seminar in California. We discussed the impacts and possible outcomes for the similarly low-socioeconomic schools with high immigrant populations in the city we were all working in. The successes described by Toronto police in similar neighborhoods reducing crime – juvenile and adult – were the first focus of the conversation. Later the learning outcomes for both adults and children were discussed.

Education Debt and New Directions

Geneva Gay (2007), speaking at the American Educational Research Association's 2007 conference, built on the idea that culturally responsive teaching requires: community culture and knowledge bases, courage, a strong will to confront resistance, skills with local cultures, and tenacity. Her words addressed both the increased multicultural movement globally and the increasing contact of multiple groups in campus settings, contact that can be an invitation to students, families, and educators for maturity and conscious negotiation of intercultural spaces. Given global fluidity, the skills that teachers, family members, educational leaders, and community members need are different than those of homogeneous pre-jet, pre-satellite and pre-web communities. If the new skills needed to address inequities in a global milieu are not developed, colonial stratification by social class, gender, language, and race will continue to determine student outcomes.

When majority educational leaders ignore the realities of minority groups, who are numerically a majority but lack the dominant cultural capital, social power, or resource autonomy, frictions result. However, when the explicit teaching of both the school curriculum, at the formal and informal levels, as well as the hidden curriculum of cultural capital and institutional savvy are all part of the student's shared understandings, then teachers can incorporate lived experiences of students and make meaning of campus life in diverse settings with their students (Delpit, 1993; Nieto, 2008; Sleeter, 2005).

Concepts like colorblindness that deny difference have the effect of *racial erasure* that bell hooks (1992) describes as the homogenizing efforts to maintain the myth of sameness and ignore the lived experience of poverty: layoffs, underemployment, differential promotions and wages, limited healthcare access, reduced housing and mortgage availability, and so on. Canadians can be proud of the availability of basic needs across groups in a comparative global sense, and yet there is still stratification in Canadian society based on class, gender, and race.

The backcover description of Sterling's 2001 title states the problem clearly: "education is largely behind other fields in developing new thinking and practice in response to the challenge of sustainability." His view for educational leadership involves restructuring the "prevailing managerial and mechanistic paradigm" to move into transformation education. The difference in "sustainable education" is that the diversity in human potential and the "interdependence of social, economic and ecological wellbeing" moves to the forefront of educators "vision and design" for learning.

Close

This chapter was written as a part of an on-going exploration of multicultural educational leadership in Canada. I invite you to look at your local context with your peers and expand the views and experiences of cross-cultural and multicultural education you are working with. I look forward to meeting you one day to exchange stories and resources.

To become educationally equitable will take a willingness to stretch and grow on the part of all Canadians. From preschool to university there are successful cross-cultural examples to explore further, participate with, and build on. Courage will be required, courage towards overcoming the colonial influences of our very different education experiences across rural and urban, race and language, gender and sexual orientation, spirituality and religion, ability and disability, and social class experiences. This very complex and deeply humanizing endeavor holds a promise for our country as a multicultural leader among nations. Let us put our minds together to see what our interdependent future holds for our children.

Questions

1. a) What efforts do you see on local campuses to integrate various populations and groups of learners?
   b) Which ethnic/racial groups live in your city, region or province?
   c) What languages are incorporated or not incorporated into classrooms in your area?
2. Consider the cross-cultural attributes and skills Grace describes as relevant to the inclusion of GLBT students. Choose a group on the margins in your area and adapt the list, then add more of your own skills and attributes for inclusion of the group you chose.
3. Describe each of Banks' four stages of multicultural teacher development as you have experienced them for yourself as an educator or through teachers around you. Give a specific example for each.
4. Interview an educational leader on cross-cultural dynamics they are working with in their current position. Have them compare the current dynamics with other work settings or campuses they have experienced.

References

Banks, J. (2002). *An introduction to multicultural education* (3rd ed.). Boston, MA: Allyn and Bacon.

Caracciolo, D. (2007, April). *Closing the distance: Partnering with the Indigenous peoples on whose lands we earn our living.* Table Session at American Educational Research Association Chicago, IL.

Daniels, Y. (2007). School administrators as public intellectuals: Rethinking leadership preparation. In W. Smale & K. Young (Eds.), *Approaches to educational leadership and practice.* Calgary, AB: Detselig Enterprises Ltd.

Darder, A. (1995). Buscando America: The contributions of critical Latino educators. In C. Sleeter & P. McLaren (Eds.), *Multicultural education, critical pedagogy and the politics of difference.* Albany: State University of New York Press.

Delpit, L. (1993). *Other people's children: Cultural conflict in the classroom.* New York: The New Press.

First Nations Education Steering Committee (FNESC). (2008). Retrieved August 29, 2008, from http://www.fnesc.ca

Fullan, M. (2001). *The new meaning of educational change* (3rd ed.). New York: Teacher's College Press.

Gay, G. (2007, April). *Tensions of theory and practice.* Presentation at American Educational Research Association annual meeting, Chicago, IL.

Grace, A. (2007). In your care: School administrators and their ethical and professional responsibility toward students across sexual minority differences. In W. Smale & K. Young (Eds.), *Approaches to educational leadership and practice.* Calgary, AB: Detselig Enterprises Ltd.

Helin, C. (2006). *Dances with dependency: Indigenous success through self-reliance.* Vancouver, BC: Orca Spirit Publishing & Communications, Inc.

hooks, b., (1992). *Black looks: Race and representation.* Cambridge, MA: South End Press.

Joshee, R., & Johnson, L. (Eds.). (2008). *Multicultural education policies in Canada and the United States.* Vancouver, BC: UBC Press.

Matthew, N., & Williams, C. (2006). First Nations jurisdiction over education. [Powerpoint presentation] Retrieved on Sept. 3, 2008 from http://www.fnesc.ca/attachments/Education%20Policy%20Framework/06-05-29%20EPF_DIALOGUE_PRESENTATION_FINAL1.ppt

Neufeld, G. (2005). *Hold on to your kids: Why parents need to matter more than peers.* Toronto: Vintage Canada.

Nieto, S. (2008). *Affirming diversity: The sociopolitical context of multicultural education* (5th ed.). Boston, MA: Pearson Education, Inc.

Shields, C., & Sayani, A. (2005). Leading in the midst of diversity: The challenge of our times. In F. English (Ed.), *The SAGE handbook of educational leadership: Advances in theory, research, and practice.* Thousand Oaks, CA: SAGE Publications.

Shields, C. (2004). Dialogic leadership for social justice: Overcoming pathologies of silence. In *Educational Administration Quarterly, 40*(1), 109-132.

Sleeter, C. (2005). *Un-standardizing curriculum: Multicultural teaching in the standards-based classroom.* New York: Teacher's College Press.

Smale, W., & Young, K. (2007). *Approaches to educational leadership and practice.* Calgary, AB: Detselig Enterprises Ltd.

Smart Source Hiring System: Creative benefits for small employers. Retrieved on September 21, 2008 from www.ypp.com/articles_creative_benefits.html

Spring, J. (2003). *Deculturalization and the struggle for equality: A brief history of the education of dominated cultures in the United States* (4th ed.). Boston, MA: McGraw-Hill Companies.

Sterling, S. (2001). *Sustainable education: Re-visioning learning and change.* Bristol, UK: Green Books Ltd.

Chapter Eight

The Evolving Teacher, Leader, and Action Researcher

Thomas G. Ryan, Ed.D.
Nipissing University

Introduction

Our world is changing and there is a need to move with this change and adapt as a society. This is not something educators need to oppose; it is something to embrace, reflect upon, and plan for. We need to be progressive and adopt a view of nature as being in flux, as ever changing. Adapting to this view allows us to enhance our knowledge, to redefine ourselves and rediscover, to keep pace with change (Ryan & Cooper, 2004). The implication for our schools and our preservice teacher education programs is to confront change and respond accordingly. However, to do this "a new paradigm of the teaching profession is needed – one that recognizes both the capacity of the profession to provide desperately needed school revitalization and the striking potential of teachers to provide new forms of leadership in schools and communities" (Crowther, Kaagan, Ferguson, & Hann, 2002, p. 3). New teachers, leading the charge to confront change, must possess knowledge, skills, and dispositions (beliefs) required to assume these fresh forms of leadership, and a "pre-service program can either set this process in motion with the appropriate tools, attitudes, and expectations, or it can set the novice up for a dizzying fall from the heights of unchallenged naive idealism" (Russell & McPherson, 2001, p. 8). Therefore, teacher preparation programs must make deliberate attempts to require the analysis of knowledge, skills, and dispositions of teacher leaders, and nurture these traits to ensure that change is embraced by new educators, leaders, and those in our profession.

Admittedly, the growth and analysis of teacher knowledge "begins with what teachers already know and enact in their practices rather than beginning with knowledge that needs to be given to teachers" (Clandinin, 2007, p. 15). To do this requires professors to uncover the elements of knowledge that student-teachers bring into a program: after all, "teacher knowledge refers to teachers' narrative knowledge, their personal practical knowledge, composed and recomposed over time and in the contexts of personal and professional knowledge landscapes" (Clandinin, 2007, p. 15). This pre-existing knowledge is deeply embedded and often tacit. Frequently this core knowledge surfaces during the intense and unpredictable practice teaching sessions via self-discovery and reflective revelation. These practicum experiences can direct and inform future actions, reflections, and revisions; hence, varied outcomes emerge and need to be discussed.

The practicum is a time of sudden growth that requires student teachers to effectively face problems and deal with dilemmas in an authoritative manner since a teacher is an authority by virtue of their position and expertise (Peters, 1959). This situation can create tension given that "student teachers are uncomfortable during these early stages because they dislike seeing themselves as authoritative figures" (Boudreau, 1999, p. 458). However, it is not entirely the challenge of being in authority that is unsettling; it is the requirement to do this in another teacher's classroom, over a short period of time (practicum), while being evaluated by mentors that heightens discomfort for these emerging teachers.

The practicum is a test of physical and mental capacities. It is an immersion in a culture that often puzzles and requires multiple leadership skills. The importance of these leadership skills becomes more evident to new teachers as they take on their new role in the classroom: "Teachers hold a central position in the ways that schools operate and in the core functions of teaching and learning, what is new are increased recognition of teacher leadership, visions of expanded teacher leadership roles, and new hope for the contributions these expanded roles might make in improving schools" (York-Barr & Duke, 2004, p. 255). This reality has produced a need to study, sort, cultivate, and scrutinize the concept of emerging teacher leadership. A natural place to begin is within the training of teachers as they become known as teachers, leaders, and action researchers. Those familiar with the idea of reflective practitioners are already familiar with the basis for action research.

Theoretical Background

Action Research

As a pre-service teacher, if your actions do not unfold the way they were imagined and planned or an unexpected behavior or event transpires, you make changes until you are satisfied with the planned outcomes. The pre-service teacher acting as "the action researcher is interested in the improvement of the educational practices in which he is engaging. He undertakes research in order to find out how to do his job better – action research means research that affects actions" (Corey 1949, p. 509). Hopkins (1993) further delineates the concept of action research: "Action research combines a substantive act with a research procedure; it is action disciplined by inquiry, a personal attempt at understanding while engaged in a process of improvement and reform" (p. 44). Action research is both working to discover self-knowledge and using that new knowledge to refine the practice of teaching:

> Action research is, therefore, a deliberate way of creating new situations and of telling the story of who we are. Action research consists of deliberate experimental moves into the future, which change us because of what we learn in the process. (Connelly & Clandinin, 1988, p. 153).

These definitions and the recursive nature of the teaching practicum are commonplace in most Faculty of Education programs. Each round of practice teaching offers the student teacher a new opportunity to refine outcomes. This recurring teaching practicum within the teacher training program complements action research as student teachers act, reflect and revise recursively. Parsons and Brown (2002) concluded:

> Action research has been found to serve not only as a means of improving teaching . . . but also in developing practitioners' flexibility and problem-solving skills . . . and their attitudes to professional development and the process of change. . . . Participation in action research resulted in increased confidence, self, esteem, willingness to embrace research, and liberated creative potential for the educator-turned-action researcher. . . . Action research has been described as a vehicle for improving pre-service . . . [and] has been found to promote a climate of professionalism and scholarship. (p. 6)

Reflection

Making sense of an action in practicum, the perspective taken on the interpretation of events following the action (stance) and related revised teaching decisions in a pre-service program requires deep reflection upon self in relation to others as a means to self-monitor (Schoonmaker, 1998), develop, and improve. Students completing a pre-service program complete both *practicum* (student teaching) and *theory classes* that delve into teacher training requisites. Some course activities are particularly well regarded by students that link pre-service teacher's reflections on the role of the teacher, course readings, and observations during students' field experiences (Pryor, Sloan, & Amobi, 2007). Links are developed often by the construction of a reflection on paper and the sharing of this written effort in class discussions. It is an essential task that can guide and affect the teaching-learning process as it contextualizes and connects educational theory to praxis (Onwuegbuzie, Witcher, James, & Minor, 2002).

Leadership

At present we see a convergence of old models and new models of leadership (for example, the push towards professional learning community) that give way to contemporary images such as the one offered by Fullan (2001). He offers an image of leadership as a circle with five "independent but mutual reinforcing forces for positive change" (p. 3): Moral purpose, understanding change, relationship building, knowledge creation and sharing, and coherence making. My colleagues in the Faculty of Education and I chose these five elements to guide and inform our study as we read written accounts and looked for evidence of these leadership qualities within the lines of reflective text. We did this because we believed, as do Kouzes and Posner (1995), that

> leadership is an observable, learnable set of practices. Leadership is not something mystical and ethereal that cannot be understood by ordinary people. Given the opportunity for feedback and practice, those with the desire and persistence to lead – to make a difference – can substantially improve their abilities to do so. (p. 4)

Therefore we believed that the five traits of leadership could be detected in the reflective accounts of evolving teachers.

Purpose

The purpose of this action-research effort was to train pre-service teachers to create written accounts of their leadership actions. Secondly, this act, reflect, and revise mode (action research) enabled and enhanced pre-service teacher's capacity to articulate their practice and improve teaching and leadership. In doing so, identity formation, growth, and the expansion of self-understanding was nurtured.

Research Questions

The following questions served as a guide:

1. Using an act, reflect, revise mode (action research) what evidence of leadership can be realized?
2. What leadership/teaching actions and reflections will cause revisions and guide growth?

Sample

A purposeful cross-sectional sample (N=320) was selected due to accessibility and convenience. All participants were pre-service teachers (students) who attended Faculty of Education classes. All were enrolled in the Bachelor of Education (BEd) program, a one-year, full-time professional program that meets the requirements of the Ontario College of Teachers for teacher certification. All participants had an approved undergraduate degree from an accredited university before enrollment. Participants were enrolled in one of two divisions in the Bachelor of Education program. Participants Included 120 students who were training to become J/I (Junior/Intermediate, Grades 4 to 10) teachers and 200 pre-service students in the I/S (Intermediate/Senior, Grades 7 to 12) levels.

Pre-service students completed recursive rounds of action research during practicum while completing courses in curriculum studies, curriculum methods, and foundations in education. There were three practice teaching sessions for a total of thirteen weeks of placement in elementary and secondary schools throughout Ontario. The age of the participants ranged from twenty-two to fifty-seven. The research included 217 female and 103 male participants.

Research Design

This qualitative endeavor required us to supply images of action research that were studied in class. Exemplars of written action research accounts from previous year students were used to layout a framework. Our intent was to facilitate the development of leadership skills through reflective practicum tasks on three separate occasions. We collected over 1000 reflective accounts which were read, sorted into themes, and checked for the act, reflect, and revise elements. The themes, as noted earlier, involved five elements: Moral purpose, understanding change, relationship building, knowledge creation/sharing, and coherence making. These beacons of leadership guided and informed this study as we read accounts and looked for evidence line by line.

Each participant enacted an action research effort by noting their actions (ACT), documenting their thoughts and feelings concerning their leadership actions (REFLECT) and detailing what they planned to do to next (REVISE). This task (ACT-REFLECT-REVISE) was but one means of collecting evidence and documenting the beginning of a long journey in education.

Results

Of the over 1000 reflective written accounts scrutinized, 158 (16%) provided evidence of moral purpose (MP), 228 (29%) demonstrated an understanding of change (UC), 542 (54%) mentioned relationship building (RB), 482 (48%) noted knowledge creation and sharing (KCS), and 127 (13%) enacted coherence making (CM). A number of traits were intertwined and common to many reflective accounts; however, we determined the predominant trait via discussion of reflective accounts in class and through rereading.

Moral Purpose

Moral purpose is about making a "difference in the lives of students. . . . If you don't treat others . . . well and fairly, you will be a leader without followers" (Fullan, 2001, p. 13). Hence, we looked for evidence of concern for the lives of students and fair treatment. Of the 158 (16%) accounts denoting moral purpose, we have included one that demonstrates a pre-service educator acting with moral purpose:

> My practicum was full of learning experiences – some more pronounced than others. The revisions that I made since October to my management strategies worked out fantastically; especially with my one behavioral student who was having some difficulties in the classroom, but was even more unmanageable in the gymnasium. After careful, personal consideration and discussion with my associate teacher, I decided to approach this situation from a different angle. I began each day by preparing this student for the gym class. I told him exactly what we were going to be doing. I explained what equipment we needed, the warm-up, the drill, and the activity I had planned for the gym class that day. After telling him step by step how the class was going to unfold, I told him because it was going to be so busy, I needed help setting up the equipment and making sure the class ran as smoothly as possible. He jumped at the chance and volunteered to help me immediately.

The pre-service teacher's individual and personal consideration motivated the student and the pre-service teacher discovered just how moral purpose and fair treatment can establish pathways and bonds that diminish acting out in this context. Leading by engaging others is not straightforward and there are a number of possible reactions to the disruptive student, yet using the right approach, a fair one, in this case pays dividends.

Understanding Change

Teacher leaders know innately, that teaching and leading requires strategizing and innovativeness (Fullan, 2001, p. 31), but these changes must be at a pace that gives the students the ability to adapt as well. The following excerpt, one of 228 (29%) identified, is the latter portion of a four page reflection upon a teaching practicum:

> During the debates I had students calm themselves and take a deep breath between each new set of debaters. There were six teams in all for a total of three debates. Those who were not immediately involved sat at the back of the class like an audience. Once the debates were over students did not want to stop discussing and suggesting their ideas and arguments. I asked students to return to their rows and that we would only continue the debate as a class if they could listen, respect each other, and speak one at a time when called on. When they began to get loud and talk over each other I had to raise my voice and say "Quiet" because I wanted to stop them before it got out of control. They were quiet right away. I felt a little embarrassed having to get stern, but I think with such a large group it was necessary to remind them of the behavior I asked for during the agreement.
>
> I will continue to experiment with group work activities and with motivating students to engage in classroom discussions, especially at the Grade 12 level because the vocalization of ideas and arguments will be expected of them in most Universities. I will try a new debate format and preparation process with the Grade 10's when I return in November. This time we will look at two sides of a topic related to WWII. I look forward to challenging them and having them try out new roles and ways of working together and presenting information.

I believe the key to innovativeness is the intention to experiment, to risk and to hope for rewarding teaching and leading within the teaching practicum.

Relationship Building

Relationship building involves being interested in others and constructing a focused collaborative community of learners: "Increasingly, leadership in schools is becoming a shared responsibility. . . . Leaders are considerably more effective if they work with and through people in their enterprise. . . . We have to talk about feelings in public" (Naested, Potvin, & Waldron, 2004, p. 30). One student teacher, of the 548 (54%) identified, provided the following reflection:

> During my first practicum, I spent a lot of time with the students with learning disabilities and behavioral issues. I watched their individual learning styles, recorded problem areas, observed their manners, and took note of times when their behavior was appropriate and times when it was out of control. I worked to establish a rapport with these students and helped integrate them into their new classroom with as much ease as possible. I anticipated these were the students that would challenge me the most when I was in front of the class teaching. I want to be able to diffuse and manage potential disturbances or out-of-control situations as efficiently as I can in order to maximize the effectiveness of my lesson for all the students in the class. I believe each student is an individual and has individual actions, reactions, and needs. It is essential for classroom management to have an extensive awareness and knowledge of these aspects with all students, but especially with students who have special needs.

Establishing a rapport is a fundamental element in classroom leadership, and we see an instance of that here as the student teacher observed, plotted, and worked to establish connectedness in an effort to build a relationship.

Knowledge Creation and Sharing

Fullan (2001) explains:

> The process of knowledge creation is no easy task. First tacit knowledge is by definition hard to get at. Second, the process must sort out and yield quality ideas; not all tacit knowledge is useful. Third quality ideas must be retrained, shared, and used throughout the [classroom]. (p. 80)

We looked for evidence of the above as teachers attempted to make their knowledge accessible and shared within their practice-teaching. One student explained how the learning is mutual, sudden, and rewarding.

> During my week of actual teaching, I was responsible for the math portion of the afternoons. Prior to my first lesson my AT asked me to work with the group of students that were not present for the first probability lesson and review with them what they had missed. This was

definitely the eye opener for me and all the challenges surrounding this individual with Asperger's. As I was working with the students; all of whom were identified, this boy could not maintain his focus. He was scribbling on his page, he was talking aloud commenting on unrelated issues that did not quite make any sense, and he was disrupting the other students and all of this was leading to him not learning my lesson. It was interesting since I have never worked with challenged individuals or children with disabilities; I was not sure how I should respond. At first I politely asked him to refocus and pay attention to the task at hand. I would ask him direct questions to make sure he was not drifting away. At one point, I picked up one of his pens to show him something on his paper and he started panicking because I was using the black pen and it was apparently poisoned. He had another pen in his hand that you could choose which colour to use and he begged me to use that pen instead. To be honest, the whole experience was frustrating. I didn't know how to respond to his odd fits and his disruptive behavior. That first day I definitely showed signs of impatience and I admit I was not quite prepared to handle this kind of student.

The next week once my actual teaching began I kept pondering about how I would handle this boy and what tactics I would use to help him learn. My AT informed me that this boy is not stupid; he is in fact quite smart. He is manipulative in the sense that he fully knows what he is doing and has preconceived notions regarding his actions. On that note I was told to be firm with him and not tolerate his episodes. The next week I started teaching probability and it actually went a lot better than I thought. I learned a lot about this boy and how he worked.

During independent work I found that he demanded a lot of my attention. He would complain that he didn't understand the work and that he was behind. At the beginning I definitely fell for it. I would sit beside him and work through the problems with him. I learned after a few classes that he actually understood the material quite well; he just believed he didn't understand or he just wanted someone to be there with him to assist with the questions so that he didn't have to do the work alone. I needed to stay on task since other students had questions and they couldn't be neglected either. It was difficult trying to adhere to the needs of my students as well as

> keep an eye on what his boy was doing. If I didn't come see him for a while, he would completely stop doing the work. If I asked him why he stopped, he would say he didn't understand. I would claim that he did all the previous questions with no problem and then he would state that it was because I helped him. I eventually told him that, yes, I was present while he did the question; however, I assisted him in no way at all besides reading that question to him. I made sure I was encouraging in telling him that he was doing a great job and was working well and to keep it up. In a supportive tone, I told him that he knew what he was doing and I would come and check to see his next question in a few minutes. I would check on him periodically to help him stay on task.
>
> One night I assigned homework and he told me that he would not complete it since he didn't understand. During language period that day I had a talk with him about math and his understanding. I was encouraging and explained to him that he knew what he was doing and to try. I was looking for effort and attempt. The next day he had completed the homework and it felt very rewarding. I also had a quiz that week and he actually did quite well. It felt good to see that he was understanding the content and actually completing his work. For me this was an example where I felt like I handled the situation well. I do realize that in a real classroom setting when I am my own teacher, I will not have that same amount of time to spend with him one on one.

A new teacher feels pulled in many directions at once. However, experience decreases these tensions as seasoned educators merely sense the occupational pressures of the classroom and respond tacitly.

Coherence Making

Coherence making refers to ones ability to facilitate, sort, and contribute to problem-solving and "the most powerful coherence is a function of having worked through the ambiguities and complexities of hard-to-solve problems" (Fullan, 2001, p. 116). Therefore, we were looking for proof of this in the reflective accounts of pre-service teachers. A non-typical reflective account suggested and noted the steps undertaken to achieve such outcomes. This elementary school student teacher/leader supplied the chart on the next page.

The student in this case elected to display the task within a chart in order to sort, organize, and layout the next steps in problem solving, which indicates another element of leadership.

Act	Reflect	Revise
Remaining silent until the students are quiet.	I felt that this worked sometimes, depending on the day. If they students were in more of an observant mood, then it worked. Otherwise, they didn't care as much, and I had to resort to other management methods.	I would perhaps wait longer next time before giving in when I do this, if they don't catch on right away.
Using a timer to motivate efficiency.	This worked as a motivator for the students. Anything that is turned into a competition for them is great, since it gives them something fun to work towards: i.e., beating their time from last time, etc.	This usually worked well, and there isn't much I'd change about this management strategy. Perhaps to maybe incorporate a tangible rewards system after so many successful attempts.
Using peer pressure to gain quietness.	This does not always work in this classroom. That is because there are many students with behavioral problems and learning disabilities who see misbehaving almost as a challenge and entertaining. Therefore, on certain days, they don't care whether they get in trouble or not (even to the extreme of being sent to the principals office).	This is not much to change about this, except to not do it. It would work in some classrooms; however, with the dynamics of this class, it is not an effective strategy to use.
Getting students to line up quietly to walk down the hallway.	This was a good strategy, in order to get them focused, since otherwise they would not be in the 'zone' to be quiet.	This usually worked fine. However, sometimes they don't really understand its value, so perhaps talk about it in class together, and get them to state why being quiet in the hallways is important.
Ensuring students put up their hand to speak in class.	This creates great structure in the classroom. It also creates respect among the peers and the peers to teacher(s).	There is not much to change about this. However, we need to continue focusing on sticking by this rule, since it is not always strictly regarded as important.
Taking my time when speaking and asking questions, ensuring students are following me.	This is important, since the students need time to process information and construct thoughts. This time allows them the chance to do this. It also allows them to think critically for themselves.	There isn't anything I would change about this strategy. The only thing I would perhaps add is to ask more probing questions to help their thought process.

Act	Reflect	Revise
Flexibility depending on how the day is going (every day is different).	This is critical. Since things are changing so much, things are coming up, and students attitudes vary day to day, being well prepared, and therefore flexible to make changes as the day goes on, is important to help the day go smoothly.	The only thing to keep in mind is to be overly prepared, to be able to make quick changes to the day.
Enforcing the rule that when someone else is speaking, no one else is (whether it is the teacher or another student).	This is very important again, to demonstrate the importance of respect for one another. Half the students got frustrated when it was not silent for them to speak, and the other half didn't care. So a real emphasis on this needs to be continuously focused on.	What I need to change for this strategy is to enforce it stronger. It isn't consistent enough with them, since they take advantage of it sometimes.
Having instructions on the board for when the students come in the classroom in the morning, or following any recess.	This helped students get settled, since it gave them a task to do when they came in, as they were waiting for all their peers to get changed and get seated as well. This way they all had something to do, and no one was sitting around with nothing to do.	This seemed to work great, since the students in this class were for the most part fairly needy, and had to have something to keep them on task at all times.
Getting the students to pick up their coats, scarves, mittens, and hats and make sure they are hung up.	This helped them realize that no one was there to pick up after them.	This seemed to work since the students went from having their stuff all over the floors in the hallway, to having 'most' of their stuff hung up.
If they are misbehaving, tell them they will owe me time from their recess. Each check they get beside their name, they get one minute removed from their recess which they own me.	This worked in most cases. However, there are those exceptions of students who enjoy staying in at recess, therefore I am selective who I will use this on.	I am not sure what I can change about this. It seems to work for some of them, since some of the students are off task easily, and it helps put them back on the right path for the time being. I find it to have a temporary effect (in the sense it works differently day to day with different students).

Act	Reflect	Revise
"Brooksy Bucks", (my associates last name is Brooks) pretend money they can collect when being good. At the end of each week, they were allowed to cash it in for real prizes.	This really helped encourage them since it was to buy prizes they all wanted (i.e., pokemon cards).	I don't think there is anything I'd want to change with this. It was very helpful since they all seemed to really enjoy it.

Initially, our purpose was to discover if using an act, reflect, revise mode of action research would produce leadership evidence. Given the above excerpts, we answered this question positively and realized that the reflective process does indeed cause revisions and guide growth within teaching. It is about evolving while enacting praxis (practice) and to do this requires ongoing openness to change. Edwards (2000) states that "teachers who are successful in changing their practices do so through their commitment to change as well as visualizing what that change looks like" (p. 32). This attempt to revise praxis required an inner desire that ultimately amends teaching beliefs, actions and stance.

Discussion

Teachers are generally communal and it is this ability to commune, collaborate and support one another that is indispensable. Naested, Potvin, and Walden (2004) suggest:

> We have to make ourselves vulnerable to others . . . Clearly this kind of expression of our inner self demonstrates who we really are. . . . [L]eaders who inquire effectively into their own values and behaviours become more reflective and credible. In effect, they become models for the integrity and interpersonal trust needed to explore a host of organization-wide issues. . . . In many of todays more enlightened schools, shared leadership is commonly understood in concept and action. Teachers are leaders in a very authentic sense. (p. 31)

As noted herein, the classroom leader needs be guided by moral purpose, capable of understanding change, able to build relationships, create knowledge, and share in a coherent manner. No one trait is above the other as it is a linear relationship. To the leader who demonstrates these traits there is a reward:

> Empowerment, also referred to as shared decision-making, is essential to school reform and to the changing demands in a global world. Empowerment translates into teacher leadership and exemplifies a paradigm shift with the decisions made by those working most closely with

> students rather than those at the top of the pyramid. (Terry, 1999, p. 1)

We have discovered that, teachers who recognize the value of the five noted leadership traits will easily empower both themselves and others. Our mode of inquiry leads to empowerment as action research is about connectedness and relationships, for "without social interaction in human learning, no conceptual learning would be possible" (Sfard, 2003, p. 371). It is important that pre-service teachers have the opportunity to act, reflect upon actions, and then propose revisions, especially when taking initial steps in their chosen profession. It is about evolving while enacting praxis and to do this requires ongoing change which is observed, examined, and connected to what was known. Some would argue that it is constructivism in its purest form "grounded in the philosophy of Dewey and the theories of Piaget (1950) and Vygotsky (1978), [since] constructivisim is based on the premise that students learn best when they are able to construct their knowledge, often from hands-on interactions" (Henniger, 2004, p. 258). Our student-teachers are learning, constructing linkages, and growing as leaders.

Revealing pre-service educators' educational experiences is essential since it can inspire, prompt, and clarify needed behavioral change and it can also expose entrenched or tacit knowledge. This improves a teachers' social functioning. Dewey's concern for social functioning within a society remains engaging today because of the daily dysfunction that reaches us via the media coverage of education and schooling. The suggestion, for our schools and our pre-service programs, is to confront change and take action. Pre-service teachers often find fault within the educational system they are plunged into each practicum suggesting it is wanting and that they intend to take a leadership role to make it better.

Our many reflective practice-teaching accounts demonstrated elements of leadership and this is important since:

> Teachers' roles are changing in fundamental and positive ways at the beginning of the twenty-first century. Greater autonomy and an expanded role in educational policy-making has led to 'unprecedented opportunities for today's teachers to extend their leadership roles beyond the classroom. (Parkay, Hardcastle-Standford, Vaillancourt, & Stephens, 2005, p. 371)

The teachers who complete practicum in this era write about their complex and broad duties, which is refreshing since this demonstrates a greater level of democracy and shared power when so much is expected of student-teachers. After all, "teachers' lives are enriched and energized in many ways when they actively pursue leadership opportunities" (Barth, 2001, p. 444). The faculty of education is no longer solely producing teachers; they are supporting the development of leaders.

Conclusion

The evolving action researchers, classroom leaders, and teachers are dealing with personal experiences that inform and steer people in the pre-service year. Our data (written accounts) provided evidence that supports our resulting inferences, discussion, and conclusions and demonstrates the leadership within the pre-service classroom during practicum. Yet it is the analysis and synthesis of practicum reflections that illuminates core beliefs, attitudes and needs of emerging action researchers, leaders, and teachers. Dewey (1916) suggested, "Meanings and purposes of education must be actively constructed by individual persons" (p. 96), and the practicum and theory classes seem to provide this opportunity. Nonetheless, Webster (2004) provides a reproving note:

> Pre-service teachers remain basically unchanged through education programs. . . . In spite of this resilience to educative change, it is argued here that facilitating authentic development of teachers' purposes of education, by changing their holistic beliefs remains a worthwhile task. (Webster, 2004, p. 82)

This cautionary note appears to have merit but may not be applicable to all since the developmental mode of teacher education is often internal, varied, and covert. The pre-service experience is about self-analysis and discovery learning; however, the requirement to clearly formulate and express ones educational experience via reflection seems understandable and necessary in order to construct well-built internal and external positions. These positions provide fuel for reflective modes which can substantively improve development and leadership.

Questions

1. Why is action research a useful qualitative mode to investigate practice?
2. Can you rank the five components of leadership from most to least important and locate a peer who shares your ranking and rationales.
3. Do you believe the five components of leadership represent independent but mutual reinforcing forces for positive change?
4. To what extent did your pre-service experience require these leadership components?

References

Barth, R. S. (2001). *Learning by heart.* San Francisco, CA: Jossey-Bass.

Boudreau, P. (1999). The supervision of a student teacher as defined by cooperating teachers. *Canadian Journal of Education, 24*(4), 454-459.

Clandinin, D.J. (2007, January). *Teacher as knowledge composer: More complex than a question of knowledge for teachers.* Paper presented at the Ontario Teachers Federation/Ontario Association of Deans of Education Conference at Toronto, ON.

Connelly, F. M., & Clandinin, D. J. (1988). *Teachers as curriculum planners: Narratives of experience.* Toronto: OISE Press.

Corey, S.M. (1949). Action research, fundamental research and educational practices. *Teachers College Record, 50*, 509-14.

Crowther, F., Kaagan, S., Ferguson, M., & Hann, L. (2002). *Developing teacher leaders: How teacher leadership enhances school success.* Thousand Oaks, CA: Corwin Press, Inc.

Dewey, J. (1916). *Democracy and education.* New York, NY: Macmillan.

Edwards, B. S. (2000). The challenges of implementing innovation. T*he Mathematics Teacher, 93*(9), 777-781.

Fullan, M. (2001). *Leading in a culture of change.* San Francisco, CA: Jossey-Bass.

Henniger, M. L. (2004). *The teaching experience: An introduction to reflective practice.* Upper Saddle River, NJ: Pearson, Merill Prentice Hall.

Hopkins, D. (1993). *A teacher's guide to classroom research* (2nd ed.). Philadelphia, PA: Open University Press.

Kouzes, J., & Posner, B. (1995). An instructor's guide to the leadership challenge [Electronic Version]. *The Jossey-Bass Management Series.* Retrieved Jan. 14, 2006 from http://media.wiley.com/assets/57/11/lc_jb_instructors_guide.pdf

Naested, I., Potvin, B., & Waldron. (2004). *Understanding the landscape of teaching.* Toronto: Pearson-Prentice Hall.

Onwuegbuzie, A. J., Witcher, A. E., James, T. L., & Minor, L. C. (2002). Changes in teacher candidates' beliefs about education. *Academic Exchange Quarterly, 6*(3), 136-140.

Parkay, F. W., Hardcastle-Stanford, B., Vaillancourt, J. P., & Stephens, H. C. (2005). *Becoming a teacher.* (2nd Canadian ed.). Toronto: Pearson.

Parsons, R. D., & Brown, K. S. (2002). *Teacher as reflective practitioner and action researcher.* Toronto: Wadsworth/Thomson Learning.

Peters, R. S. (1959). *Authority, responsibility and education.* London: Falmer Press.

Piaget, J. (1950). *Origins of intelligence in children.* New York: Norton.

Pryor, C. R., Sloan, K., & Amobi, F. (2007). Three professors' teaching philosophy of education: Strategies and considerations for undergraduate courses. *The Journal of Scholarship of Teaching and Learning, 7*(1) 77-101.

Russell, T., & Mcpherson, S. (2001, May). *Indicators of success in teacher education: A review and analysis of recent research.* Paper presented at the Pan-Canadian Education Research Agenda Symposium Teacher

Education/Educator Training: Current Trends and Future Directions, Laval University, Quebec City, PQ.

Ryan, K., & Cooper, J. M. (2004). *Those who can, teach.* (10th ed.). New York: Houghton Mifflin.

Schoonmaker, F. (1998). Promise and possibility: Learning to teach. *Teachers College Record, 99*, 559-591.

Sfard, A. (2003). Balancing the unbalanceable: The NCTM standards in light of theories of learning mathematics. In J. Kilpatrick, W. G. Martin, & D. Schifter (Eds.), *A research companion to Principles and Standards for School Mathematics* (pp. 353-392). Reston, VA: National Council of Teachers of Mathematics.

Terry, P. (1999). Empowering teachers as leaders [Electronic Version]. *National Forum of Teacher Education Journal, 10*(3). Retrieved on May 11, 2006 from http://www.nationalforum.com/Terryte8e3.html>

Vygotsky, L. S. (1978). Thinking and speech. In R. W. Rieber & A. S. Carton (Eds.), *The collected works of L. S. Vygotsky* (pp. 239-243). New York: Plenum Press.

Webster, S. R. (2004). Changing pre-service teachers' purposes of education through existential crises. *Australian Journal of Education, 48*(1), 82-95.

York-Barr, J., & Duke, K. (2004). What do we know about teacher leadership? Findings from two decades of scholarship [Electronic Version]. *Review of Educational Research, 3*, 255-316.

Chapter Nine

Community, Cooperation, and Inclusion: An Alternative Future for Leading Ontario's Community Schools

Jason Price, Ph.D.
University of Victoria

> Leadership without morality is simply bureaucratic technique. (F. W. English. 1994, p. 231)

> The goal of education is to give a sense of the value of things other than domination, to help create wise citizens of a free community, to encourage combination of citizenship with liberty, individual creativeness, which means that we regard each child as a gardener regards a young tree, as something with an intrinsic nature that will develop into an admirable form if given proper soil and light. (Bertrand Russell, 1994, p. 41)

Preface

Educational leadership in the twenty-first century will, in my mind, be as multifaceted as the school systems that I anticipate developing in the province of Ontario and throughout Canada during the next few decades. I expect the continuation of school systems comprised of brick and mortar for profit private schools, public schools, charter schools (unfortunately, mostly profit-driven corporate vehicles), religious and community-based schools, as well as more public and private virtual schools to develop. Without question there will be big winners and big losers in this competitive and increasingly commodified education *market* of the future. Many communities lack the resources with which to support independent non-profit, community-based schools or lack boards of education with the will and resources to develop and support public schools with empowered site-based community management. Privileged communities have more money and more time, both commodities which institutional public schools devour with a voracious appetite.

Although public schools may continue to be the most dominant means with which to attempt to pursue equity and social justice educationally, they are under sustained pressure and scrutiny from their increasingly diverse and dissatisfied stakeholders. Marginalized and economically and culturally dominant communities alike are increasingly frustrated with the inability of public schools to prepare citizens of a democratic nation for meaningful participation in the democratic and civic life of the nation beyond the new low-wage, service-based workplace. Moreover, many parents of non-dominant racial, religious, and class affiliations and identities are challenging the relevance, cultural insensitivity, and effectiveness of the curricular and co-curricular programming of the public system. More and more parents and students are feeling alienated and intimidated by a fast-paced instrumentalist school system, focused on student results rather than students. Schools that teach common curriculum not uncommon students. Further, parents and students are recognizing that despite these intensive utilitarian efforts to prepare students for employment in competitive global markets, most students from outside the middle and elite class are being left behind to fill the rolls of the new poverty employment opportunities offered by low-wage jobs in the service industry. There is increasing awareness that the public system is essentially reproducing a social and economic order that continues to privilege white middle-class Canadians.

This opposition combined with the deteriorating services and quality from shrinking budgets will mean that urban public school boards of education like the Toronto, Halton, Durham, and Peel District School Board will be especially vulnerable to challenges from new community-based approaches to schooling. This must be viewed by educationists and activitists as important opportunity, calling for new forms and unprecedented cooperation, collaboration, and joint actions, or, in other words, new forms of community leadership and leadership for communities.

These new schools will require new forms of leadership and new kinds of leaders that can transcends paradigms: a post-paradigmatic leader, or, more accurately, post-paradigmatic collective form of leadership: A people-centred model of leadership inspired by Indigenous leadership approaches and premised upon values, consensus of agreements, and community rather than authoritarian bureaucratic management systems and market forces; a Leadership exercised by an empowered collective of formal and informal leaders, rather than by an individual?

Background to a Future that might be

After regaining control of Queen's Park in 2012, the New Democratic Party caucus, in the NDP minority government led by Premier Sun Rae Brant and Education Minister Amer John Shujah, successfully introduced charter schools legislation. In response to a spirited opposition led by the Ontario College of Teachers, which had been muscularized by the previous short-lived minority Liberal Government of Dalton McGuinty; the Ontario Public School Teachers Federation; Ontario Secondary School Teachers Federation; the Catholic church; the Muslim Community Schools Association; and a group of education activists led by Heather Jane Robertson, who made front page news by chaining herself to the doors of Queen's Park; Bill 207 was amended to exclude for-profit charter schools. The bill as it passed third reading provided strong financial and legislative support for charter schools formed by Ministry approved community-based partnerships. The first Charter schools in Ontario were located in the Greater Toronto Area and were founded by partnerships of community-based non-government organizations, parent groups, and interested educators.

As previously stated, much of the early motivation for charter schools was provided by the deterioration of the Toronto District Public School Board (TDSB), a result of the draconian funding formula reforms introduced in the 1990s by Premier Eckerd's mentor, former Premier Mike Harris, which the soft liberal governments of Dalton McGuinty continued, and the perceived dominant cultures inertia and insensitivity of the public system to the needs and desires of non-white, non-middle class Canadians. TDSB's schools were becoming larger and more diverse, at the same time as operating resources continued to shrink requiring the elimination or downsizing of special needs, technology, ESOL, and co-curricular programming. An informed and empowered cadre of parents in some communities, experienced with educational management as a result of participation in school committees and community organizations, were strong supporters of the Charter schools movement. These parents were instrumental in lobbying for and working towards the development of Ontario Community Charter Schools.

The first school founded under Bill 207 was the result of a partnership formed between the Ontario Institute for Studies Centre for Leadership and Diversity Studies, and the Toronto Parents for Relevant and Experiential Education, a diverse multi-cultural, multi-racial group of parents drawn form a range of socioeconomic backgrounds experienced in site-based school management. On December 29th, 2012 the Ministry of Education of the Province of Ontario accredited the Paulo Freire Community Learning Centre of Relevant and Experiential Education (PFCLC). The school was loosely based on the Community Learning Centre (CLC) model, which was part of the New American Schools initiative of the early 1990s, and the critical pedagogical ideas of Paulo Freire. Surprisingly, the school was accredited under Bill 207 without having to articulate in anything but the broadest terms the vision, objectives, activities and programmes the school would implement. According to the plan submitted by PFCLC Implementation Committee, the specific vision, curriculum, activities, policies, and procedures of the school would be articulated by consensus after an intensive process of dialogue and consultation between committee members, the principal, professional faculty, paraprofessionals, parents, students, and community and local business leaders.

The student body of PFCLC was required to be composed of a diverse cross-section of students. As part of the accreditation plan the school was required to be representative of the socioeconomic, racial, and academic abilities of the community it serves. No student would be assigned to PFCLC. Any resident of the GTA was free to choose the PFCLC as an alternative school. Believing small is better; the PFCLC implementation committee limited enrollment to 300 students (Sergiovanni, 1996). Upon admission students were *grandfathered* and could leave and re-enter PFCLC as many times as necessary until graduation. PFCLC alumni would also be welcome to participate in the schools management and programmes.

Community Leadership of PFCLC: Hiring as Cultural Formation in the Post-Modern School

The Implementation Committee of PFCLC hired a highly experienced Coordinator after a nationwide recruitment effort and exhaustive interview process conducted with voting representatives of all school stakeholders.[1] Winslow Johns was the unanimous choice of the Implementation Selection Committee, and he began to interview teacher, assistant teachers, and community resource liaisons, and technology facilitators as his first task. Johns was an experienced educator, from an urban, working-class, Irish and Anishnabe background with

[1] In keeping with Sergiovanni's belief that changing the metaphor changes the theory, the term *principal*, with its hegemonic etymology, and ties to theories of individual-based organizational leadership will not be utilized. In its place, I have chosen to use *coordinator*, which more accurately describes the function and the role of the lead facilitator at PFCLC.

twenty years of successful urban high school teaching experience, and five years experience as the coordinator of a cooperative/experiential programme for a large progressive First Nations school board in Northern Ontario. Johns was well travelled, and had served as an observer for Amnesty International of which he had been a member for twenty-five years. Johns, it was noted in his final interview, viewed his role at PFCLC to be roughly analogous to that of an administrator in a teaching hospital, or a good Chief or Headman in Indigenous community in Canada, South America, Asia, or Africa. Johns envisioned himself coordinating a range of services provided by empowered, self-directed, and self-monitoring, and peer-monitored professionals and paraprofessionals. Beyond that, he would attend to the day-to-day administrivia of a large community project. Johns was given hiring and salary-negotiating discretion within parameters broadly defined by the Implementation Committee.

Johns set out to identify individuals with a shared interest in breaking the lines between the school and the community in order to turn the school into a hub in social service package delivery. He looked for a commitment to inclusiveness, cooperative education, and consensus-based, democratic decision making. He believed these shared values established a firm foundation for a shared culture or community of the mind (Sergiovanni, 1996). He also assumed that there would be less resistance to innovation and the institutionalization of change in a group selected on the basis of shared values and experiences (Fullan, 1991). Johns expectations were that one could expect a higher degree of professional flexibility and responsiveness to be practiced by a learning team hired on such a basis (Fullan, 1994; Prestine, 1994). Johns informed the committee in his first report that through the careful coordination of hiring based on shared values and experiences, PFCLC would be expected to have less tension between the school's implicit and explicit culture, allowing for a more comprehensive and easier embedding of core technological, organizational, curriculum and instructional changes (Fullan, 1993, 2007; Prestine, 1994; Miles & Ekholm as cited in Prestine, 1994; Senge, 1990)

In association with the Implementation Committee, Johns had defined the specific criteria he would use for identifying a highly qualified and motivated learning team. Johns was looking for educationists dedicated to facilitating and engineering learning rather than those most comfortable in the *banking model* of education. He wished to attract educationists equipped to work (with extensive PD and monitoring support) coordinating the efforts of assistants, volunteers, students, and community liaisons. Further, Johns was especially looking for self-confident educators prepared to work with parents as partners, and who viewed students as unique and valuable people who are important contributors and empowered decision makers. Johns was conscious that the need for formal leadership will decline in importance as consensus on values is shared. In a sense, he planned for his own obsolescence. Community leadership was his overall goal, as it would ensure the moral, ethical, and pedagogical relevance of the school. Johns' foremost goal was that the school's leadership would outlive his tenure or that of any other titular head teacher. By hiring teachers with shared values and experiences, he knew he would overcome the greatest challenge facing PFCLC. Johns was confident the challenge of implementation and the administration of the new school would not involve finding resources; instead, the challenge lay in identifying and hiring a professional and support staff that believed in the goals of the school and made the school goals their goals. Most of all Johns wanted to coordinate the assembly of a community of the mind, made up of educationists, parents, and students committed to the *humanization* of education through consensus-based community leadership.

During interviews for teachers or *facilitators of learning*, Johns and a panel of members of the Implementation Committee dialogued with prospects for evidence that they shared the normative assumptions of the CLC model school, a respect and working knowledge of the liberatory pedagogical ideas of Paulo Freire, and enthusiasm for working towards the articulation of an individualized approach to the model through participation in an intensive consensus and school-building process. When checking references and going through curriculum vitae of prospective faculty, Johns looked for evidence of both risk taking, team work, and collaboration. Johns looked for demonstrable success utilizing a repertoire of different teaching techniques, strategies and approaches. Johns also deliberately set out to identify facilitators that reflected the racial, ethnic, religious, class, and sexual orientation composition of the student and parent body of the school. Johns also kept an eye open for applicants with experience working on projects in consultation or cooperation with activist community leaders, movements, and marginalized and disenfranchised segments of society. He also looked for facilitators he believed would be sensitive to parent's needs and previous educational experience. Facilitators also needed a critical awareness of the connection between community-based issues and the wider economic and social world. He was also interested in applicants travel history and looked for candidate's with experience in development and aid activities. He looked for a history of collaboration, kindness, perseverance, eagerness in tackling tough problems with no easy or one-size-fits-all solutions. In his words, "They must love the work, and love working hard at it."

After the interview process and the selection of the facilitators, they interviewed and hired the paraprofessional – aides, technologists, and community liaisons – along with Johns on a consensus basis. Consensus on hiring practices was determined through dialogue between the Coordinator and facilitators. Together they determined that the criteria for hiring paraprofessionals and support personnel must once again be supportive of the basic model of the CLC, core values, and principals drawn from critical theory, especially the work of Paulo

Freire. They sought staff with a commitment to utilizing the students and community as essential learning resources. The staff needed experience or simply enthusiasm for working both independently and as part of a learning team coordinated by the learning facilitators. They also looked for support for the concept of the school as a social service coordination hub and, hence, wanted people with experience and knowledge of local community, NGO, and business resources. Once again, Johns and the facilitators believed it was important to hire paraprofessionals and support staff that reflected the ethnic, sexual orientation, religious, class, and racial composition of the student and parent body of the school. The final hiring decisions were made by a Hiring Committee of four facilitators elected by the facilitation team and four parents elected through a parent caucus. Specific placements were made by the Hiring Committee in consultation with Johns, who independently established the salary and benefit packages for the respective positions according the guidelines established by the Implementation Committee and the recommendations of the Hiring Committee.

Post-Paradigmatic Vision & Covenant Building at PFCLC

After assembling the PFCLC learning teams, Johns planned a series of formal and informal meetings/dialogue sessions (*Circulo de Cultura*) involving the faculty team, prospective parents, students, community activists, academics, and local business leaders. Johns did not perceive these meetings as a radical exercise, in fact he saw them in his minds as town meetings, facilitated by critically informed guides (Sergiovanni, 1994). Johns' goal was not to immediately create a formal vision for the school, but to initiate the important process of thinking about, reflecting on, and talking about the development of a context sensitive vision for the school. Johns broad goal in Freirian terms was both *conscientization* and *problematization*. First, these stakeholder and community leadership dialogues where designed to set in motion a critical process whereby awareness of the vehicles and sources of oppression in the community and education process are identified, codified, and then critically scrutinized through consciousness raising dialogue (conscientization). The second purpose of these dialogues was to engage and empower the school community group in opposing and altering the oppressive forces and removing the social and cultural impediments within the school and community. Johns hoped this process would inspire faculty, parents, and especially students to engage in participatory research directed towards the elimination of dependency and its symptoms, poverty, illiteracy, malnutrition, an so on. The goal of this vision-building process for Johns was to develop statements, agreements, or a covenant based on the purposes and values of the school.This shared understanding and commitment would then validate and incorporate the conceptions and beliefs of informed individual stakeholders about the purpose of the school and their individual roles within it. Although all members of the faculty team were aware of the specifications of the CLC model they would be seeking to develop within the school, they were challenged by Johns to think about the problems they were facing while developing their curriculum, defining learning plans with parents and students, exploring cooperative education opportunities in the community, and learning to work with one another as part of a collaborative learning team. As previously stated, Johns initial analogous thinking regarding his role was of the model of the hospital, where an administrative leader coordinates a range of service providers and specialists. Out of his meeting with all stakeholders, Johns and the facilitators drew up a list of questions to guide the reflection and discussion during the articulation of the formal school covenant by the faculty, students, and parents. Heterogeneous committees made up of parents, facilitators, paraprofessionals, support staff, and community resource people were formed to develop formal vision statements. Further, committee chairs and members were encouraged to value divergent ideas and dissent, and to value the process of debate and dialogue even at the cost of expediency. Johns believed that dissent must be institutionalized if differences were to be the source of inspiration and innovation rather than dissent and conflict. Each committee was asked to consider each of the following questions and any others they considered salient when considering the school's covenant. They would be asked to utilize this set of "telling" questions during the design and implementation of all programmes, regulations, policies, and procedures (Dalin & Rust, 1996; Sergiovanni, 1996).

Questions for Covenant Building and Programme & Policy Development at PFCLC

- Do our programmes prepare students for a meaningful role as contributing members of their communities and active citizens of a fair and democratic nation?
- Do our programmes prepare students to lead through partnership, consensus, and collaboration, rather than from dominance and authority?
- Do our programmes use technology in the service of human growth and benefit?
- Do our programmes teach life skills that will assist learners in being happier and healthier?
- Do our programmes and activities stress creativity and problem solving over standardization?
- Do our programmes meet the needs of all of our students?
- Is our school a school for all the children and youth in our community?
- Is our programme inclusive or exclusive?
- Have we programmed for the academic needs of a select few students?

- How do we design our programme models so that they are flexible and change as the needs of students change?
- Does our programming measure up to our promise contained in our accreditation agreement that we will ensure universality of access and equity of opportunity?
- Does our programme address the physical, social, emotional, cultural, and moral needs of our students?
- Does our programme equip and assist students in identifying and altering structures, forces, and vehicles of oppression in their community and society?
- How do we want students to live their lives in our school and community, to care for each other, to help each other, to respect each other?
- "What will our obligations be to each other?" (Sergiovanni, 1996, p. 64)
- How will our programmes, policies, and procedures support our goal of consensual governance?
- "What obligations and commitments do we need to make to parents, and what obligations and commitments should we expect from them?"(Sergiovanni, 1996, p. 64)

After the initial round of meetings were completed and the committees had each generated a number of statements or ideas regarding the school's vision, Johns gathered the committees together in a plenary session. Johns and the facilitators organized the session to take place during a three-day, out-of-town retreat in May of 2013, with the goal of engineering a living covenant mission statement draft that could be shared with the community, adjusted, tweaked, amended, and formally ratified by all stakeholders. Johns believed the formal covenant mission statement was needed to guide the school, staff, parents, and students day to day in all school related planning and activities. A Draft Committee was elected by the committee members, after an extended open and sometimes heated dialogue and at the end of the retreat session a tentative draft vision statement was published in the school newsletter, on the school's web site, in the student paper, and was posted through out the school for community wide comment. The covenant would then be ratified through consensus at a full school community meeting and signed by all stakeholders. Johns would constantly refer to this *living* vision statement during all weekly meetings, which were incidentally dedicated strictly to professional development, and meaningful dialogue. Johns also encouraged his facilitators to make the same-grounded reference to the covenant in their daily team meetings and to use the covenant for grounded reflection. Further, Johns asked facilitators and committees to look at individual statements in the school's covenant and utilize them as a kind of self-administered litmus test for decisions, programmes and initiatives. This formal mission agreement took one year to develop and it will never be finalized if the school expects to continue to grow, and adapt.

PFCLC is not attempting to massage education to fit existing structure and conditions of schools but, instead, to create an evolutionary alternative school that could be designed around a central programmatic focus, *experiential learning*. Understanding that knowledge is time specific, PFCLC will need to constantly and collaboratively reflect upon and alter their mission, strategies, and content of the curricular, co-curricular, cooperative, and social service programming. The post-paradigmatic coordinators of the school will have to remain active in keeping the school's vision relevant, and in touch with the values and aspirations of the stakeholders. PFCLC is a learning organization where leadership is diffused, but not defused.

Postscript: Post-Paradigmatic Educational Leadership in the Post-Modern World

Post-modern society is the context of the preceding speculative non-fiction. The post-modern world, is at a fundamental level a complex world of relationships, meaning, connections, and processes. A theory of educational administration for the post-modern age must not simply be a recipe for implementing the reform flavor of the day, it must be sensitive to the needs of a complex, diverse population, the rapid changes society is undergoing as a result of the information technology explosion, and the undeniable trends towards transnational corporate control of a world marketplace. The accompanying changes in employment, new forms of poverty, and increasing racial and ethnic diversity in once supposedly homogeneous nation states call for new approaches to schooling and new methods of organizing schools.

Even with the changes the central question for educationists remains what is the purpose of schooling? In this new age, students are required to prepare for citizenship at multiple levels, local, community, regional, and global, and national. (Block as cited in Spears, 1998) Further, they are required to meet instrumental and accountability requirements that purportedly measure reasoning capabilities but limit the indicators of rationality so severely that they discount or even abuse students' affective, aesthetic, and cultural developmental needs. Schools and educationist are increasingly taking responsibility for investing in students with social capital necessary to secure the necessities of life including love and a sense of belonging, along with shelter, food, and meaningful employment. Exploring the relationship between educational practice to the development of democracy is becoming even more pressing in the age of globalization. Indeed, H. G. Wells (1925) may well have been inspired when he cautioned his modernist audience that "history is a race between education and catastrophe." He might have appropriately added community and cooperation versus competition and commodification to this race. Common curriculum and testing, standardized teaching and leadership is a modern answer to a post-modern problem of assuring effective education in an incredibly complex and diverse context – the twenty-first-century school.

References

Dalin, P., & Rust, V.D. (1996). *Towards schooling for the twenty-first century.* London: Cassell.

English, F. W. (1994). *Theory in educational administration.* New York: Harper Collins.

Fullan, M. (1991). *The Best Faculty of Education in the Country: A Fable.* Submitted to the Strategic Planning Committee. Faculty of Education, University of Toronto.

Fullan, M. (1993). *Change forces: Probing the depths of educational reform.* London: Falmer Press.

Fullan, M. (1994). *The school as a learning organisation: Distant dreams.* University of Toronto, Canada.

Fullan, M. (2007). *The new meaning of educational change.* (4th ed.). New York: Teachers College Press.

Prestine, N. A. (1994). *Sorting it Out: A tentative analysis of essential school change Efforts in Illinois.* Paper Presented at the American Educational Research Association Meeting. New Orleans, LA.

Russell, B. (1994). *On education.* London & New York: Routledge.

Senge, P. (1990). *The fifth discipline: The art and practice of the learning organization.* Milsons Point, US: Random House.

Sergiovanni, T. J. (1994) *Building community in schools.* California: Jossey-Bass Publishers.

Sergiovanni, T. J. (1996). *Leadership for the schoolhouse.* Jossey-Bass: San Francisco.

Spears, L. (Ed.). (1998). *Insights on leadership: Service, stewardship, spirit, and servant-leadership.* Toronto: John Wiley & Sons, Inc.

Wells, H. G. (1925). *The new Machiavelli.* London: Fisher Unwin.

Helpful Resources

In October of 1844, Sir Charles Metcalfe, the head of administrative affairs in the province, appointed **Rev. Dr. Egerton Ryerson** to the position of Chief Superintendent of Education for Upper Canada, the highest position in the Department of Public Instruction for Upper Canada at the time. This moment marks the founding of formal educational leadership in Canada.

http://www.archives.gov.on.ca/English/exhibits/education/ryerson.htm

The **UCEA Center for the Study of School Site Leadership** is co-hosted by University at Buffalo/State University of New York and the Ontario Institute for Studies in Education (OISE), University of Toronto.

http://www.oise.utoronto.ca/research/schoolleadership/ssl_usa.html

The Canadian Journal of Educational Administration and Policy (CJEAP) is a peer reviewed online journal based at the Faculty of Education, University of Manitoba.

http://www.umanitoba.ca/publications/cjeap/currentissues.html

Canadian Association of Principals (CAP) is the advocate for principals and vice-principals at the national level. Working with other national educational groups, CAP presents the views and opinions of principals and vice-principals regarding a variety of issues and in many different forums.

http://www.cdnprincipals.org/

NSELC has targeted educators already in positions of senior leadership (principals, vice principals, and central office personnel) and/or teachers who were aspiring to move into an administrative role. The NSELC is now expanding our Modules/Workshops specifically with teachers as the audience: i.e. classroom teachers interested in becoming curriculum leaders, student teachers and beginning teachers who want to learn how to be more effective classroom managers, seasoned teachers who want to develop their instructional strategies to better meet the needs of their students, teachers who are fulfilling the role of coach/mentor in their schools or board.

http://nselc.ednet.ns.ca/

The **Saskatchewan Educational Leadership Unit** is a non-profit agency which serves as a coordinator, developer and administrator of leadership development activities.

http://www.usask.ca/education/selu/whatis.html

Each year **Action Canada** will select up to twenty exceptional young Canadians—those in the early years of their careers or following a course of graduate studies—to participate in a program focusing on leadership development and public policy projects of significance to Canada.

http://www.actioncanada.ca/english/program.htm